M. M. Macomb

Tables of geographic Positions, Azimuths, and Distances

M. M. Macomb

Tables of geographic Positions, Azimuths, and Distances

ISBN/EAN: 9783337140090

Printed in Europe, USA, Canada, Australia, Japan

Cover: Foto ©ninafisch / pixelio.de

More available books at **www.hansebooks.com**

ENGINEER DEPARTMENT, U. S. ARMY.

TABLES

OF

GEOGRAPHIC POSITIONS, AZIMUTHS, AND DISTANCES,

TOGETHER WITH

LISTS OF BAROMETRIC ALTITUDES, MAGNETIC DECLINATIONS,
AND ITINERARIES OF IMPORTANT ROUTES,

PREPARED PRINCIPALLY BY

First Lieut. M. M. MACOMB, 4th U. S. Artillery,
ASSISTANT,

FROM

DATA GATHERED BY PARTIES OF THE UNITED STATES GEOGRAPHICAL SURVEYS WEST OF THE 100TH MERIDIAN, OPERATING IN THE STATES AND TERRITORIES OF CALIFORNIA, COLORADO, NEBRASKA, NEVADA, OREGON, ARIZONA, IDAHO, MONTANA, NEW MEXICO, AND WYOMING,

UNDER THE DIRECTION OF

Captain GEO. M. WHEELER, Corps of Engineers, U. S. Army,
IN CHARGE.

1883.

WASHINGTON:
GOVERNMENT PRINTING OFFICE.
1885.

10040 G P

LETTER OF TRANSMITTAL.

UNITED STATES GEOGRAPHICAL SURVEYS
WEST OF THE ONE HUNDREDTH MERIDIAN,
Washington, D. C., October 31, 1883.

SIR: I have the honor to forward herewith "Tables of Geographic Positions, &c.," with the request that authority be granted for the printing of 1,000 copies.

These tables contain important unpublished data (final results of the Survey), and should prove of much practical value in map compilation and for reference.

Very respectfully, your obedient servant,
GEO. M. WHEELER,
Captain of Engineers in charge.

The CHIEF OF ENGINEERS, U. S. ARMY,
Washington, D. C.

OFFICE CHIEF OF ENGINEERS, U. S. ARMY,
November 2, 1883.

Respectfully submitted to the honorable the Secretary of War, with the recommendation that the report be printed at the Government Printing Office, and that 1,000 copies be furnished on requisition from this office.

H. G. WRIGHT,
Chief of Engineers, Brig. & Brt. Maj. Gen.

Approved. By order of the Secretary of War.
JOHN TWEEDALE,
Chief Clerk.

WAR DEPARTMENT, *November 3, 1883.*

TABLE OF CONTENTS.

	Page.
Introductory Note	7

PART I.

ASTRONOMIC AND GEODETIC POSITIONS.

TABLE I.—Primary astronomical stations	10–11
II.—Secondary astronomical stations	12
III.—Base lines	13, 14
IV.—Positions of mountain peaks alphabetically arranged by States and Territories	15–35
V.—Positions of cities, towns, and settlements, &c., alphabetically arranged by States and Territories	36–40
VI.—Positions of military posts, alphabetically arranged	41–44

PART II.

AZIMUTHS AND DISTANCES FROM PRIMARY TRIANGULATION STATIONS.

TABLE I.—Los Angeles base, California and Nevada	49–62
II.—Sutro base, California, Nevada, and Oregon	63–83
III.—Ogden base, Idaho and Utah	85–96
IV.—Santa Fé base	97–105
V.—Fort Bayard base	107–114
VI.—Fort Bliss (or El Paso) base	115–120

PART III.

BAROMETRIC ALTITUDES.

List of reference stations	124–126
TABLE I.—Military posts	127–128
II.—Mountain peaks	129–141
III.—Cities, towns, and settlements	142–171
IV.—Lakes, springs, &c.,	172–180
V.—Mountain passes	181–191

PART IV.

ITINERARIES OF IMPORTANT ROUTES.

Routes Nos. 1–41, inclusive	194–261

NOTE.

Through the following tables there are presented, in accessible form, such portions of the more important numerical results of this Survey, from the year 1873 to 1879, inclusive, as it has been found necessary to compute *pari passu* with the plottings made from the field notes, together with such additional determinations as may have been required in the construction of the final atlas sheets.

The speed with which results were demanded and produced during the years that field observations were in progress, and the subsequent paucity in office assistance, have rendered it impossible to exhaust the subject under any one of the headings found in the contents. Such results, however, as would seem to be of the greatest general interest and usefulness have been collected in this volume, which is submitted to take a place among the miscellaneous publications of the Survey, wherein its importance will correspond in a measure to the number of positions, elevations, distances, &c. (of which there are many), not hitherto in print.

These tables, independent of showing the larger part of the framework upon which the atlas sheets rest, should prove of practical assistance to parties hereafter operating in the same areas, and of value in all general map compilations of this portion of our western territory.

Many of the results which have already appeared in various annual or preliminary reports, for convenience are repeated here, with additions and corrections where necessary.

In any case of difference the figures herein, having been recompared with the final records, should be given the preference over any contained in earlier publications.

Other than Lieutenant Macomb, among those assisting in preparing the within tables, should be mentioned especially Mr. F. W. Floyd, also Messrs. Gilbert Thompson, Anton Karl, and Francis Klett, who have performed valuable services in collating from the original records.

G. M. W.

U. S. ENGINEER OFFICE,
GEOGRAPHICAL SURVEYS WEST OF THE 100th MERIDIAN,
Washington, D. C., October 31, 1883.

On account of the prolonged illness and consequent continued absence from duty of Captain Wheeler, this publication was still further delayed till commencement of the year 1885.

PART I.

ASTRONOMIC AND GEODETIC POSITIONS.

TABLE I.—PRIMARY ASTRONOMICAL STATIONS.
II.—SECONDARY ASTRONOMICAL STATIONS.
III.—BASE LINES.
IV.—MOUNTAIN PEAKS.
V.—CITIES, TOWNS, AND SETTLEMENTS.
VI.—MILITARY POSTS.

NOTE.—Only such positions as have received distinctive names, and which have undergone final computation at the date of going to press, have been included in the following tables. All longitudes in this volume are west from Greenwich, and all latitudes are North.

TABLE I.—PRIMARY ASTRONOMICAL STATIONS.

[CLASSES OF STATIONS.—(1) Main astronomical; (2) Secondary astronomical; (3) Secondary triangulation; (4) Base-line; (5) Primary triangulation; (6) Three-point; (7) Cross-sight.]

Station.	Atlas sheet.	Latitude.	Longitude.	Altitude.	Magnetic variation, E.	Expeditionary year.	Remarks.
		° ′ ″	° ′ ″		° ′ ″		
Austin, Nev	48D	39 29 21.92	117 03 41.70	7,521		1871	No triangulation dependent upon this determination.
Battle Mountain, Nev	48B	40 38 18.74	116 56 13.50	14,508		1871	Do.
Beaver, Utah	59A	38 16 23.28	112 38 35.90	5,916	15 56 00	1872	Do.
Boz-man, Mont	14D	45 40 51.92	111 02 36.64	4,839		1873	Do.
Camp Independence, Cal	65A	36 50 10.00	118 12 45.00	3,956	15 33 43	1871	Longitude by lunar culminations. No triangulation dependent upon this determination.
Carlin, Nev	40C	40 42 26.67	116 07 20.60	14,908		1871	No triangulation dependent upon this determination.
Cheyenne, Wyo	44C	41 07 46.62	104 48 51.30	16,041		1872	Do.
Cimarron, N. Mex	70A	36 30 10.01	104 54 59.04	6,384		1874	
Colorado Springs, Colo	62A	38 49 41.67	104 49 15.10	6,010		1873	
Dalles City, Oreg	20A	45 36 17.78	121 12 20.47	180		1878	
Fort Bayard, N. Mex	84C	32 47 40.35	108 09 08.77	6,097	12 56 00	1878	Base measured and development begun.
Fort Bliss (El Paso), Tex	90B	31 45 31.14	106 29 05.37	3,630	12 25 15	1878	
Fort Fred Steele, Wyo	43A	41 46 40.24	106 56 48.80	6,850	16 27. 10	1873	
Fort Sidney, Nebr	44D	41 08 36.75	102 58 13.32	4,106		1874	
Fort Union, N. Mex	70C	35 54 24.86	105 00 51.15	6,744	14 14 00	1873	
Fort Whipple, Ariz	75A	34 33 06.12	112 27 10.20	5,318		1871	Longitude by lunar culminations; latitude by zenith telescope.
Fresno, Cal	64B	36 43 31.22	119 47 19.50	314		1878	Base measured; no connection made with main triangulation.
Georgetown, Colo	52D	39 42 36.36	105 41 27.60	8,588		1873	
Green River, Wyo	42B	41 31 38.12	109 28 06.57	6,096		1872	
						1873	

NOTE.—The letters *a*, *l*, and *t* in altitude column indicate determinations from aneroid observations, by level lines, and vertical angles, respectively. All other altitudes are cistern barometer re-sults.

TABLE I.—PRIMARY ASTRONOMICAL STATIONS—Continued.

Station.	Atlas sheet.	Latitude.	Longitude.	Altitude.	Magnetic variation, E.	Expeditionary year.	Remarks.
		° ′ ″	° ′ ″		° ′ ″		
Gunnison, Utah	50D	39 09 25.62	111 49 15.00	5,145		1872	
Hughes, Colo	53A	39 59 24.09	104 48 58.80	5,022		1873	
Julesburg, Colo	45C	40 59 07.63	102 21 32.30	3,500		1874	
Labran, Colo	62A	38 23 08.97	105 06 17.78	5,218		1873	
Laramie, Wyo	43D	41 18 51.80	105 35 33.60	7,123		1872	
Las Vegas, N. Mex	78A	35 35 27.66	105 13 27.57	6,418		1874	
North Platte, Nebr	45D	41 08 18.33	100 45 53.14	2,789		1874	
Ogden Astronomical Observatory, Utah	41D	41 13 08.56	111 59 54.64	4,374	18 27 06	1873 1874	Variation in 1877; top of east meridian stone, west observing room; center of dome, 111° 59′ 54″.47. in longitude.
Pioche, Nev	58D	37 55 26.07	114 26 18.27	5,942	15 58 00	1872	
Saint George, Utah	67A	37 06 29.38	113 35 00.30	2,611	16 27 00	1871	
Salt Lake City, Utah (Mormon Observatory).	41D	40 46 03.76	111 53 42.90	4,330	17 01 00		Latitude and longitude from Coast Survey determinations; variation in 1872.
Santa Fe, N. Mex	69D	35 41 19.29	105 56 45.22	6,965	13 09 32	1873	Longitude by trigonometrical connection.
South Pueblo, Colo	62A	38 15 42.84	104 36 57.53	4,732		1874	
Trinidad, Colo	70A	37 10 46.53	104 30 01.42	5,990		1873	
Virginia City, Nev	47D	39 17 35.92	119 39 06.35	6,339		1873	
Walla Walla, Wash	12C	46 03 55.89	118 20 50.14	1,034	20 15 00	1878	Main triangulation of California and Nevada, from latitude 37° 15′ to 42° 30′ N., and from longitude 117° to 121° 30′ depends upon this determination. No triangulation dependent upon this determination.
Winnemucca, Nev	39D	40 58 19.97	117 43 54.16	4,355		1873	Do.

TABLE II.—SECONDARY ASTRONOMICAL STATIONS.

[Latitude by sextant; longitude by telegraph and transit.]

Station.	Atlas sheet.	Latitude.	Longitude.	Altitude.	Magnetic variation, E.	Expeditionary year.	Remarks.
		° ′ ″	° ′ ″		° ′ ″		
Camp Ruby, Nev	49A	40 03 38.63	115 31 06.75	6,153	17 09 04	1869	
Deep Creek, Utah	49B	40 06 01.71	113 57 16.05	5,237		1872	
Elko, Nev	40C	40 49 38.44	115 45 37.20	5,148	17 35 03	1869	
Fillmore (near), Utah	59B	38 57 14.94	112 16 54.93	6,120	16 22 30	1872	
Fort Hallock, Nev	40C	40 48 34.35	115 19 34.05	5,790	16 21 24	1869	
Hamilton (near), Nev	49C	39 15 48.87	115 25 58.38	7,601	16 43 29	1869	
Kanab, Utah	67A	37 02 25.43	112 31 39.00	4,909	14 23 00	1872	
Monte Christo Mill, Nev	49C	39 13 16.83	115 34 49.20	7,596	17 05 06	1869	
Pekо, Nev	40C	40 55 46.35	115 30 14.50	5,180		1869	
Pipe Springs, Ariz	67A	36 51 36.34	112 42 57.00	5,397		1872	
Provo, Utah	50B	40 13 47.84	111 40 27.00	4,567	17 01 00	1872 / 1873	} Variation in 1872.
Richfield, Utah	59B	38 46 11.40	112 02 27.00	5,283		1873	
Toquerville, Utah	67A	37 15 19.88	113 16 20.90		16 11 05	1872	

TABLE III.—BASE-LINE STATIONS AND LENGTH OF BASES.

[Measurements depend upon Coast Survey standard rods. To change feet to meters, log factor 9.4840273; meters to feet, 0.5159677; meters to miles, 6.7933338.]

Station.	Class of station.	Atlas sheet.	Latitude.	Longitude.	Measured length of base reduced to sea-level.	Expeditionary year.
			° ′ ″	° ′ ″	*Meters.*	
Bozeman, Montana:						
North Base	4	14D	45 42 45.35	111 06 26.14	} 7,352.500	} 1877
South Base	4	23B	45 39 09.61	111 04 02.10		1877
Cimarron, New Mexico:						
Northwest Base	4	70A	36 30 22.26	104 54 28.66	} 1,758.429	} 1874
Southeast Base	4	70C	36 29 50.14	104 53 30.26		1874
Colorado Springs, Colorado:						
North Base	4	62A	38 51 13.99	104 49 05.82	} 3,683.369	} 1876
South Base	4	62A	38 49 14.64	104 49 12.49		1876
Dalles, Oregon:						
North Base	4	20A	45 37 35.26	121 14 14.99	} 2,633.568	} 1878
South Base	4	20A	45 36 15.02	121 13 33.68		1878
Fort Bayard, New Mexico:						
North Base	4	84C	32 40 42.13	108 07 16.15	} 8,306.263	} 1878
South Base	4	84C	32 36 24.88	108 08 56.74		1878
Fort Bliss, Texas:						
East Base	4	90B	31 47 11.43	106 24 40.72	} 2,453.421	} 1878
West Base	4	90B	31 47 59.78	106 25 54.85		1878
Fort Union, New Mexico:						
North Base	4	70C	35 55 17.24	105 00 11.01	} 4,469.638	} 1874
South Base	4	70C	35 52 54.06	104 59 42.68		1874
Los Angeles, California:						
Northeast Base	4	80A	33 56 02.95	118 18 16.71	} 6,642.529	} 1875
Southwest Base	4	80A	33 54 12.86	118 21 59.08		1875
Ogden, Utah:						
North Base	4	41D	41 15 48.62	111 58 24.33	} 7,072.931	} 1877
South Base	4	41D	41 11 59.36	111 58 29.73		1877

TABLE III.—BASE-LINE STATIONS AND LENGTH OF BASES—Continued.

Station.	Class of station.	Atlas sheet.	Latitude.	Longitude.	Measured length of base reduced to sea-level.	Expeditionary year.
			° ′ ″	° ′ ″	Meters.	
Panamint, California:						
North Base	4	65D	36 10 28.32	117 17 11.38	} 10,912.231	} 1875
South Base	4	65D	36 04 37.72	117 16 10.79		1875
Santa Fe, New Mexico:						
Northeast Base	4	77B			} 5,910.626	} 1874
Southwest Base	4	77B				1874
Sutro, Nevada:						
East Base	4	47D	39 18 45.67	119 30 09.38	} 7,137.603	} 1876
West Base	4	47D	39 16 24.86	119 34 05.82		1876
Terrace-Lucin, Nevada:						
Terrace, East Base	4	41A	41 30 41.24	113 29 51.18	} 36,967.670	} 1878
Lucin, West Base	4	40D	41 21 30.11	113 53 24.90		1878
Trinidad, Colorado:						
East Base	4	70A	37 13 56.86	104 29 54.37	} 9,020.506	} 1874
West Base	4	70A	37 14 54.35	104 23 55.48		1874
Verdi, Nevada:						
East Base	4	47D	39 30 16.72	119 56 57.92	} 2,597.036	} 1887
West Base	4	47D	39 30 57.38	119 58 33.13		1877
Weldon, California:						
East Base	4	73A	35 39 15.88	118 19 34.93	} 5,171.275	} 1875
West Base	4	73A	35 39 14.39	118 23 00.53		1875

TABLE IV.—MOUNTAIN PEAKS.

Name of peak.	Class of station.	Atlas sheet.	Range or group.	Latitude.	Longitude.	Altitude.	Expeditionary year.	Astronomical initial point.
ARIZONA.				° ′ ″	° ′ ″			
Graham	7	83C	Pinaleño	32 41 58.9	109 52 18.9	a10,516	{ 1874 1878 }	Ft. Bayard, N. M.
Thomas	4	83B	White Mountain	33 54 24.1	109 34 16.0	a11,275	1878	Do.
CALIFORNIA.								
Abbot	7	57C	Sierra Nevada	37 22 24.8	118 47 58.0	a13,582	{ 1878 1879 }	Virginia, Nev.
Adams	5	47B	do	39 54 32.2	120 05 43.2	8,432	1876	Do.
Agua Caliente	6	80B	San Jacinto	33 19 18.3	116 37 12.6	a7,034	1876	Los Angeles, Cal.
Alder Hill	6	56B	Sierra Nevada	38 37 40.0	120 14 08.4	a7,731	1877	Virginia, Nev.
Alpine (or Woods—Round-Top, U. S. C. and G. S.).	4	56D	do	38 39 40.5	119 59 53.9	10,426	1877	Do.
Alturas Hill	5	38D	Argus	41 28 56.7	120 32 43.2	4,459	1877	Do.
Argus	5	65D	Warner	35 50 52.2	117 26 56.5	t6,333	1875	Los Angeles, Cal.
Bidwell	5	38B	Panamint	41 56 52.6	120 07 49.8	8,551	1877	Virginia, Nev.
Birds	7	65B	Sierra Nevada	36 52 56.2	117 27 19.4		1875	Los Angeles, Cal.
Black Mountain	5	65A	do	36 48 46.5	118 21 44.1	13,009	1875	Do.
Black Mountain, point south of	4	56D		37 32 07.7	119 22 20.01		1879	Virginia, Nev.
Blue Mountain	7	56B	Foot-hills of Sierra Nevada	38 20 23.0*	120 21 46.1*	6,076	{ 1879 1879 }	Do.
Breckenridge	5	73A	Sierra Nevada	35 25 40.0	118 34 16.0	7,418	1875	Los Angeles, Cal.
Browns	4	65D	Panamint	35 40 49.4	117 01 29.1	5,392	1875	Do.
Buena Vista	7	56D	Sierra Nevada	37 35 27.8	119 30 54.0	t9,707	{ 1878 1879 }	Virginia, Nev.
Butt Mountain	5	47A	do	40 12 58.2	121 23 02.1	7,831	1878	Do.
Cary	5	56B	Hope Valley group, Sierra Nevada	38 44 10.2	119 52 10.7	9,970	1877	Do.
Castle (Stanford)	4	47D	Sierra Nevada	39 21 48.6	120 20 47.3	9,014	{ 1876 1877 }	Do.

* Preliminary result; final adjustment not made.

TABLE IV.—MOUNTAIN PEAKS—Continued.

Name of peak.	Class of station.	Atlas sheet.	Range or group.	Latitude.	Longitude.	Altitude.	Expeditionary year.	Astronomical initial point.
CALIFORNIA—Continued.				° ′ ″	° ′ ″			
Castle Rock	7	56B	Sierra Nevada	38 14 43.1*	119 50 07.5*	9,872	{1877 / 1878}	Virginia, Nev.
Ceca	4	73C	Ceca Mountains	34 30 29.7	119 04 30.7		1875	Los Angeles, Cal.
Cedar	4	38B	Warner	41 36 31.9	120 16 00.2	8,308	1877	Virginia, Nev.
Cerro El Paso	4	73B		35 28 16.3	117 50 46.5		1875	Los Angeles, Cal.
Cerro Gordo	4	65B	Cerro Gordo Mountains	36 32 01.8	117 47 15.0		1875	Do.
Chiquito	4	56D	Sierra Nevada	37 20 46.8	119 25 31.8	18,257	{1878 / 1879}	Virginia, Nev.
Clarks (Gothic, also the Obelisk)	4	56D	Merced group, Sierra Nevada	37 41 36.4	119 25 33.0	111,512	1878	Do.
Claremont Hill	6	47A	Sierra Nevada	39 52 54.7	120 56 37.3	6,999	1878	Do.
Cloud Rest	5	56D	Yosemite group, Sierra Nevada	37 45 53.2	119 29 11.8	19,912	{1878 / 1879}	Do.
Coahuila	6	80B	San Jacinto	33 34 37.0	116 48 55.0	a5,606	1876	Los Angeles, Cal.
Conness	4	56D	Sierra Nevada	37 57 51.2	119 19 06.2	112,552	{1878 / 1879}	Virginia, Nev.
Cooks Point	5	73A	do	35 37 09.0	118 26 30.4	16,336	1875	Los Angeles, Cal.
Corcoran (Whitney, No. 1)	5	65A	do	36 31 14.0	118 14 23.8	14,094	1875	Do.
Coso	5	65D	Coso Mountains	36 11 56.6	117 42 56.9	18,425	1875	Do.
Cottonwood	7	56D	Sierra Nevada	37 55 26.6	119 43 57.6	17,633	{1878 / 1879}	Virginia, Nev.
Crystal	5	47D	do	39 28 20.9	120 02 13.5		1877	Do.
Dalton Hill	7	64B	do	37 05 24.0	119 58 43.0		1878	Do.
Dana	4	57C	do	37 53 49.2	119 13 05.3	113,043	{1878 / 1879}	Do.
Dardanelle Cone	6	56B	do	38 24 07.7	119 52 10.0		1877	Do.
Dead	7	74A		35 31 38.2	116 21 16.4	10,829	1875	Los Angeles, Cal.

* Preliminary result; final adjustment not made.

TABLE IV.—MOUNTAIN PEAKS—Continued.

Name of peak.	Class of station.	Atlas sheet.	Range or group.	Latitude.	Longitude.	Altitude.	Expeditionary year.	Astronomical initial point.
CALIFORNIA—Continued.				° ′ ″	° ′ ″			
Deadwood	4	64B	Sierra Nevada	37 18 36.7	119 41 00.2	14,451	1878 / 1879	Virginia, Nev.
Denels	5	65A	...do...	36 30 46.1	118 17 50.1	13,376	1875	Los Angeles, Cal.
Devils	4	56D	South Fork group, Sierra Nevada	37 31 34.2	119 44 16.8	16,985	1878 / 1879	Virginia, Nev.
Disappointment	5	73C	San Gabriel Mountains	34 14 49.8	118 06 54.8	8,541	1875	Los Angeles, Cal.
Downieville Butte	4	47C	Sierra Nevada	39 35 29.8	120 38 39.3	12,289	1877	Virginia, Nev.
Dundrberg (locally, Castle)	5	56D	...do...	38 03 43.2	119 16 16.6	7,369	1878	Do.
Dyer	5	47A	...do...	40 14 15.2	121 01 48.4	9,934	1877	Do.
Eagle	5	38D	Warner	41 16 56.0	120 11 51.4		1878	Do.
Eagle Point	7	56D	Sierra Nevada	37 44 34.9	119 36 43.7	17,751	1878 / 1879	Do.
Echo	5	56D	Cathedral group, Sierra Nevada	37 49 54.9	119 23 35.1	111,184	1878 / 1879	Do.
Ellis	5	47D	Sierra Nevada	39 04 00.2	120 11 44.2	8,675	1876	Los Angeles, Cal.
F (Nell)	5	65B	Darwin	36 32 44.3	117 31 59.6	7,361	1875	Do.
Fossil Butte	4	65B	Cerro Gordo	36 34 00.8	117 48 48.7		1875	Do.
Fredonyer	4	38D		40 41 11.0	120 35 44.4	7,995	1877 / 1878	Virginia, Nev.
Freels	4	56B	Lake Tahoe group, Sierra Nevada	38 51 18.8	119 53 50.4	10,849	1876 / 1877	Do.
Fishermans Peak, or Mount Whitney	4	65A	Sierra Nevada	36 34 33.0	118 17 32.0	14,470	1875	Los Angeles, Cal.
Funeral	4	65D	Funeral Mountains	36 19 25.7	116 44 47.8		1875	Do.
Gold Lake Peak (B)	5	47C	Sierra Nevada	39 42 26.1	120 41 13.5		1876	Virginia, Nev.
Granite Chief	7	47D	...do...	39 11 47.4	120 17 06.3		1876	Do.
Green Mountain	7	64B	Foot-hills of Sierra Nevada	37 15 43.6	119 59 19.6	1,352	1878	Do.
Green Mountain, No. 1 of	4	65A	...do...	37 17 27.7	119 10 57.5		1878	Do.
Green Mountain, No. 2 of	7	65A	...do...	37 11 35.4	119 06 43.4		1878	Do.
Grizzly	4	73D	Sierra Nevada	34 05 52.7	116 50 54.7	11,723	1878	Los Angeles, Cal.

1874 WH——2

TABLE IV.—MOUNTAIN PEAKS—Continued.

Name of peak.	Class of station.	Atlas sheet.	Range or group.	Latitude.	Longitude.	Altitude.	Expeditionary year.	Astronomical initial point.
CALIFORNIA—Continued.				° ′ ″	° ′ ″			
Hahn	7	65A	Inyo	36 42 14.7	117 57 42.5	f11,030	1875	Los Angeles, Cal.
Half or South Dome	6	56D		37 44 35.2	119 31 49.8	8,823	1878	Virginia, Nev.
Harkness	6	47A	Sierra Nevada	40 25 48.7	121 17 59.7	a8,875	1878	Do.
Haskells	5	47D	do	39 39 40.7	120 33 01.0	8,126	1876	Do.
Hat	5	38D	Warner	41 03 57.0	120 05 47.9	7,676	1877	Do.
Highland	4	56B	Silver Mountain group, Sierra Nevada.	38 32 28.4	119 45 09.7	10,956	1877	Do.
Hoffman	4	56D	Sierra Nevada	37 50 38.5	119 30 28.3	f10,747	{1878, 1879}	Do.
Hot Springs	4	47B		40 22 24.8	120 07 07.3	7,692	1877	Do.
Houghs	6	47A	Sierra Nevada	40 02 34.4	120 53 01.8	a7,391	1878	Do.
Humphrey	7	65A		37 16 01.7	118 40 10.9		1878	Do.
I (Nell)	7	66C	Kingston	36 01 48.8	116 04 51.1		1875	Los Angeles, Cal.
Ingalls	4	47B	Sierra Nevada	39 59 33.3	120 37 28.8	8,472	{1876, 1878}	Virginia, Nev.
Inyo	7	65A	Inyo	36 43 47.8	117 59 05.9	f10,972	1875	Los Angeles, Cal.
Jackson	5	47D	Sierra Nevada	39 26 40.5	120 32 55.1	8,390	{1876, 1877}	Virginia, Nev.
Kaweah	7	65A		36 32 28.7	118 30 45.8		1878	Do.
Kettle Rock	7	47A	do	40 08 42.0	120 43 03.1	7,843	1878	Do.
Kingston	5	66C	Kingston	35 43 37.8	115 55 47.0		1875	Los Angeles, Cal.
Lassens Butte	4	47C	Sierra Nevada	40 29 12.4	121 30 09.7	10,437	1878	Virginia, Nev.
LM (Nell)	7	66C	Kingston	36 15 24.2	116 15 36.0		1875	Los Angeles, Cal.
Lookout Hill	5	65D		36 14 16.4	117 26 00.8	a4,214	1875	Do.
Los Cerritos (E)	4	80A		33 47 51.9	118 09 48.1	357	1875	Do.
Lyell	4	56D	Sierra Nevada	37 44 11.0	119 16 07.3	f13,104	{1878, 1879}	Virginia, Nev.
McBride	4	57C	White Mountain	37 50 08.0	118 21 12.6	f13,415	{1878, 1879}	Do.
McDonald	5	38D		40 56 23.2	120 24 35.7	7,954	1877	Do.

TABLE IV.—MOUNTAIN PEAKS—Continued.

Name of peak.	Class of station.	Atlas sheet.	Range or group.	Latitude.	Longitude.	Altitude.	Expeditionary year.	Astronomical initial point.
CALIFORNIA—Continued.				° ′ ″	° ′ ″			
McGill	4	73C	Sierra Nevada	34 48 43.9	119 08 52.6	9,214	1875	Los Angeles, Cal.
McKesicks	5	47B	Sierra Nevada	40 05 22.9	120 14 43.1	7,083	1876	Virginia, Nev.
M (Nell)	7	65D		35 46 57.0	116 46 24.7		1875	Los Angeles, Cal.
Markleeville	6	56B	Sierra Nevada	38 39 32.1	119 53 39.9	9,431	1877	Virginia, Nev.
Matterhorn	7	56D	Sierra Nevada	38 05 25.1	119 22 43.6		1878	Do.
Matnrango	4	65D	Argus	36 06 56.3	117 29 49.9	†8,844	1875	Los Angeles, Cal.
Merced	5	56D	Merced group, Sierra Nevada	37 37 54.9	119 23 30.6	†11,442	{1878 1879}	Virginia, Nev.
Millerton Hill, No. 1	7	64B	Sierra Nevada	36 55 34.5	119 38 20.6		1878	Do.
Millerton Hill, No. 2	7	64B	...do...	36 55 43.2	119 38 37.1		1878	Do.
Moccasin	4	56D	Moccasin	37 48 08.1*	120 19 34.7*	3,003	{1878 1879}	Do.
Mokelumne	4	56B	Sierra Nevada	38 32 08.5	120 05 30.5	9,385	1877	Do.
Morgan	4	57C	...do...	37 24 07.2	118 43 46.9	†13,791	{1878 1879}	Do.
Needle	5	47D	Sierra Nevada	39 11 54.8	120 17 54.2	8,833	1877	Los Angeles, Cal.
New York Butte	4	65A	Inyo	30 38 40.8	117 55 56.4	†10,675	1875	Do.
Nichols Point	5	73A	Sierra Nevada	35 37 00.5	118 18 05.2	†6,233	1877	Virginia, Nev.
Observation	4	38D		40 46 22.2	120 10 06.9	8,009	1877	Los Angeles, Cal.
Olancha	4	65C	Sierra Nevada	36 15 43.8	118 07 10.2	12,251	1875	Virginia, Nev.
Omjunni	5	47B	...do...	39 56 16.8	120 16 55.6	8,293	1876	Los Angeles, Cal.
Ophir	5	65D		36 17 19.1	117 36 05.6	†6,063	1875	Do.
Owens	4	65C	Sierra Nevada	35 44 05.4	118 00 00.5		1875	Do.
Pah-ute	5	73A	...do...	35 28 37.6	118 21 49.8	8,342	1875	Virginia, Nev.
Palisades, N. W.	5	65A	...do...	37 00 57.3	118 25 09.6	†14,275	1878	Do.
Palisades, S. E.	7	65A	...do...	37 05 26.9	118 30 40.0	14,200	1878	Do.
Pilot	7	56D	Foot-hills of Sierra Nevada	37 45 35.5	119 56 01.1	†6,024	{1878 1879}	Do.

* Preliminary result ; final adjustment not made.

TABLE IV.—MOUNTAIN PEAKS—Continued.

Name of peak.	Class of station.	Atlas sheet.	Range or group.	Latitude.	Longitude.	Altitude.	Expeditionary year.	Astronomical initial point.
CALIFORNIA—Continued.				° ′ ″	° ′ ″			
Pilot Knob	4	73B		35 23 32.1	117 13 49.7	5,525	1875	Los Angeles, Cal.
Pyramid	4	56B	Sierra Nevada	38 50 32.6	120 09 20.6	10,127	{1876 1877}	Virginia, Nev.
Pyramid	7	65D	Amargosa	36 23 07.9	116 36 47.1	16,754	1875	Los Angeles, Cal.
Raphael	7	73C		34 37 15.5	119 00 03.0		1875	Do.
Red	7	56D	Sierra Nevada	37 39 02.9	119 24 24.1	f11,686	{1878 1879}	Virginia, Nev.
Red Crater	4	65A	do	37 06 40.4	118 17 51.7		1875	Los Angeles, Cal.
Red Slate	7	57C	do	37 30 15.7	118 51 58.0	f13,067	{1878 1879}	Virginia, Nev.
Richardsons, or Sixteen Mile	7	56D	do	38 04 52.2	119 41 24.2	9,794	{1878 1879}	Do.
Ritter	7	57C	do	37 41 09.9	119 11 48.6	f13,130	{1878 1879}	Do.
Robbs	6	56B		38 55 21.8	120 24 04.3	6,746	1876	Do.
Rotten	5	73B		35 39 44.6	116 37 26.2		1875	Los Angeles, Cal.
San Antonio	4	73D	Sierra Nevada	34 17 06.2	117 39 14.1	10,120	{1875 1878}	Do.
San Bernardino	7	73D	do	34 07 07.1	116 56 17.8		1875	Do.
San Fernando	4	73C	Coast	34 19 39.3	118 36 01.9	3,793	1875	Do.
San Gabriel	4	73C	San Gabriel	34 14 27.5	118 05 54.5	6,232	{1875 1878}	Do.
San Jacinto	4	80B	San Jacinto	33 49 07.9	116 42 22.3	10,987	1875	Do.
San Pedro Hill	5	80A		33 44 39.2	118 20 07.8	1,462	1875	Do.
Saddle (formerly Malaga)	4	73C	Coast	34 04 33.5	118 39 17.2	2,897	1875	Do.
Santiago Mountain (highest point)	7	80B	do	33 42 31.1	117 32 03.9		1875	Do.
Santiago Mountain (northwest point)	7	80B		33 43 01.0	117 32 42.8	f5,730	{1875 1878}	Do.
Schultz	4	56D	Sierra Nevada foot-hills	37 26 33.1	120 08 32.9	2,275	1878	Virginia, Nev.
Sentinel Dome	7	59D	Sierra Nevada	37 43 12.3	119 34 54.2	8,122	1878	Do.

TABLE IV.—MOUNTAIN PEAKS—Continued.

Name of peak.	Class of station.	Atlas sheet.	Range or group.	Latitude.	Longitude.	Altitude.	Expeditionary year.	Astronomical initial point.
CALIFORNIA—Continued.				° ′ ″	° ′ ″			
Sevastopol	7	56D	Sierra Nevada	37 35 49.0	120 10 06.6		1878	Virginia, Nev.
Shaffer	5	47B	do	40 26 43.1	120 21 18.6	6,864	1877	Do.
Signal (Red)	6	47D	Sierra Nevada	39 20 13.3	120 31 58.4	7,857	1877	Do.
Silver Lake (Oreana)	4	56B	do	38 51 45.2	119 28 33.8	9,381	1877	Do.
Sister Else	4	73C	San Gabriel Mountains	34 16 00.0	118 14 19.6		1875	Los Angeles, Cal.
Smiths	7	80B	San Jacinto	33 22 24.9	116 51 39.7	16,852	{1876 1878}	Do.
Sonora (Little Pyramid)	4	56B	Sierra Nevada	38 21 04.2	119 37 57.5	11,479	1877	Virginia, Nev.
South Fork	4	38D	do	41 09 14.3	120 33 39.5	7,409	1877	Do.
South Sweetwater	7	56B	Sweetwater	38 24 57.9	119 17 08.6	11,123	1878	Do.
Stanislaus	6	56B	Sierra Nevada	38 22 53.3	119 39 51.0		1877	Do.
Starr King	7	56D	Yosemite group, Sierra Nevada	37 41 59.6	119 30 53.5	19,080	{1878 1879}	Do.
Stevens	5	56B	Sierra Nevada	38 43 52.9	119 58 44.4	10,011	1877	Do.
Summit	4	47D	do	39 42 04.0	120 08 25.0	8,311	1876	Los Angeles, Cal.
Sunday	4	65C	do	35 46 48.5	118 35 17.3	8,335	1875	Virginia, Nev.
Sweetwater	4	56B	Sweetwater	38 26 03.3	119 18 07.2	11,778	1877	Do.
Tallac	5	56B		38 54 12.2	120 05 48.1		1876	Los Angeles, Cal.
Tehachapai	5	73A	Tehachapai	35 02 21.3	118 34 35.6	8,056	1875	Do.
Tehachapai Double	5	73A	do	35 01 47.0	118 29 25.5	8,263	1875	Do.
Telescope	4	65D	Telescope	36 09 52.4	117 05 27.2	110,938	1875	Virginia, Nev.
Tells	6	56B	Tells Peak group, Sierra Nevada	38 56 46.6	120 14 25.4	9,042	1877	Do.
Thompsons	4	47B	Sierra Nevada	40 15 34.1	120 33 17.4	7,752	{1876 1878}	Do.
Thunder	5	65C	do	36 04 52.2	118 34 40.7	9,122	1875	Los Angeles, Cal.
Tinkers Knob	7	47D	do	39 14 33.5	120 16 58.0		1876	Virginia, Nev.
Torros Cone	6	81A		33 32 23.4	116 28 07.6		1875	Los Angeles, Cal.
Tower	7	56D	Sierra Nevada	38 08 30.5	119 32 41.6	111,719	{1878 1879}	Virginia, Nev.

TABLE IV.—MOUNTAIN PEAKS—Continued.

Name of peak.	Class of station.	Atlas sheet.	Range or group.	Latitude.	Longitude.	Altitude.	Expeditionary year.	Astronomical initial point.
CALIFORNIA—Continued.				° ′ ″	° ′ ″			
Twin	4	47D	Sierra Nevada	39 06 37.1	120 13 47.0	8,824	1876	Virginia, Nev.
Volcano	6	81A	San Jacinto	33 19 19.1	116 14 00.4		1876	Los Angeles, Cal.
Volcano (Crater) (17)	4	65D		35 57 08.2	117 50 01.9	5,434	1875	Do.
Wades	5	56D		37 51 08.5	119 47 16.9	7,154	1878	Virginia, Nev.
Wahguyhe	4	65B		36 56 03.5	117 06 15.6	8,528	1875	Los Angeles, Cal.
Warren	4	38D	Warner	41 22 38.7	120 12 59.6	9,668	1877	Virginia, Nev.
Waucoba	4	65A	Inyo	37 01 07.8	118 00 23.2	11,267	1875	Los Angeles, Cal.
Wellington	5	47B	Sierra Nevada	39 51 59.9	120 31 40.6	7,665	1876	Virginia, Nev.
White Granite	5	73C		34 36 34.0	119 07 55.1	7,069	1875	Los Angeles, Cal.
White Mountain	4	57C	White Mountain	37 37 51.4	118 15 07.9	[14,245	{1878, 1879}	Virginia, Nev.
Williarrison	7	65A	Sierra Nevada	36 39 11.0	118 18 39.8	[14,360	1875	Los Angeles, Cal.
Workmans Hill	4	73C		34 00 48.4	118 01 14.5	1,364	1875	Do.
COLORADO.								
Aeolus	5	61C	San Juan	37 37 39.4	107 36 15.4	[14,211	1875	Trinidad, Colo.
Agency Knob (Popes nose)	5	61B	Sierra Madre	38 16 23.8	106 51 53.9	12,273	{1874, 1877}	Pueblo, Colo.
Antelope Butte	5	62C	Wet Mountains	38 03 30.0	105 17 44.3	9,287	1876	Trinidad, Colo.
Antoro	6	61B	Sierra Madre	38 19 28.3	106 12 55.5	13,497	1875	Pueblo, Colo.
Baldy (Fort Garland)	5	62C	Sangre de Cristo	37 35 01.8	105 26 29.6		1874	Trinidad, Colo.
Banded	4	69B	San Juan	37 06 24.5	106 37 19.9		1875	Do.
Basaltic	5	61B		38 43 05.1	105 41 04.1	12,824	{1873, 1876}	Pueblo, Colo.
Bear	5	62A	Wet Mountains	38 10 20.9	105 16 25.6	11,565	1876	Do.
Blaine (Sueffels)	7	61C	Unaweep	38 00 13.6	107 47 22.0	[14,249	{1874, 1875}	Trinidad, Colo.
Bristol Head	5	61C	San Juan	37 47 34.5	107 03 17.9	a12,638	1874	Do.
Buffalo (Hunchback)	5	61C	do	37 36 24.4	107 29 26.8	13,755	1873	Do.

TABLE IV.—MOUNTAIN PEAKS—Continued.

Name of peak.	Class of station.	Atlas sheet.	Range or group.	Latitude.	Longitude.	Altitude.	Expeditionary year.	Astronomical initial point.
				° ′ ″	° ′ ″			
COLORADO—Continued.								
Canby	5	61C	San Juan	37 46 54.6	107 30 50.0	13,356	1874	Trinidad, Colo.
Cap Butte	5	62A	Front	38 40 09.3	105 23 57.5	9,317	1876	Pueblo, Colo.
Carbon	5	61A	West Elk	38 47 38.6	107 02 23.9	12,078	1877	Do.
Cerro Blanco	4	62C	Sangre de Cristo	37 34 43.5	105 28 53.3	14,270	1874 1875 1876	Trinidad, Colo.
Cheops Pyramid (Signal Butte)	5	53C	Front	39 03 29.7	105 13 11.1	9,487	1876	Pueblo, Colo.
Christ	5	53C	do	39 10 18.6	105 11 20.7	9,689	1876	Do.
Craig	5	53C	Kenosha	39 18 19.6	105 17 50.9	a10,261	1876	Do.
Cuerno Verde	4	62C	Wet Mountains	37 52 54.9	105 07 37.2	12,305	1875	Trinidad, Colo.
Culebra	4	70A	Sangre de Cristo	37 07 19.1	105 10 58.2	14,049	1875	Do.
Deer	4	53C	Wet Mountains	39 13 13.6	105 22 28.8	11,537	1876	Pueblo, Colo.
Del Norte	4	61D	San Juan	37 29 05.8	106 25 45.6	13,084	1874	Trinidad, Colo.
Del Norte Hill	5	61D	do	37 40 13.8	106 21 25.5	8,218	1875	Do.
Dunns	4	61C	San Miguel	37 50 24.2	108 05 37.2	13,502	1874	Do.
Engineer	5	61C	San Juan	37 41 57.1	107 48 14.1	13,277	1875	Do.
Evans	5	52D	Front	39 35 16.9	105 38 25.2	14,321	1873 1879	Pueblo, Colo.
Fairplay, Mountain near	6	52D	Park	39 11 36.0	105 59 11.6	12,264	1879	Do.
Farnum (Tarryall)	5	51C	Kenosha	39 14 17.9	105 29 44.5	9,639	1876	Do.
Fishers	4	70A	Raton Plateau	37 06 00.08	104 27 30.8	9,656	1874	Trinidad, Colo.
Fourth of July Hill	5	61A		38 18 12.1	107 14 45.4	13,729	1876	Pueblo, Colo.
Gibson	5	61B	Sangre de Cristo	38 06 07.6	105 39 27.6		1876	Do.
Gilbert	7	61B	do	38 22 57.9	105 56 33.0		1875	Do.
Glacier	7	61C	San Miguel	37 50 20.7	107 59 20.0	14,243	1874	Trinidad, Colo.
Goat	4	52D	Park	39 13 57.4	106 10 00.1		1879	Pueblo, Colo.
Grand Mesa (Nells 50)	5	61A		38 53 33.9	108 10 25.9		1876 1877	Do.
Grays	4	52D	Front	39 38 02.1	105 48 52.6	14,411	1876	Do.
Gunnison	5	61A	West Elk	38 48 43.1	107 22 46.1	12,242	1876 1877	Trinidad, Colo.

TABLE IV.—MOUNTAIN PEAKS—Continued.

Name of peak.	Class of station.	Atlas sheet.	Range or group.	Latitude.	Longitude.	Altitude.	Expeditionary year.	Astronomical initial point.
COLORADO—Continued.				° ′ ″	° ′ ″			
Handie	5	61C	San Juan	37 54 46.2	107 30 05.5	14,149	1875	Trinidad, Colo.
Harvard	5	61B	Sierra Madre	38 55 26.6	106 19 03.4	14,152	1873	Pueblo, Colo.
Holy Cross	5	52D	Park	39 28 00.0	106 28 43.3		1879	Do.
Hosefly	5	61A	Uncompahgre Plateau	38 11 42.5	107 55 38.6	10,504	1875	Trinidad, Colo.
Humboldt	4	61D	Sangre de Cristo	37 58 33.4	105 33 07.1	14,041	1876	Pueblo, Colo.
Hunts	4	61B	Sierra Madre	38 25 23.4	106 13 10.4	14,055	1874	Do.
Landsend	5	61A	West Elk	38 46 12.6	107 32 56.8	10,772	1877	Trinidad, Colo.
La Plata	4	61C	La Plata group	37 26 40.9	108 05 10.5	13,316	1875	Do.
Leon	4	52C	Grand Mesa	39 04 45.4	107 50 27.2	11,218	1877	Do.
Lincoln	4	52D	Park	39 21 04.4	106 06 30.1	14,456	1873	Pueblo, Colo.
Little Crestones	5	61D	Sangre de Cristo	37 58 42.4	105 36 28.2	13,190	1876	Trinidad, Colo.
Macomb	5	61C	San Juan	37 34 25.4	106 58 43.0	a13,154	1875	Do.
Mears	4	61C	San Miguel	38 01 50.1	107 54 23.4	13,009	1875	Do.
Meigs (Summit)	5	61D	San Juan	37 21 01.5	106 41 38.8	13,393	1875	Do.
Mosquito	7	52D	Park	39 18 19.0	106 10 55.0		1879	Pueblo, Colo.
Observatory Cone	5	61B		38 34 40.6	106 51 36.7		1876	Do.
Owens	5	61D	Sangre de Cristo	38 08 23.0	105 42 40.1	13,309	1875	Trinidad, Colo.
Pagosa	5	61C	San Juan	37 26 37.0	107 03 49.8	12,676	1875	Do.
Pikes	4	62A	Front	38 50 22.7	105 02 25.0	h14,147	1876	Pueblo, Colo.
Pisgah	5	62A	do	38 45 20.5	105 12 53.5	10,487	1876	Trinidad, Colo.
Pisgah, Little	5	62A	do	38 38 23.2	105 07 20.2	10,027	1876	Do.
Pole Creek	5	61C	San Juan	37 47 30.5	107 25 25.7	r13,804	1874	Do.
Pyramid (Topaz Butte)	5	62A	Front	38 59 45.1	105 17 11.3	9,750	1876	Do.
Quadrilateral	7	61B		38 48 46.4	105 31 04.2		1876	Pueblo, Colo.
Red Cloud	5	61C	San Juan	37 56 26.7	107 25 07.8	14,093	1875	Trinidad, Colo.

U. S. GEOGRAPHICAL SURVEYS. 25

TABLE IV.—MOUNTAIN PEAKS—Continued.

Name of peak.	Class of station.	Atlas sheet.	Range or group.	Latitude.	Longitude.	Altitude.	Expeditionary year.	Astronomical initial point.
COLORADO—Continued.				° ′ ″	° ′ ″			
Rito Alto	5	61B	Sangre de Cristo	38 13 08.5	105 45 12.1	13,561	1876	Pueblo, Colo.
Sheep	7	52D	Park	39 11 25.9	106 06 33.0		1879	Do.
Silesia	5	61D	Sangre de Cristo	38 09 48.4	105 39 47.8	13,599	1876	Do.
Silverheels	7	52D	Park	39 20 21.2	106 00 02.2		{1873, 1879}	Do.
Simpsons Pyramid	4	61C	San Juan	37 40 53.7	107 23 11.3	14,056	1874	Trinidad, Colo.
Snow Mass	7	52C		39 07 06.4	107 03 48.7		1876	Pueblo, Colo.
Spanish Peaks (Eastern)	4	62C	Sangre de Cristo	37 23 33.9	104 55 02.1	12,790	{1874, 1875}	Trinidad, Colo.
Spanish Peaks (Western)	4	62C	do	37 22 30.7	104 59 27.4	13,718	1874	Do.
Stewarts	4	61C	San Juan	38 01 22.2	106 55 17.7	14,032	1874	Do.
Sultan	5	61C	do	37 47 09.6	107 42 03.6	13,501	1875	Do.
Torrey	5	52D	Park	39 38 34.1	105 49 05.8	14,360	1879	Pueblo, Colo.
Trinchera	4	70A	Culebra	37 17 19.3	105 09 41.7	13,611	1875	Trinidad, Colo.
Trois Tetons	5	61D	Sangre de Cristo	37 58 05.1	105 34 45.8	14,198	1876	Pueblo, Colo.
Twin Cone	5	52D	Park	39 24 57.3	105 40 46.8		1876	Do.
Tyndall	5	62C	Wet Mountains	38 07 55.4	105 19 47.8	9,482	1876	Do.
Uncompahgre	4	61C	San Juan	38 04 23.7	105 27 21.1	14,408	1877	Trinidad, Colo.
Veta (Abeyta)	4	62C	Sangre de Cristo	37 34 56.4	105 08 39.2	11,654	1874	Do.
Washington Monument	7	61C	Florida Crags	37 37 56.6	107 38 36.0		1874	Do.
West Elk	4	61A	West Elk	38 43 03.7	107 11 47.3	13,102	{1876, 1877}	Pueblo, Colo.
West Point	7	60D	San Miguel	37 53 16.5	108 15 10.4	12,635	1875	Trinidad, Colo.
Wetterhorn	5	61C	San Juan	38 03 45.6	107 30 30.9	14,062	1874	Do.
IDAHO.								
Antelope	7	41A	Wahsatch	42 15 28.8	112 51 47.4	7,282	1877	Ogden, Utah.
Badger	5	32C		42 33 00.9	113 04 01.2	6,389	1877	Do.
Bannock	4	32C		42 36 08.8	112 42 43.0	8,359	1877	Do.

26 ASTRONOMIC AND GEODETIC POSITIONS—TABLE IV.

TABLE IV.—MOUNTAIN PEAKS—Continued.

Name of peak.	Class of station.	Atlas sheet.	Range or group.	Latitude.	Longitude.	Altitude.	Expeditionary year.	Astronomical initial point.
IDAHO—Continued.				° ′ ″	° ′ ″			
Big Butte	4	32A		43 23 42.2	113 01 38.0	7,659	1877	Ogden, Utah.
Black Pine (1)	4	41A		42 07 08.5	113 07 27.9	9,386	1877	Do.
Black Pine Cone	6	41A		42 04 56.2	113 03 57.5		1877	Do.
Bloomington	6	41B	Bear River	42 10 08.7	111 35 34.7		1877	Do.
Butte No. 3 (W)	7	32A		43 29 46.9	112 40 11.4	9,354	1877	Do.
Cache	4	41A	Raft River	42 11 04.1	113 39 54.8	10,451	1877	Do.
Castle Rock	5	41B	Bear River	42 12 09.0	111 33 08.0	9,611	1877	Do.
Cedar Creek	5	32C		42 26 46.1	111 03 34.6	7,586	1877	Do.
Deep Creek	4	32C		42 28 13.1	112 39 37.7	8,818	1877	Do.
Elkhorn (North Point)	4	32D		42 20 00.3	112 19 56.6		1877	Do.
Elkhorn (South Point)	4	41B		42 19 57.8	112 19 58.2		1877	Do.
Eyrie	6	41A	Wahsatch	42 17 38.2	112 57 43.5	9,458	1877	Do.
Meades	4	32D		42 29 41.4	111 15 10.7	a10,541	1877	Do.
Oxford	5	41B	Port Neuf	42 16 07.6	112 06 05.4	9,386	1877	Do.
Pillar Butte	4	32C		42 52 57.7	111 13 08.7	5,301	1877	Do.
Pisgah (Caribou)	4	32D		43 05 34.5	111 18 57.7	a9,695	1877	Do.
Putnam	4	32D	Port Neuf	42 57 08.0	112 10 09.8	8,905	1877	Do.
"S"	6	32C		42 28 58.6	113 34 09.3		1877	Do.
Sedgwick	5	32D	Port Neuf	42 30 54.0	111 55 39.9	9,207	1877	Do.
Sherman	5	32D	Bear River	42 27 52.2	111 33 11.2	9,572	1877	Do.
South Putnam	6	32D	Port Neuf	42 55 03.4	112 07 58.6		1877	Do.
NEVADA.								
Alida	7	57D		37 29 41.3	117 02 14.0		1875	Virginia, Nev.
American Flat	6	47D	Washoe Mountains	39 16 20.4	119 41 13.3	6,659	1877	Do.
B. (Kahler)	6	38B		41 53 30.7	119 50 44.3	7,172	1878	Do.
Badger Flat	6	48C		39 24 26.8	118 03 10.9	a7,038	1876	Do.
Hald Mountain	5	48D		39 00 16.8	117 33 20.5		1876	Do.
Bare	4	65B	Bare Mountains	36 51 35.0	116 42 23.0	6,039	1875	Los Angeles, Cal.

TABLE IV.—MOUNTAIN PEAKS—Continued.

Name of peak.	Class of station.	Atlas sheet.	Range or group.	Latitude.	Longitude.	Altitude.	Expeditionary year.	Astronomical initial point.
NEVADA—Continued.				° ′ ″	° ′ ″			
Basalt	4	57A		38 59 09.8	118 25 59.0	6,599	1876	Virginia, Nev.
Birchim	5	48D	Reese River	39 08 53.6	117 28 33.5	10,408	{1876 1877 1878}	Do.
Brown Knob	5	48C	Toyabe	39 03 47.2	118 42 19.3	6,202	1876	Do.
Bunker Hill	4	48D	Toyabe	39 15 02.9	117 07 18.2	11,404	1876	Do.
Butler	6	47D	Washoe Mountains	39 18 10.8	119 40 03.9	7,525	1877	Do.
C. (Kahler)	6	38B		41 56 29.0	119 50 52.1	7,239	1878	Do.
Carroll	5	57D		37 41 25.8	117 21 32.5			
Chalk Wells	5	48D	Spring Mountain	39 08 51.6	117 48 00.3	7,604	1876	Los Angeles, Cal.
Charleston	7	66C	Spring Mountain	36 15 46.7	115 41 48.2	10,874	1869	Virginia, Nev.
Churchill Butte	5	48C		39 20 16.3	119 17 32.2	6,009	1876	Do.
Cleaver	6	47D	Pine Nut or Como	39 12 58.7	119 07 48.9	16,682	1876	Do.
Como	5	47D	Pine Nut or Como	39 01 07.5	119 28 14.4	9,017	1876	Do.
Cone	5	48C		39 06 09.4	118 20 46.8			
Cory (Mount Grant of U. S. C. S.)	4	57A	Walker River	38 33 57.4	118 47 15.9	11,326	1876	Do.
Cowles	5	48D		39 03 14.4	117 33 24.9	9,980	1876	Do.
D. (Kahler)	6	38B		41 46 02.5	119 32 18.4		1878	Do.
Davidson	5	47D	Washoe Mountains	39 18 21.9	119 39 37.2	7,941	1876	Do.
Desatoya	4	48D	Desatoya	39 21 46.9	117 45 18.7	9,921	1876	Do.
Division	4	38D	Granite	41 05 46.1	119 15 31.5	8,585	1877	Do.
East McClellan	6	47D	Washoe Mountains	39 15 17.0	119 40 04.4	6,181	1877	Do.
Emigrant	5	48D		39 24 10.2	117 23 20.1		{1877 1878}	Do.
Emma	5	47D	Flowery Ridge of Washoe Mts	39 17 39.3	119 36 00.9	6,439	1876	Do.
F. (Nell)	7	57D	Monitor	37 37 34.7	116 45 14.8		1875	Do.
Fairview	4	48C	Toano	39 13 22.4	118 08 55.4	8,412	1876	Do.

TABLE IV.—MOUNTAIN PEAKS—Continued.

Name of peak.	Class of station.	Atlas sheet.	Range or group.	Latitude.	Longitude.	Altitude.	Expeditionary year.	Astronomical initial point.
				° ′ ″	° ′ ″			
NEVADA—Continued.								
Flowery	6	47D	Flowery Ridge	39 19 04.6	119 36 29.4	6,650	{1876, 1877}	Virginia, Nev.
"Forty-nine"	6	38B		41 33 28.7	119 55 21.8	7,498	1877	Do.
Frenchs	5	48D	Toyabe	39 00 34.7	117 15 36.4	10,779	1876	Do.
G. (Nell)	7	57D	Monitor	37 29 33.8	116 44 17.3		1875	Do.
Geneva	5	48D	Toyabe	39 21 27.0	117 04 14.9	10,708	{1876, 1878}	Do.
Genoa	4	47D	Lake Tahoe Group, Sierra Nevada	39 02 26.4	119 52 43.0	9,156	1876	Do.
Gold Mountain	4	65B		37 14 51.3	117 18 14.0		1875	Do.
Granite	4	38D		40 47 22.6	119 25 47.7	8,990	1877	Do.
Gant	4	48C		39 32 16.6	117 54 56.2	9,965	1876	Do.
Grapevine	4	65B	Grapevine Mountains	36 57 36.0	117 08 56.3	8,528	1875	Do.
I. (Nell)	7	58C	Monitor	37 30 25.0	116 19 13.5		1875	Do.
K. (Nell)	7	58C	do	37 33 41.0	116 04 21.0		1875	Los Angeles, Cal.
Kate	6	47D		39 16 03.6	119 36 57.0	6,141	1877	Virginia, Nev.
Kumiva	7	47B		40 24 16.1	119 15 35.4		1877	Do.
La Plata Hills	5	48C		39 27 50.2	118 20 02.8		1876	Do.
Lodi	6	57A		38 59 44.8	117 54 36.0	6,486	1876	Do.
Lone Butte	6	48C		39 29 14.0	118 44 57.2	a4,201	1876	Do.
Lone Mountain	7	57D		38 01 21.7	117 29 24.5		1875	Do.
Lyon	4	47D	Pine Nut or Como	39 07 33.2	119 28 12.4	8,794	1877	Do.
McClellan	4	47D	Washoe Mountains	39 15 26.1	119 41 46.2	7,532	1876	Do.
Mahogany	4	38D	Granite	41 01 26.4	119 33 17.9	8,363	1877	Do.
Marlette	4	47D	Lake Tahoe Group, Sierra Nevada	39 11 11.5	119 53 31.2	8,631	1876	Do.
Monument	5	56B		38 55 13.3	119 53 41.8		1876	Do.
Mount Airy Mesa (Boundary Mesa)	5	48D		39 31 12.0	117 22 20.7	a7,590	1876	Do.
New Pass	7	48D		39 38 44.5	117 28 45.8		1876	Do.
Oasis Valley Hill	5	65B		37 02 30.9	116 45 06.8		1876	Los Angeles, Cal.
North East Base		47D		39 25 43.0	119 25 39.0	7,100	1877	Virginia, Nev.
Pahrum	7	47B	Lake	40 23 19.9	119 34 19.4		1877	Do.

U. S. GEOGRAPHICAL SURVEYS 29

TABLE IV.—MOUNTAIN PEAKS—Continued.

Name of peak.	Class of station.	Atlas sheet.	Range or group.	Latitude.	Longitude.	Altitude.	Expeditionary year.	Astronomical initial point.
				° ′ ″	° ′ ″			
NEVADA—Continued.								
Painted Mesa	5	48C		39 06 39.8	118 49 03.4	6,027	1876	Virginia, Nev.
Paradise	4	57B		38 48 15.9	117 49 22.7	8,662	1876	Do.
Park (Bald)	5	57B		38 56 03.7	117 46 11.0	8,670	1876	Do.
Peavine	4	47D	Sierra Nevada	39 35 06.9	119 55 44.0	8,281	1876 1877 }	Do.
Pilot Knob	4	40D	Gosiute	41 01 12.2	114 04 51.5	10,758	1878	Ogden, Utah.
Piute, or Pah-Ute	4	39C		41 16 42.8	119 03 23.1	8,618	1877	Virginia, Nev.
Porters	6	48D		39 30 01.3	117 35 03.4		1876	Do.
Poston (Davies)	4	57B	Toyabe	38 49 48.4	117 20 56.0	11,978	1876 1877 1878 }	Do.
Prometheus	5	48D	Toyabe	39 29 38.9	117 02 26.4	8,144	1876 1878 }	Do.
Rawe (Monument)	5	47D	Pine Nut or Como	39 11 56.5	119 28 40.4	8,404	1876	Do.
Red	5	57A		38 58 22.0	118 08 03.6		1876	Do.
Rocky Point	4	47D	Flowery Ridge, Washoe Mountains	39 20 50.2	119 34 02.4		1876	Do.
Rose	6	47D		39 16 52.6	119 36 29.1	6,314	1877 1878 }	Do.
Rose (Mount Rose)	4	47D	Lake Tahoe Group, Sierra Nevada	39 20 30.3	119 54 54.1	10,820	1876	Do.
Rose Knob	6	47D	do	39 17 01.9	119 59 03.7	9,492	1876	Do.
Sandy Butte	6	48C		39 32 06.9	118 58 40.3		1876	Do.
Silver City	6	47D	Washoe Mountains	39 19 24.4	119 41 30.1	6,739	1877	Do.
Slate	5	48C	Fairview	39 06 25.1	118 12 08.8	7,115	1876	Do.
Snow Valley	7	47D	Tahoe	39 09 08.4	119 52 49.2		1876	Do.
Spanish	7	47D	Virginia	39 39 00.6	119 27 36.0	7,402	1876	Do.
State Line	5	47B	Sierra Nevada	40 01 43.9	119 58 32.4	8,405	1876	Do.
Tarogqua	4	48C	Pah-ute	39 34 51.7	118 13 54.2	8,772	1876	Do.

30 ASTRONOMIC AND GEODETIC POSITIONS—TABLE IV.

TABLE IV.—MOUNTAIN PEAKS—Continued.

Name of peak.	Class of station.	Atlas sheet.	Range or group.	Latitude.	Longitude.	Altitude.	Expeditionary year.	Astronomical initial point.
				° ′ ″	° ′ ″			
NEVADA—Continued.								
Tibbie	4	47D	Flowery Ridge, Washoe Mts	39 22 08.6	119 31 54.6	7,383	1876	Virginia, Nev.
Tolicha	4	65B		37 15 43.6	116 48 30.2	7,022	1875	Los Angeles, Cal.
Tohakum	4	47B	Virginia	40 10 40.2	119 27 07.6	8,174	1877	Virginia, Nev.
Tutib	4	48C	Natchez	39 42 52.8	119 09 46.6	7,062	1876	Do.
Twin Butte (1)	7	66A		37 05 34.7	116 12 39.0		1875	Los Angeles, Cal.
Twin Butte (2)	7	66A		37 05 09.5	116 13 01.2		1875	Do.
Wassuck Spur	5	48C		39 01 11.9	118 57 00.4		1876	Virginia, Nev.
Wells	5	66C	Kingston	35 50 35.0	116 07 10.7		1875	Los Angeles, Cal.
White Cliff	7	46D	Tahoe	39 12 03.1	119 54 45.0		1876	Virginia, Nev.
Yellow Mesa	7	38B		41 50 05.0	119 37 15.8		1877	Do.
NEW MEXICO.								
Alamocita	5	76D	Datil	34 11 58.6	108 27 56.2		1878	Ft. Bayard, N. M.
Animas	6	84C	Mimbres	32 58 21.6	107 31 18.1	6,106	1878	Do.
Baldy (Elizabethtown)	4	70A	Costilla	36 37 45.9	105 12 37.5	12,491	1874	Cimarron, N. M.
Baldy (Santa Fe)	4	69D	Santa Fe	35 49 51.5	105 45 26.4	12,661	1874	Santa Fe, N. M.
Bare Point, south of Cimarron	7	70C		36 28 35.0	105 09 18.9		1874	Ft. Bayard, N. M.
Bear	4	83D	Diablo	32 50 00.7	108 21 31.6	8,081	1878	Santa Fe, N. M.
Bernal Hill	4	78A		35 22 33.0	105 19 38.4	7,029	1875	Ft. Bayard, N. M.
Black	5	70C	Cimarron	36 26 55.7	105 04 40.2	10,900	1874	Cimarron, N. M.
Black	5	84C	Mimbres	32 54 26.0	108 04 46.9	8,910	1878	Ft. Bayard, N. M.
Black Island	4	90A		32 19 50.5	107 53 03.0		1878	Do.
Block Hill	4	84B	Chupadero Mesa	32 44 25.3	108 05 53.8	7,217	1877	Do.
Broken Back (Crater)	6	83D		33 49 49.1	106 04 22.3		1878	Do.
Burro	7	84C	Sierra de los Caballos	32 35 17.9	108 25 59.4		1878	Do.
Caballo Cone (1)	7	84C	do	32 57 42.8	107 14 13.2	7,751	1877	Do.
Caballo Cone (2)	7	84C		33 06 01.8	107 13 40.4	6,057	1878	Do.
Capilla	5	77D	Manzano	34 42 00.0	106 24 30.6		1876	Santa Fe, N. M.
Capitan	4	85A	Capitan	33 35 24.4	105 16 20.3	10,023	1877	Do.
Capullin	7	70B		36 46 55.5	103 57 50.4		1874	Cimarron, N. M.
Carrizo	7	84B	Carrizo	33 41 29.4	105 44 06.2		1877	Ft. Bayard, N. M.

TABLE IV.—MOUNTAIN PEAKS—Continued.

Name of peak.	Class of station.	Atlas sheet.	Range or group.	Latitude.	Longitude.	Altitude.	Expeditionary year.	Astronomical initial point.
NEW MEXICO—Continued.				° ′ ″	° ′ ″			
Cerro Colorado	4	84B		33 50 42.5	106 42 06.2	5,654	1877	Ft. Bayard, N. M.
Cerro Escobas	4	77B	Santa Fe	35 32 02.6	105 42 45.2	8,278	{1874, 1875}	Santa Fe, N. M.
Cerro Pelon	6	77B	Placer Mountains	35 20 07.0	105 59 40.0	6,939	1875	Do.
Cerro Potrillo	7	90A		31 55 23.8	107 03 47.0		1878	Ft. Bayard, N. M.
Cerro Roblado	7	84C		32 25 59.9	106 54 58.3	15,798	1878	Do.
Cerro Tecolote	4	77D		34 04 37.2	105 41 44.2	7,254	1877	Santa Fe, N. M.
Cone	5	77B		35 33 39.0	106 36 33.0	7,031	1873	Do.
Cooke	4	84C	Cooke	32 32 01.4	107 43 53.9	a8,330	1878	Ft. Bayard, N. M.
Costilla	4	70A	Cimarron	36 49 59.2	105 13 12.4	12,615	1875	Cimarron, N. M.
Crater	6	84B		33 49 49.1	106 04 22.3		1877	Ft. Bayard, N. M.
Crater (59)	5	77B		35 08 23.0	106 46 34.0		1874	Santa Fe, N. M.
Cuchillo Negro	7	84C	Mimbres	33 09 16.9	107 18 27.5		1878	Ft. Bayard, N. M.
Eagle	4	83B	Tulerosa	33 40 33.2	108 34 41.3	9,791	{1873, 1878}	Do.
East Carrizo	5	84B	Carrizo	33 38 59.6	105 37 17.5	7,976	1877	Do.
El Monte	5	84C	Mimbres	32 57 24.1	107 46 44.8		1878	Do.
Florida	7	90A	Florida	32 07 18.3	107 37 19.2	7,295	1878	Do.
Fra Cristobal	4	84A	Fra Cristobal	33 25 35.0	107 07 10.1	6,646	1877	Do.
Hacheta	4	89B	Sierra Hacheta	31 37 58.3	108 23 57.0	8,352	1878	Do.
Horse	5	84A		33 58 38.2	108 27 29.9	9,434	1878	Do.
Hurricane Rock	5	84C		32 37 28.2	107 42 47.3	6,479	1878	Do.
Jicarilla, cone east of	5	69D	Santa Fe	35 58 37.1	105 36 32.6		1874	Santa Fe, N. M.
Jemez	7	77B	Nacimiento	35 39 39.7	106 50 45.6	8,569	1874	Do.
Ladrones	7	77C	Ladrones	34 26 01.0	107 05 29.5	9,214	1876	Do.
La Lacha	5	89B	Las Animas	31 50 21.2	108 27 13.6	6,527	1878	Ft. Bayard, N. M.
Las Truchas	4	69D	Santa Fe	35 57 40.7	107 33 39.1	13,150	1874	Santa Fe, N. M.
Leitendorf	7	89R		35 14 08.9	108 43 11.2		1878	Ft. Bayard, N. M.
Loma Parda	4	70C		35 49 17.2	105 05 22.4		1874	Ft. Union, N. M.
Lone Mountain	4	84C		32 41 59.4	108 11 00.5	5,986	1878	Ft. Bayard, N. M.

TABLE IV.—MOUNTAIN PEAKS—Continued.

Name of peak.	Class of station.	Atlas sheet.	Range or group.	Latitude.	Longitude.	Altitude.	Expeditionary year.	Astronomical initial point.
NEW MEXICO—Continued.				° ′ ″	° ′ ″			
Luera Knoll	6	84A		33 51 05.6	107 51 48.8		1878	Ft. Bayard, N. M.
M. (Maxson)	5	70C		35 53 47.1	104 53 47.3		1875	Ft. Union, N. M.
Magdalena	4	84A	Turkey Mountains	33 59 23.2	107 11 39.1	10,798	1876	Ft. Bayard, N. M.
Manzano	4	77D	Magdalena	34 35 23.2	106 27 12.2	a10,086	1876	Santa Fe, N. M.
Mexican Boundary, hill near	6	90A	Manzano	31 47 10.7	107 57 56.6		1878	Ft. Bayard, N. M.
MF., in Mimbres Plains	7	83D		32 21 18.2	108 19 49.5		1878	Do.
Mogollon	7	83B	Mogollon	33 16 50.3	108 41 59.3	9,725	1873 1878 }	Do.
Monument	7	69D	Santa Fe	35 54 27.3	105 39 55.4		1875	Santa Fe, N. M.
Mora	7	70C	Mora	36 14 03.0	105 24 23.1	12,020	1874	Cimarron, N. M.
Mosca	4	77D	do	34 48 36.5	106 24 34.5	9,723	1876	Santa Fe, N. M.
Needles	7	68B		36 41 28.0	108 50 18.1		1874	Trinidad, Colo.
Nogal	4	84B	Sierra Blanca	33 29 47.5	105 48 36.2	9,983	1877	Santa Fe, N. M.
North Oscuro	4	84B	Oscuro	33 47 31.8	105 22 53.0		1877	Do.
Ocate Crater	4	70C		36 05 29.1	105 03 26.1	8,903	1874	Ft. Union, N. M.
Organ	7	84D	Organ	32 20 34.4	106 33 40.5	19,108	1878	Ft. Bayard, N. M.
Organ Cone	7	90B		32 19 45.4	106 32 42.0		1878	Do.
Oscuro (South Oscuro)	7	84B	Oscuro	33 37 49.0	106 22 48.4	8,732	1877	Santa Fe, N. M.
Osha	4	77D	Manzano	34 38 09.3	106 26 43.6	10,023	1876	Do.
Pedernal	4	77B		34 50 38.5	106 39 04.2	7,580	1876	Do.
Picacho	4	90A		32 19 48.8	106 52 55.5	4,824	1878	Ft. Bayard, N. M.
Placer	6	77B	Placer	35 20 03.4	106 10 36.0	8,965	1874	Santa Fe, N. M.
Point far South	7	84C		32 31 12.9	107 35 16.0		1877	Ft. Bayard, N. M.
Rattlesnake Hill	4	77D	Animas Hills	34 34 07.5	105 49 41.4	6,616	1876	Santa Fe, N. M.
Red Cone	4	76D		34 17 52.4	108 53 42.5		1878	Ft. Bayard, N. M.
Round Mountain	4	84A	Mimbres	33 40 28.7	108 06 06.7		1878	Do.
Rodadero	5	90B		31 47 10.3	106 32 31.7		1878	Do.
Salinas	4	84B	San Andreas	33 17 50.6	106 32 15.0	9,039	1877	Santa Fe, N. M.

U. S. GEOGRAPHICAL SURVEYS. 33

TABLE IV.—MOUNTAIN PEAKS—Continued.

Name of peak.	Class of station.	Atlas sheet.	Range or group.	Latitude.	Longitude.	Altitude.	Expeditionary year.	Astronomical initial point.
NEW MEXICO—Continued.				° ′ ″	° ′ ″			
Sandia	5	77B	Sandia	35 14 00.0	106 27 49.0	10,609	1873	Santa Fe, N. M.
San Mateo	4	84A	San Mateo	33 33 07.3	107 26 04.9	10,209	1876, 1877, 1878	Ft. Bayard, N. M.
Santa Clara	4	69D	Valles	36 00 25.8	106 22 54.0	11,507	1874, 1875	Santa Fe, N. M.
Sierra Blanca	4	84B	Sierra Blanca	33 22 24.3	105 48 54.9	11,892	1876, 1877	Do.
Solitario	4	70C	Las Vegas	35 44 27.7	105 24 49.8	10,258	1874	Ft. Union, N. M.
South Oscuro	7	84B	Oscuro	33 36 09.8	106 21 49.2	8,732	1877	Santa Fe, N. M.
South Sandia	(*)	77B	Sandia	35 07 09.0	106 26 15.0	8,567	1876	Do.
Sunday Cone	5	84C		32 37 08.5	107 26 54.0	6,030	1873, 1878	Ft. Bayard, N. M.
Taos	5	70A	Taos	36 33 32.0	105 24 46.0	13,098	1875	Cimarron, N. M.
Taos, cone east of	5	70A		36 32 41.1	105 24 08.4	13,052	1874	Do.
Taylor	4	77A	San Mateo	35 14 15.6	107 36 54.8	11,391	1873	Santa Fe, N. M.
Tetilla	5	77B		35 36 24.3	106 13 00.8	7,060	1873	Do.
Thompsons Cone	7	84C	Mimbres	32 49 33.9	105 45 20.6		1877	Ft. Bayard, N. M.
Tuerto	6	77B	Placer	35 14 58.0	106 11 43.0		1874	Santa Fe, N. M.
Ute	5	69B		36 56 13.0	105 40 52.1	10,152	1874, 1877	Do.
Urraca	4	70C	Jicarilla Mountains	36 24 23.2	105 03 45.5		1877	Cimarron, N. M.
West Jicarilla Cone	6	84B		33 51 05.5	105 41 27.0	7,727	1877	Santa Fe, N. M.
West Turkey Cone	6	77D	Turkey Mountains	34 14 49.2	105 48 21.6			
OREGON.								
Beatties Butte	7	29D		42 23 06.1	119 19 41.0		1877	Virginia, Nev.
Celilo Hill	4	11C	Klikatat	45 40 48.0	120 55 53.2		1878	The Dalles, Oreg.
Dalles Hill	4	20A	Cascade	45 35 14.9	121 07 08.3	1,210	1878	Do.
Hood	7	20A	do	45 22 24.3	121 42 49.6		1878	Do.

*Trigonometric connection.

1874 WH——3

34 ASTRONOMIC AND GEODETIC POSITIONS—TABLE IV.

TABLE IV.—MOUNTAIN PEAKS—Continued.

Name of peak.	Class of station.	Atlas sheet.	Range or group.	Latitude.	Longitude.	Altitude.	Expeditionary year.	Astronomical initial point.
				° ′ ″	° ′ ″			
OREGON—Continued.								
Jefferson	7	20C	Cascade	44 40 26.1	121 48 59.9		1878	The Dalles, Oreg.
Klikatat Hill	4	11C	Klikatat	45 41 47.5	121 11 16.6		1878	Do.
Little Hood	7	20A	Cascade	45 20 33.5	121 32 29.9	3,070	1878	Do.
Lolochewis	4	38B	Drews Valley Mountains	42 18 22.6	120 37 37.7	7,957	1878	Virginia, Nev.
Mutton	5	20A		45 00 46.4	121 06 15.6	5,792	1878	The Dalles, Oreg.
North End	5	38B	Warner	42 03 54.0	120 14 13.1	8,472	1877	Virginia, Nev.
Sugarloaf	4	38B	....do	42 17 57.6	120 07 12.4	8,416	1877	Do.
Tygh Hill	5	20A		45 17 56.6	121 06 20.6		1878	The Dalles, Oreg.
Warner	4	29D		42 27 32.6	119 44 13.1	5,730	1877	Virginia, Nev.
TEXAS.								
Franklin (2)	7	90B	Franklin	31 51 48.3	106 29 13.7		1878	Fort Bliss, Tex.
Franklin (3)	7	90B	....do	31 57 30.4	106 29 40.4		1878	Do.
Graveyard Hill	5	90B		31 45 52.0	106 29 40.7		1878	Do.
North Franklin	4	90B	Franklin	31 54 06.8	106 29 23.4	7,070	1878	Do.
South Franklin	4	90B	....do	31 48 14.6	106 28 46.3		1878	Do.
UTAH.								
A (Party 2, Great Salt Lake, Utah)	6	41A	Clear Creek	41 55 02.0	113 13 55.7	7,907	1877	Ogden, Utah.
Antelope Island	4	41D	(In Great Salt Lake)	40 57 40.4	112 13 12.1	6,660	1877	Do.
Barton	5	41D	Wahsatch	41 04 51.8	111 51 19.9	9,854	1877	Do.
Black Butte	7	41B		41 55 36.0	112 07 37.0		1877	Do.
Blue Springs (formerly North Promontory).	4	41A	Promontory	41 47 36.0	112 32 54.4	7,131	1877	Do.
Box Elder (Logan)	5	41B	Wahsatch	41 38 05.9	112 01 07.3	9,542	1877	Do.
Clear Creek	4	41A	Raft River	41 41 22.5	113 44 44.0	9,132	1877	Do.
Conner (formerly "T")	5	50B	Oquirrh	40 39 41.8	112 12 02.2	9,997	1877	Do.
Desert	4	40D	Desert	40 57 02.4	113 47 36.2	8,175	1878	Do.
E (Party 2, Utah)	6	41A	Clear Creek	41 49 56.7	113 33 20.0	7,211	1877	Do.
Grant	4	50		40 27 31.50	112 37 49.0		1878	Do.

U. S. GEOGRAPHICAL SURVEYS.   35

TABLE IV.—MOUNTAIN PEAKS—Continued.

Name of peak.	Class of station.	Atlas sheet.	Range or group.	Latitude.	Longitude.	Altitude.	Expeditionary year.	Astronomical initial point.
UTAH—Continued.				° ′ ″	° ′ ″			
Hansel	6	41A	Clear Creek	41 50 55.3	112 40 39.2	6,266	1877	Ogden, Utah.
K (Party 2, Utah)	6	41A	Bear River	41 53 46.4	113 40 59.2	8,354	1877	Do.
Kimballs	5	41B	Bear River	41 57 40.0	111 13 57.0	7,778	1877	Do.
Naomi	4	41B	Desert	41 54 38.9	111 40 46.3	9,951	1877	Do.
Newfoundland	4	41C	Wahsatch	41 11 06.7	113 22 19.2	7,046	1878	Do.
Observatory (formerly Ogden)	4	41D	do	41 11 56.8	111 53 09.6	9,589	1877	Do.
Ogden (formerly North Ogden)	4	41D	do	41 21 44.8	111 57 53.1	9,696	1877	Do.
Ogden No. 2 (formerly North Ogden No. 2; also Willard).	(*)	41D		41 23 01.0	111 58 42.0	4,276	1877	Do.
Porcupine	5	41D	do	41 01 07.0	111 07 06.8		1877	Do.
Promontory (formerly South Promontory; also Benada).	4	41C	Promontory	41 29 21.8	112 30 44.9	7,460	1877	Do.
South Promontory (formerly Promontory [A]).	7	41C	do	41 18 45.8	112 27 04.9	7,075	1877 1878	Do.
Stansbury Island	4	41C	(In Great Salt Lake)	40 50 45.8	112 30 10.7		1878	Do.
Tangent	4	41C		41 28 50.6	113 10 42.2		1877	Do.
West Twin (higher)	7	50B		40 35 44.4	111 43 41.8		1877	Do.
WASHINGTON.								
Adams	7	11C	Cascade	46 12 14.1	121 31 08.3		1878	The Dalles, Oreg.
Saint Helens	7	10D	do	46 11 52.3	122 12 37.0		1878	Do.
WYOMING.								
Burnt Hill	5	42C		41 15 25.8	110 59 18.5		1877	Ogden, Utah.
Medicine Butte	4	42C		41 21 04.1	110 55 02.3		1877	Do.
South Meridian Hill	5	42C		41 14 10.8	110 58 43.4		1877	Do.
MEXICO.								
Boca Grande	7	90A		31 37 48.6	107 59 38.9		1878	Fort Bliss, Tex.
Mexico	7	90B		31 43 13.4	106 34 53.3		1878	Do.
E (Mexico)	4	90B		31 40 11.1	106 30 56.3		1878	Do.

*Measured on a plot.

36 ASTRONOMIC AND GEODETIC POSITIONS—TABLE V.

TABLE V.—CITIES, TOWNS, SETTLEMENTS, SPRINGS, &c.

Name.	Class of station.	Atlas sheet.	Latitude.	Longitude.	Altitude.	Magnetic variation, E.	Expeditionary year.
CALIFORNIA.			° ′ ″	° ′ ″		° ′	
Armstrongs Ranch	6	56B	38 49 44.1	119 47 08.9	5,083	16 45 00	1876
Blackwood Creek, mouth of (Lake Tahoe)	6	47D	39 06 17.9	120 09 23.0	6,202		1877
Boundary monument between California and Nevada*	5	65B	36 56 12.3	117 06 03.8			1876
Boundary monument between California and Nevada, southeast shore of Lake Tahoe†	6	56B	38 57 21.5	119 56 56.2		15 51 00	1876
Boundary monument between California and Nevada, State-line point, north shore Lake Tahoe‡	6	47D	39 13 12.7	120 00 00.6		15 51 00	1876
Boundary monument between California and Nevada, south of Antelope Mountain	6	47D	39 39 54.1	119 59 49.9	5,133		1876
C-huenga Pass	6	73C	34 08 10.3	118 21 52.2	750		1875
Cerro Gordo Landing (Owens Lake)	6	65D	36 27 56.8	117 51 31.8	3,656	15 18 42	1875
Darwin City	6	65D	36 15 58.8	117 35 37.4	4,840		1875
Furnace Creek Station	5	65D	36 26 15.9	116 50 47.0	405	15 41 00	1875
Hot Springs (Lake Tahoe)	5	47D	39 13 31.4	120 00 39.1	6,237	§18 01 00	1876
Indian Wells	6	73A	35 39 57.5	117 52 40.7	2,608	15 12 31	1875
Land-Office monument, township 20 south, range 42 and 43 east	5	65D	36 11 53.5	117 22 11.9			1875
Lone Pine Camp	6	65A	36 36 18.3	118 03 54.9	3,810	15 20 00	1875
Los Angeles, rendezvous camp	6	73C	34 03 35.0	118 12 48.0	312	14 27 00	1876
Lusks (Lake Tahoe)	6	47D	39 02 11.6	120 07 13.6	6,212	15 37 00	1876
Merced Court-House, County seat (Central Pacific Railroad)	7	64B	37 18 11.8	120 28 55.5	171		1878
Observatory Point (Lake Tahoe)	6	47D	39 10 59.6	120 05 25.3			1875
Passmore Post-Office	5	65C	36 16 45.8	118 00 23.6		14 54 00	1878
Prattville	6	47A	40 12 44.7	121 08 52.0	4,394		1878
Rowlands (Lake Tahoe)	6	56B	38 56 28.4	119 59 13.1	6,222	15 51 00	1876
Rubicon Point (Lake Tahoe)	6	56B	38 59 47.2	120 05 38.0	6,202	15 37 00	1876
San Fernando Mission	7	73C	34 16 18.1	118 27 41.1	1,013		1875
Saratoga Springs	5	66C	35 40 57.2	116 26 14.1	264	15 05 00	1871

*Oregon, 414 miles + 75 chains. †Granite stone, Oregon, 191 miles + 0 chains.
†Granite stone, Oregon, 210 miles + 76 chains. §Probable local attraction—magnetite abounds here.

TABLE V.—CITIES, TOWNS, SETTLEMENTS, SPRINGS, &c.—Continued.

Name.	Class of station.	Atlas sheet.	Latitude.	Longitude.	Altitude.	Magnetic variation, E.	Expeditionary year.
CALIFORNIA—Continued.			° ′ ″	° ′ ″		° ′ ″	
Shakespeare Cliff	6	47D	39 04 41.4	119 56 07.7			1876
Sugar Pine Point (Lake Tahoe)	6	47D	39 03 30.6	120 06 39.7	6,202		1876
Susanville	6	47A	40 24 58.4	120 39 46.4	4,195	18 21 00	1877
Tahoe City	6	47D	39 10 10.1	120 08 17.7	6,252		1877
Wamelo Rock	7	56D	39 27 04.4	119 31 59.7			1878
Yanks Landing (Tallac post-office) (Lake Tahoe)	6	56B	38 56 20.3	120 02 59.9	6,202	15 51 00	1876
COLORADO.							
Colonas Ferry (Rio Grande)	6	69B	37 05 03.1	105 44 45.4	7,443	11 04 15†	1877
Colorado Springs (Coast Survey astronomical monument)	5	62A	38 50 01.0	104 49 04.8			1876
Conejos Ferry	6	61D	37 20 03.8	105 43 50.8	7,835		1877
Fair-play (center of town)	7	52D	39 13 18.6	105 59 55.5	10,026	14 26 00	1879
Gardners Post Office	5	62C	37 46 55.0	105 10 16.8	6,956		1874
Russia Mine	6	52D	39 20 54.5	106 05 58.6			1879
San Luis	5	70A	37 11 50.2	105 25 14.9	7,596		1874
Star Ranch	6	61D	37 51 21.1	105 51 05.1	7,327		1877
IDAHO.							
Danilsons Springs	6	32C	43 04 56.7	112 41 48.8	4,350		1877
Land Office stake	6	32C	42 58 42.2	112 31 15.4			1877
Rices Ferry (Snake River)	6	31D	42 31 34.7	113 50 20.0	4,192		1877
Ross Fork, near agents house	6	32C	43 01 30.0	112 26 03.5	4,545		1877
Shadow Lake	6	32C	42 43 01.2	113 05 05.8	4,310	16 04 00	1877
Snake River, camp on	6	32C	42 59 10.5	112 45 12.3			1877
NEVADA.							
Ash Meadows (Kings)	5	66C	36 23 41.3	116 16 27.3			1871
Carson City (dome of Capitol)	7	47D	39 09 42.4	119 45 47.6	*4,660	16 47 00	1876
Cave Rock, east shore Lake Tahoe	5	47D	39 02 39.0	119 56 43.6			1876

*Altitude of Friend's Observatory.   †Variation in 1874.

38   ASTRONOMIC AND GEODETIC POSITIONS—TABLE V.

TABLE V.—CITIES, TOWNS, SETTLEMENTS, SPRINGS, &c.—Continued.

Name.	Class of station.	Atlas sheet.	Latitude.	Longitude.	Altitude.	Magnetic variation, E.	Expeditionary year.
			° ′ ″	° ′ ″		° ′ ″	
NEVADA—Continued.							
Centre Station (American Flat)	6	47D	39 16 14.0	119 40 01.8	5,541	*16 30 00	1876
Coxs Station	6	48C	39 10 03.5	118 22 36.6	a4,379		1877
Dayton, near	6	47D	39 13 21.3	119 34 20.2	4,369		1876
Dead Horse Wells	5	57A	39 53 41.8	118 22 36.7	4,117	16 30 05	1878
Friday Creek, mouth of (Lake Tahoe)	6	56B	38 57 49.8	119 56 52.6	6,202		1876
Glenbrook Wharf (Lake Tahoe)	5	47D	39 05 09.5	119 56 19.4	6,202	15 59 00	1876
Land Office monument, northeast corner township 16 north, range 21 east	5	47D	39 17 17.5	119 33 25.1			1876
McMahons Ranch	6	57B	38 59 23.9	117 27 50.2	6,552	15 41 17	1876
Pah-rimp Spring	6	66C	36 11 51.8	116 00 00.7			1872
Pattersons Ranch	5	48D	39 30 56.1	117 44 57.8	5,213	16 27 24	1876
Reno	6	47D	39 31 51.5	119 48 48.3	4,484	17 25 00	1876
Sheridan	6	56B	38 53 56.0	119 49 12.8	a4,794		1876
Sutro Tunnel (entrance)	6	47D	39 16 40.2	119 34 50.8	64,482		1876
Washington Mine	6	48D	39 09 12.3	117 15 11.5			1876
Washoe Grade (Station 7)	6	47D	39 15 47.1	119 41 36.1	7,202		1877
NEW MEXICO.							
Albuquerque (flagstaff in plaza)†		77B	35 05 41.0	106 40 36.0	4,919	†13 45 00	1876
Antelope Spring	6	77D	34 49 59.0	106 04 26.0	6,291	13 26 00	1875
Apache Tejo	6	84C	32 37 49.7	108 07 34.6	5,478	12 42 00	1878
Crow Creek Stage Station	5	70A	36 41 46.5	104 36 14.1			1874
Estancia Ranch and Spring	7	77D	34 45 22.5	106 04 09.3	6,177	12 43 00	1876
Fort Bayard (flagstaff)	7	84C	32 47 42.6	108 09 01.8	6,068	12 56 00	1878
Galisteo (latitude and longitude for station, ¼ mile east of)	6	77B	35 24 06.0	105 56 08.0	6,117		1875
Gran Quivira Ruins	6	77D	34 15 38.8	106 05 55.7	6,407		1877
Hudson's Hot Springs (Mimbres)	6	84C	32 33 08.9	107 59 43.1	5,008	12 30 00	1878
Mexican boundary monument	5	90B	31 46 58.3	106 32 00.5	4,444		1878
Mexican boundary, near initial monument	5	90B	31 46 58.3	106 31 33.5			1878

*Variation in 1876.   †Trigonometric connection.   ‡Variation in 1873.

U. S. GEOGRAPHICAL SURVEYS.   39

TABLE V.—CITIES, TOWNS, SETTLEMENTS, SPRINGS, &c.—Continued.

Name.	Class of station.	Atlas sheet.	Latitude.	Longitude.	Altitude.	Magnetic variation, E.	Expeditionary year.
NEW MEXICO—Continued.			° ′ ″	° ′ ″		° ′ ″	
San Ignacio, near	6	77B	35 26 05.6	106 36 57.7			1874
Santo Domingo	6	77B	35 31 37.0	106 20 59.0	5,191		1877
OREGON.							
Dalles Brewery	6	20A	45 35 50.8	121 13 11.2			1878
Oak Grove	6	20A	45 09 01.7	121 09 04.2	2,414		1878
TEXAS.							
El Paso, Franklin (Astronomical Monument)	1	90B	31 45 31.1	106 29 05.4	3,630	12 25 15	1878
Fort Bliss, Old (flagstaff)	7	90B	31 46 31.4	106 26 41.0			1878
UTAH.							
Alma post-office, north of	6	41D	41 15 35.9	111 05 46.7			1878
Alma (school-house)	6	41D	41 14 55.1	112 04 54.0	4,262		1877
Bountiful (meeting-house)	6	41D	40 53 17.4	111 53 00.9			1877
Centreville (meeting-house)	6	41D	40 54 53.9	111 52 41.8	4,275		1877
Coles Farm (on mesa)	5	41D	41 09 57.6	112 01 09.2			1878
Corinne*	6	41B	41 32 54.8	112 07 06.7	4,233		1877
Farmington (court-house)	6	41D	40 58 49.7	111 53 21.6			1877
Farmington (railroad station)	6	41D	40 58 46.5	112 54 05.2			1877
Fowers Point, left shore of Weber River	6	41D	41 11 17.2	112 09 31.2			1873
Fremonts Point	6	41C	41 12 12.2	112 25 59.5			1877
Hale Point (Salt Lake Cape)	6	41D	41 08 30.1	112 10 37.4			1877
Hot Springs, 6 miles north of Salt Lake City	6	41D	40 48 54.0	111 55 22.4			1877
Hooperville (school-house)	6	41D	41 09 22.6	112 07 38.0	4,239		1878
Kaysville (Mormon synagogue)	6	41D	41 02 04.6	111 56 46.9			1877
Kelton	6	41A	41 44 47.4	113 06 33.8	4,226		1877

*Altitude C. P. R. R.

ASTRONOMIC AND GEODETIC POSITIONS—TABLE V.

TABLE V.—CITIES, TOWNS, SETTLEMENTS, SPRINGS, &c.—Continued.

Name.	Class of station.	Atlas sheet.	Latitude.	Longitude.	Altitude.	Magnetic variation, E.	Expeditionary year.
UTAH—Continued.			° ′ ″	° ′ ″		° ′ ″	
Kingston Fort (school-house)	6	41D	41 08 41.1	111 58 24.7			1877
Lakelet Promontory	6	41D	41 08 09.1	112 10 45.7			1878
Lakeside (farm-house)	6	41D	41 00 15.1	111 56 56.4			1877
Land Office stake (a), southwest corner southeast quarter, section 18, township 5 north, range 1 west, Salt Lake Meridian	5	41D	41 09 38.9	112 00 04.4			1877
Land Office stake (b), southwest corner section 18, township 5 north, range 1 west, Salt Lake Meridian	5	41D	41 09 39.2	112 00 38.8			1877
Land Office stake (c), northwest corner, township 5 north, range 1 west, Salt Lake Meridian	6	41D	41 11 35.6	112 00 37.4			1877
Little Mountain (Salt Lake Cape)	6	41D	41 14 54.4	112 15 34.7	4,264		1878
Lynn (school-house)	6	41D	40 15 30.4	111 59 02.9			1877
Miller Point (Salt Lake Cape)	6	41D	40 57 52.96	111 55 48.8			1878
North Ogden (meeting-house)*	6	41D	41 18 19.2	111 57 54.0	4,509		1877
Pilot Springs	6	41A	41 56 34.1	113 03 13.7	4,704		1877
Plain City (school-house)	6	41D	41 18 00.9	112 05 20.4	4,224		1878
Riverdale (school-house)	6	41A	41 10 56.3	112 00 32.0			1877
Skeens Ranch	6	41A	41 36 38.2	112 28 41.6			1877
Slaterville (school-house)	6	41D	41 15 48.0	112 02 12.2			1877
Ten-mile Station	6	41A	41 52 33.1	113 09 40.6	5,086		1878
Weber River, mouth of	6	41D	41 12 29.6	112 08 05.2	6,202		1877
WYOMING.							
Evanston (Richards Astronomical Monument)†	5	42C	41 15 59.9	110 58 43.4	16,757		1877
MEXICO.							
El Paso Church (cross on bell tower)	7	90B	31 44 14.8	106 28 59.2			1878

*Altitude at co-operative store.   †U. P. R. R.

U. S. GEOGRAPHICAL SURVEYS.

TABLE VI.—MILITARY POSTS.

No.	Name of post.	Atlas sheet.	Latitude.	Longitude.	Altitude.	Magnetic variation.	Expeditionary year.	Authority.	Remarks.
			° ′ ″	° ′ ″		° ′ ″			
1	Abraham Lincoln, Fort, Dakota.	18B	44 46 10.00	100 50 57.00	2,211		1874	Capt. Wm. Ludlow, Corps of Eng.; W. H. Wood, Assistant Eng.	Longitude by chronometer and sextant; latitude by sextant.
2	Apache, Fort, Arizona	83A	33 47 18.70	109 57 00.00†	5,001	14 10 42	1871	Wheeler	Do.
3	Baker, Camp, Montana	14B	46 40 44.00	111 11 00.00	4,538		1875	W.H.Wood,Ass't Eng., Yellowstone Expedition.	Do.
4	Bayard, Fort, New Mexico (Astronomical Monument).	84C	32 47 40.35	108 09 08.77	6,097	12 56 00	1878	Wheeler	Longitude by telegraph and transit; latitude by zenith telescope.
5	Benton, Fort, Montana	6C	47 49 38.00	110 39 48.00			1875	Lt. F. V. Greene, Corps of Eng.	Northern Boundary Commission Survey.
6	Bidwell,Fort,California (flagstaff)	38B	41 51 30.84	120 09 15.56	4,647	17 53 00	1877	Wheeler	Trigonometric connection with triangulation.
7	Bliss,Fort, Texas (Astronomical Monument).	90B	31 45 31.14	106 29 05.37	3,630	12 25 15	1878	Wheeler	Longitude by telegraph and transit; latitude by zenith telescope.
8	Bowie, Fort, Arizona	89B	32 10 16.20	(Not reduced.)	4,872	13 47 53	1873	Wheeler	Latitude by sextant.
9	Cameron, Fort, Utah (first building erected 1872).	59A	38 16 53.34	111 44 00.31	6,058	16 24 00	1873	Wheeler	Connection by triangulation with astronomical station at Beaver, Utah.
10	Cheyenne Depot,Wyoming.	44C	41 07 57.77	104 49 11.65	6,041		1872	Wheeler	Trigonometric connection with Cheyenne astronomical monument; altitude of astronomical monument.
11	Craig, Fort, New Mexico (flagstaff).	84A	33 38 00.99	107 01 07.96	4,448	12 59 09	1873	Wheeler	Trigonometric connection with triangulation.

ASTRONOMIC AND GEODETIC POSITIONS—TABLE VI.

TABLE VI.—MILITARY POSTS—Continued.

No.	Name of post.	Atlas sheet.	Latitude.	Longitude.	Altitude.	Magnetic variation.	Expeditionary year.	Authority.	Remarks.
			° ′ ″	° ′ ″		° ′ ″			
12	Douglas, Fort, Utah (Astronomical Monument).	41D	40 45 47.58	111 50 14.07	*4,905	17 01 00	1872	Wheeler	By traverse line to Coast Survey station at Salt Lake City.
13	Ellis, Fort, Montana (flagstaff).	15C	45 40 13.45	110 58 30.97	4,747	19 13 00	1877	Wheeler	Trigonometric connection with astronomical monument at Bozeman, Mont.; magnetic declination for Bozeman; altitude from Northern Boundary Survey.
14	Fetterman, Fort, Wyoming.	35C	42 50 26.26	105 29 11.92			1876	Capt. W. S. Stanton, Eng. Corps.	Longitude by telegraph and sextant, from Detroit, by Capt. H. M. Adams, Eng. Corps; latitude by sextant.
15	Fred Steele, Fort, Wyoming (flagstaff).	43A	41 46 50.63	106 56 54.27	16,850	16 27 10	1873	Wheeler	Trigonometric connection with astronomical monument.
16	Garland, Fort, Colorado (flagstaff).	62C	37 25 27.22	105 25 33.73	17,937	14 07 08	1873	Wheeler	Trigonometric connection.
17	Grant, Fort, Arizona.	83C	32 36 56.70	*112 11 40.00	4,833	13 49 00	1873	Wheeler	Latitude by sextant.
18	Hall, Fort, Idaho (flagstaff)	32D	43 08 54.80		4,752	18 13 00	1877	Wheeler	Do.
19	Hallock, Fort, Nevada (Astronomical Monument).	40C	40 48 34.35	115 19 34.05	5,790	16 21 24	1869	Wheeler	Longitude by telegraph and sextant; latitude by sextant.
20	Hancock, Camp, Dakota (flagstaff).	18B	46 58 17.90	100 47 14.42			1873	T. H. Safford	Trigonometric connection with Bismarck observing pier.
21	Independence, Camp, California.	65A	36 50 10.00	118 12 45.00	3,956	15 33 43	1871	Wheeler	Longitude by lunar culmination.
22	Klamath, Fort, Oregon.	29C	42 41 07.70		4,108	19 41 00	1878	Wheeler	Latitude by sextant.
23	Laramie, Fort, Wyoming (flagstaff).	44A	42 12 01.31	104 33 27.12	4,241	15 24 50	1877	Capt. W. S. Stanton, Eng. Corps.	Trigonometric connection at camp on Larmie River.

* Taken from plot.

TABLE VI.—MILITARY POSTS—Continued.

No.	Name of post.	Atlas sheet.	Latitude.	Longitude.	Altitude.	Magnetic variation.	Expeditionary year.	Authority.	Remarks.
			° ′ ″	° ′ ″		° ′ ″			
24	Lewis, Camp, Montana	15B	47 03 47.00	109 26 30.00	3,890		1875	W. H. Wood, Ass't Eng.	Longitude by chronometer and sextant; latitude by sextant.
25	McKinney, Fort, Wyoming.	34B	43 47 05.60	106 15 12.75	4,291		1877	Capt. W. S. Stanton, Eng. Corps.	Do.
26	Marcy, old Fort, New Mexico (Astronomical Monument).	69D	35 41 19.29	105 56 45.22	6,965	13 09 32	1874 1875 1877	Wheeler	Longitude by telegraph and transit; latitude by zenith telescope.
27	Mohave, Fort, Arizona.	74B	35 02 09.00	114 35 54.00	756	14 45 00	1875	Wheeler	By connection with iron monument of California boundary.
28	North Platte, Station, Nebraska.	45D	41 08 18.33	100 45 53.14	2,789		1874	Wheeler	Longitude by telegraph and transit; latitude by zenith telescope.
29	Robinson, Fort, Nebraska (Astronomical Monument).	35D	42 39 23.73	103 27 59.70			1877	Capt. W. S. Stanton, Eng. Corps.	Longitude by telegraph and sextant from Detroit, by Lieut. P. M. Price, Engineer Corps; latitude by sextant.
30	*Ruby Camp, Nevada (Astronomical Monument).	49A	40 03 38.63	115 31 06.75	6,153	17 09 04	1869	Wheeler	Longitude by telegraph and transit; latitude by sextant.
31	Russell, Fort D. A., Wyoming (flagstaff).	44C	41 08 38.83	104 50 24.47	6,041		1872	Wheeler	Trigonometric connection with Cheyenne; astronomical monument.
32	Sanders, Fort, Wyoming (flagstaff).	43D	41 17 26.89	105 34 59.56	17,168	15 30 00	1873	Wheeler	Connection by trasverse line with astronomical monument at Laramie City.
33	Shaw, Fort, Montana	5D	47 30 33.00	111 48 19.05			1875	Lt. F. V. Greene, Eng. Corps.	Northern Boundary Commission Survey.
34	Sheridan Camp, Nebraska.	36C	42 51 09.56	102 38 46.70			1876	Capt. W. S. Stanton, Eng. Corps.	Longitude by chronometer and sextant; latitude by sextant.
35	Sidney, Fort, Nebraska (Astronomical Monument).	44D	41 08 36.75	102 58 13.32	4,106		1874	Wheeler	Longitude by telegraph and transit; latitude by zenith telescope.

* Abandoned.

TABLE VI.—MILITARY POSTS—Continued.

No.	Name of post.	Atlas sheet.	Latitude.	Longitude.	Altitude.	Magnetic variation.	Expeditionary year.	Authority.	Remarks.
			° ′ ″	° ′ ″		° ′ ″			
36	Stanton, Fort, New Mexico (flagstaff).	84B	33 29 35.72	105 31 59.72	6,152	12 24 00	1878	Wheeler	Trigonometric connection.
37	Union, Fort, New Mexico (Astronomical Monument).	70C	35 54 24.86	105 00 51.15	6,744	14 40 00	1874	Wheeler	Longitude by telegraph and transit; latitude by zenith telescope.
38	Verde, Fort, Arizona	75D	34 34 20.19	111 53 00.00	3,160		1871	Wheeler	Latitude by sextant.
39	Whipple Barracks, Arizona (Astronomical Monument).	75C	34 33 06.12	112 27 10.20	5,318		1871	Wheeler	Longitude by lunar culminations; latitude by zenith telescope.
40	Wingate, Fort, New Mexico (flagstaff).	76B	35 28 49.47	108 32 20.00	7,038	14 51 27	{ 1873 1875	} Wheeler	Latitude by sextant.

NOTE.—Blanks in "Altitude" and "Variation" columns do not necessarily imply lack of field observations, the compilation not being complete.

PART II.

AZIMUTHS AND DISTANCES
BETWEEN
PRIMARY TRIANGULATION STATIONS.
1874–1878.

TABLE I.—LOS ANGELES BASE, CAL., 1875.
    II.—SUTRO BASE, NEVADA, 1876.
    III.—OGDEN BASE, UTAH, 1877-'78.
    IV.—SANTA FE BASE, N. M., SOUTHERN DEVELOPMENT, 1877-'78.
    V.—FORT BAYARD BASE, N. M., 1878.
    VI.—FORT BLISS (OR EL PASO) BASE, TEX., 1878.

U. S. GEOGRAPHICAL SURVEYS. 47.

NOTE.

In the following tables are given the azimuths and distances between the primary triangulation stations as computed and used in constructing the maps of this office.

Each primary station is given a separate place in the list with the azimuths and distances to every other station of the same class, with which connection was made and computed. Azimuths to prominent points of a lower order are occasionally given, in which case the class of the station is indicated by the number in brackets after its name, the back azimuths being given just beneath the direct, as there is no special list prepared showing the azimuths from such points.

Full data regarding the astronomical work of the survey, upon which, as initial points, the triangulation rests, has been given in Vol. II of the quarto series and in the various annual reports.

The primary triangulation was executed with theodolites of from eight to ten inches diameter of horizontal limb, reading by vernier to ten seconds. Except in the vicinity of the base lines, natural points were of necessity sighted, as the work was carried along rapidly in conjunction with, or but little in advance of, the topography. The highest points of the peaks to be occupied were, as a rule, sighted and marked after occupation by stone cairns six to ten feet in height. Where the peaks were bare and well-defined, as in the California Sierras and the mountain regions of Colorado, it was found possible to keep the error of closure to within ten or twenty seconds. The observations were adjusted and computed by the method of least squares and an outline of the routine pursued in the case of primary and secondary stations has been laid down in the annual report for 1878, p. 28. While it is evident from the above that these results cannot lay full claim to the critical accuracy of a more expensive and slowly-conducted scheme of triangulation, having in view a comparison between the theoretical and measured values of the earth's figure, for instance, yet experience has shown that map work for these thinly-settled regions of sufficient detail for all present needs can be safely based upon them, and the values obtained are of permanent value.

They will be found of great assistance and value to other surveys working in the same country, and will be sufficient, it is thought, to enable the work of this office to be connected with, intelligently, and used to the best advantage. The bases were, as a rule, measured with specially-constructed twenty-foot wooden rods with scales, vernier attachments, and reading apparatus and also Stackpole compensated steel tapes, which were always carefully compared with Coast Survey standard five-feet rods.

The following are the constant logarithms used in changes from meters to feet and miles and the reverse:

For reducing meters to miles............................ 6.7933338
For reducing meters to feet 0.5159677
For reducing feet to meters 9.4840323

It has been found impossible, from want of available funds and office force, to complete for publication the plots projected to show the extent and relations of the triangulation, a portion of the elements of which appear in the following pages.

These plots, as far as finished, have been turned over to the Engineer Department with all other manuscript maps.

M. M. M.

ENGINEER OFFICE,
U. S. GEOGRAPHICAL SURVEYS.

U. S. GEOGRAPHICAL SURVEYS.

TABLE I.—AZIMUTHS AND DISTANCES BETWEEN PRIMARY STATIONS IN SOUTHERN AND EASTERN CALIFORNIA AND SOUTHWESTERN NEVADA, DEPENDING UPON LOS ANGELES BASE, CAL., 1875.

NOTE.—The triangulation of Southern California is dependent upon a base measured on the plain south of Los Angeles and connected with the stations of the United States Coast Survey, known as West Beach, Cahuenga, and Dominguez Hill.

The geographical position of these points as determined from Coast Survey data were taken as correct, thus rendering a special astronomical determination at Los Angeles unnecessary. The following are the extreme points of the scheme of triangulation resting upon the base:

North-Tolicha Peak, latitude, 36° 51′ 35″.0.
South-Santiago Peak, latitude, 33° 42′ 31″.1.
West-Mount McGill, longitude, 119° 08′ 52″.6.
East-San Jacinto Peak, longitude, 116° 42′ 22″.3.

The scheme includes Fishermans Peak or Mount Whitney, the highest point of the Sierra Nevada, and the highest peak of the White Mountains was also observed upon and computed.

White Mountain Peak that had been connected with Sutro Base was occupied in 1878, and observations taken to more southerly points, but no final adjustment was made between the two schemes, as the office force was broken up before this could be done.

The position of White Mountain Peak as dependent upon the Sutro Base and as an occupied point is as follows: Latitude 37° 37′ 51″.4; longitude 118° 15′ 07″.9; as computed from the Los Angeles Base by intersections, its position is, latitude 37° 37′ 40″.7; longitude 118° 15′ 00″.6; a difference of 1.7 seconds in latitude, and 7.3 seconds in longitude. As the astronomical bases are entirely independent of each other and over five degrees of latitude apart, this is as close an agreement as can be expected. The primary stations, with the azimuths and distances therefrom, have been given from north to south, thus grouping together the more nearly related parts. An alphabetical list of the stations by name, with reference to pages, is also given.

M. M. M.

ENGINEER OFFICE,
U. S. GEOGRAPHICAL SURVEYS.

1874 WH——4

ALPHABETICAL LIST.
CALIFORNIA.

	Page.
Black Mountain	61
Cahuenga Peak	54
Cerro El Paso	58
Cerro Gordo Peak	59
Cooks Point	58
Domingnoz Hill	53
Fishermans Peak, or Mount Whitney	60
Fossil Butte	59
Grizzly Peak	56
Los Angeles (South West Base)	53
Los Angeles (North East Base)	53
Los Cerritos	53
Maturango Peak	59
McGill Mountain	56
Nichols Point	59
New York Butte	60
Olancha Peak	59
Owens Peak	57
Panamint Check Base (north)	60
Panamint Check Base (south)	60
Pilot Knob	58
Red Crater	61
Saddle, or Malaga Peak	55
San Antonio Peak	55
San Fernando Peak	56
San Gabriel Peak	54
San Jacinto Peak	56
San Pedro Hill	54
Santiago Peak (or Temescal)	56
Sister Else Peak	55
Sunday Peak	57
Tehachapai Peak	57
Telescope Peak	60
Volcano Peak	58
Waucoba Peak	61
Wauguybe Peak	62
Weldon Check Base (east)	58
Weldon Check Base (west)	58
West Beach	53
Workmans Hill	54

NEVADA.

Bare Mountain	62
Gold Mountain	62
Tolicha Peak	62

TABLE I.

LOS ANGELES (Southwest Base).

[Latitude, 33° 54′ 12″.86; longitude, 118° 21′ 59″.08; altitude, 108.]

To—	Azimuth.	Log. distances.
	° ′ ″	*Meters.*
West Beach	39 50 11.1	3.6110272
Northeast Base	239 16 43.7	3.8223335
Dominguez Hill	290 27 23.8	4.1068676
San Pedro Hill	350 47 41.9	4.2529128

LOS ANGELES (Northeast Base).

[Latitude, 33° 56′ 02″.95; longitude. 118° 18′ 16″.71; altitude, 247.]

San Pedro Hill	7 43 48.4	4.3274974
West Beach	51 55 57.5	4.0245182
Southwest Base	59 18 47.8	3.8223335
Dominguez Hill	321 27 13.0	4.0025572

WEST BEACH (U. S. Coast and Geodetic Survey Station).

[Latitude, 33° 52′ 31″.07; longitude, 118° 23′ 40″.88 (from U. S. Coast and Geodetic Survey)].

Cahuenga	191 26 13.7	4.4660014
Southwest Base	219 49 14.4	3.6110272
Northeast Base	231 52 56.7	4.0245182
Workmans Hill	245 59 23.3	4.5776404
Dominguez Hill	275 12 25.0	4.1661359
Los Cerritos	291 49 24.5	4.3631094
San Pedro Hill	339 19 46.7	4.1913068

DOMINGUEZ HILL.

[Latitude, 33° 51′ 47′′′.52; longitude, 118° 20′ 07″.80 (from U. S. Coast and Geodetic Survey)].

San Pedro Hill	34 42 28.3	4.2053510
West Beach	95 17 41.6	4.1661359
Southwest Base	110 31 43.8	4.1068676
Northeast Base	141 29 29.0	4.0025572
Cahuenga	163 44 00.5	4.4949348
Workmans Hill	230 06 57.0	4.4153284
Los Cerritos	316 49 33.4	3.9978914

LOS CERRITOS (East).

[Latitude, 33° 47′ 51″.9; longitude, 118° 09′ 48″.1; altitude, 357.]

San Pedro Hill	69 37 53.6	4.2307845
West Beach	111 57 08.2	4.3631094
Saddle	124 19 30.3	4.7397236
Dominguez	136 52 00.8	3.9978914
Cahuenga	157 22 16.6	4.6061902
San Gabriel	186 55 48.5	4.6948107
Workmans Hill	208 49 56.6	4.4364917
San Antonio	220 53 23.5	4.8552138
Santiago, highest point	279 27 04.6	4.7715564

Table I—Continued.

SAN PEDRO HILL.

[Latitude, 33° 44′ 39″.2; longitude, 118° 20′ 07″.8; altitude, 1,462.]

To—	Azimuth.	Log. distance.
	° ′ ″	Meters.
Saddle	141 20 41.1	4.6737178
West Beach	159 21 45.3	4.1913068
Southwest Base	170 48 43.9	4.2529128
Cahuenga	180 27 01.8	4.6354530
Northeast Base	187 40 46.5	4.3274974
Sister Else	188 44 18.0	4.7681027
San Gabriel	201 36 29.2	4.7729529
Dominguez Hill	214 39 10.8	4.2053510
Workmans Hill	224 11 40.0	4.6202236
Los Cerritos	249 32 09.1	4.2307845
Santiago, highest point	272 49 16.0	4.8712181

WORKMANS HILL.

[Latitude, 34° 00′ 48″.4; longitude, 118° 01′ 14″.5; altitude, 1,364.]

Los Cerritos	28 54 43.0	4.4364917
San Pedro	44 22 11.7	4.6202236
Dominguez Hill	50 14 11.5	4.4153284
West Beach (Los Angeles Base)	66 11 55.0	4.5776404
Saddle Peak	96 55 59.9	4.7704941
Cahuenga	114 59 56.7	4.5005119
Sister Else	144 27 12.3	4.5383469
Disappointment	161 26 19.2	4.4369002
San Gabriel	164 09 04.8	4.4188810
San Antonio	228 12 28.7	4.6560279
Santiago, highest point	306 47 07.0	4.7503340

CAHUENGA PEAK—CASTRO RANGE.

[Latitude, 34° 08′ 01″.3; longitude, 118° 19′ 54″.5 (from U. S. Coast and Geodetic Survey).]

San Pedro Hill	00 27 09.1	4.6354530
West Beach	11 28 20.2	4.4660014
Saddle Peak	77 57 59.5	4.4839695
San Gabriel Peak	240 58 48.4	4.3905619
Workmans Hill	294 49 29.2	4.5005119
Los Cerritos	337 16 37.9	4.6061902
Dominguez Hill	343 40 49.4	4.4949348

SAN GABRIEL PEAK—SAN GABRIEL RANGE.

[Latitude, 34° 14′ 27″.5; longitude, 118° 05′ 54″.5; altitude, 6,232.]

Los Cerritos	6 57 59.2	4.6948107
San Pedro	21 44 26.3	4.7729529
Cahuenga	61 06 40.4	4.3905619
Saddle	70 31 15.6	4.7360687
San Fernando	101 52 57.8	4.6740144
Sister Else	102 28 17.1	4.1215956
Ceca (?)	108 32 25.1	4.9758438
Back	287 59 19.8	

U. S GEOGRAPHICAL SURVEYS.   55

TABLE I—Continued.

SAN GABRIEL PEAK—Continued.

[Latitude, 34° 14' 27".5; longitude, 118° 05' 54".5; altitude, 6,232.]

To—	Azimuth.	Log. distance.
	° ′ ″	*Meters.*
McGill	123 37 42.2	5.0618521
Tehachapai	153 48 10.6	4.9947596
Owens	183 04 21.3	5.2199894
San Antonio	263 03 55.5	4.6152259
Grizzly	277 29 07.4	5.0656467
Santiago	{ 318 24 19.5 138 43 14.3 }	4.8962755
Workmans Hill	344 06 27.7	4.4188810

SADDLE OR MALAGA PEAK, CASTRO RANGE.

[Latitude, 34° 04' 33".5; longitude, 118° 39' 17".2; altitude, 2,897.]

Tehachapai	183 49 20.6	5.0297479
Ceca (7)	141 12 29.6	4.7896947
Back	320 58 16.9	
San Fernando	190 08 39.1	4.4525693
Sister Else	241 00 32.8	4.6414299
San Gabriel	250 12 31.2	4.7360687
San Antonio	255 36 38.1	4.9783097
Cahuenga	257 47 07.6	4.4839695
Workmans Hill	276 34 42.0	4.7704941
Los Cerritos	304 03 02.6	4.7397236
San Pedro Hill	321 09 59.9	4.6737178

SISTER ELSE, SAN GABRIEL MOUNTAINS.

[Latitude, 34° 16' 00".0; longitude, 118° 14' 19".6.]

San Pedro	8 47 32.7	4.7681027
Saddle	61 14 39.9	4.6414299
San Fernando	101 34 28.2	4.5311946
San Antonio	267 39 56.0	4.7315102
San Gabriel	282 23 32.8	4.1215956
Workmans Hill	324 19 51.7	4.5383469

SAN ANTONIO PEAK, SIERRA NEVADA.

[Latitude, 34° 17' 06".2; longitude, 117° 39' 14".1; altitude, 10,120.]

Los Cerritos	41 10 30.1	4.8552138
Workmans Hill	48 24 50.0	4.6560279
Saddle	76 10 22.3	4.9783097
San Gabriel	83 18 56.5	4.6152259
Sister Else	87 59 41.7	4.7315102
San Fernando	93 21 58.2	4.9407896
McGill	113 31 03.3	5.1733610
Tehachapai	134 57 17.3	5.0753663
Double (5)	137 22 10.0	5.0519202
Back	316 53 37.4	
Sunday	153 03 56.9	5.2706103
Owens	168 58 56.5	5.2145733
Pilot	197 22 48.0	5.1098432
Grizzly	285 23 26.7	4.8869002
San Jacinto	300 18 59.1	5.0070091

TABLE I—Continued.

SANTIAGO PEAK, HIGHEST POINT (Temescal No. 1).

[Latitude, 33° 42′ 31″.1; longitude, 117° 32′ 03″.9; altitude, 5,730.]

To—	Azimuth.	Log. distance.
	° ′ ″	Meters.
San Pedro Hill	93 15 57.1	4.8712181
Los Cerritos	99 48 02.6	4.7715564
Cahuenga	122 49 05.1	4.9420538
Workmans Hill	127 03 22.4	4.7503340
San Gabriel	138 43 14.3	4.8962755
San Antonio	170 14 18.0	4.8120841
Grizzly	235 52 46.2	4.8863012
San Jacinto	260 51 06.2	4.8946923

SAN JACINTO PEAK, SAN JACINTO MOUNTAINS.

[Latitude, 33° 49′ 07″.9; longitude, 116° 42′ 22″.3; altitude, 10,987.]

Santiago, highest point	81 59 44.8	4.8946923
San Antonio	120 50 49.5	5.0070091
Grizzly	157 00 55.1	4.5268116

GRIZZLY PEAK, SIERRA NEVADA.

[Latitude, 34° 05′ 52″.7; longitude, 116° 50′ 54″.7; altitude, 11,723.]

Santiago, highest point (Temescal No. 1)	56 56 54.5	4.8863012
San Gabriel	98 11 14.7	5.0656467
San Antonio	105 50 36.1	4.8869002
Pilot Knob	166 25 09.3	5.1695683
San Jacinto	336 56 08.1	4.5268116

SAN FERNANDO PEAK, SAN FERNANDO MOUNTAINS.

[Latitude, 34° 19′ 39″.3; longitude, 118° 36′ 01″.9; altitude, 3,793.]

Saddle	10 10 28.8	4.4525693
Tehachapai	181 35 15.2	4.8974777
San Antonio	272 49 58.0	4.9407896
Sister Else	281 22 14.4	4.5311946
San Gabriel	281 35 59.7	4.6740144

McGILL MOUNTAIN.

[Latitude, 34° 48′ 43″.9; longitude, 119° 08′ 52″.6; altitude, 9,214.]

Sunday	205 12 21.8	5.0749531
Tehachapai	244 04 40.6	4.7631384
San Antonio	292 40 13.1	5.1733610
San Gabriel	303 02 00.8	5.0618521
White Granite (5)	356 16 30.6	4.3528982
Back	176 17 03.4	

U. S. GEOGRAPHICAL SURVEYS. 57

TABLE I—Continued.

TEHACHAPAI PEAK, TEHACHAPAI MOUNTAINS.

[Latitude, 35° 02′ 21″.3; longitude, 118° 34′ 35″.6; altitude, 8,056.]

To—	Azimuth.	Log. distance
	° ′ ″	*Meters.*
San Fernando	1 46 03. 8	4. 8974777
Saddle	4 01 59. 8	5. 0297479
White Granite (5)	46 58 39. 1	4. 8430697
Back	226 39 37. 3	
McGill	64 24 18. 2	4. 7631384
Sunday	179 16 10. 6	4. 9148581
Olancha	196 49 50. 6	5. 1518033
Owens	213 59 39. 1	4. 9696561
Double (5)	277 39 05. 7	3. 8992686
Back	97 42 03. 7	
San Antonio	314 25 48. 2	5. 0753663
San Gabriel	333 31 52. 2	4. 9947596

SUNDAY PEAK, SIERRA NEVADA.

[Latitude, 35° 46′ 48″.5; longitude, 118° 35′ 17″.3; altitude, 8,335.]

McGill	25 31 46. 1	5. 0749531
Whitney	196 41 26. 6	4. 9647619
Corcoran (5)	200 46 25. 9	4. 9440956
Olancha	218 09 47. 1	4. 8334501
Owens	275 13 45. 4	4. 7276007
East Base (Weldon)	300 25 09. 7	4. 4390918
Nichols	304 50 45. 5	4. 5003026
Cooks Point	323 23 39. 7	4. 3469850
Pah-ute (5)	328 47 28. 1	4. 5941647
San Antonio	332 31 46. 1	5. 2706103
Tehachapai	359 15 46. 4	4. 9148581

OWENS PEAK, SIERRA NEVADA.

[Latitude, 35° 44′ 05″.4; longitude, 118° 00′ 00″.5.]

San Gabriel	3 21 24. 8	5. 2199894
Tehachapai Double (5)	29 47 58. 9	4. 9543086
Back	209 30 57. 0	
Tehachapai	34 19 40. 7	4. 9696561
Pah-ute (5)	49 09 28. 4	4. 6397404
Back	228 56 46. 1	
Nichols		4. 4807607
East Base (Weldon)	73 16 55. 9	4. 4891280
Cooks Point	72 20 07. 1	4. 6230883
Sunday	95 34 22. 3	4. 7276007
Olancha	169 36 50. 8	4. 7744337
Volcano	211 51 27. 9	4. 4536117
Maturango	226 54 06. 9	4. 7924412
Telescope	239 33 55. 2	4. 9771510
Argus (5)	255 42 36. 2	4. 7107030
Back	76 01 56. 5	
Pilot Knob	298 21 13. 2	4. 9000873
Cerro El Paso	334 27 47. 9	4. 5105597
San Antonio	348 47 01. 3	5. 2145733

Table I—Continued.

CERRO EL PASO PEAK.
[Latitude, 35° 28′ 16″.3; longitude, 117° 50′ 46″.5.]

To—	Azimuth.	Log. distance.
	° ′ ″	Meters.
Owens	154 33 10.5	4.5105597
Volcano	181 11 52.4	4.7274091

VOLCANO PEAK (Crater).
[Latitude, 35° 57′ 08″.2; longitude, 117° 50′ 01″.9; altitude, 5,434.]

Cerro El Paso	1 12 18.4	4.7274091
Owens	31 57 18.4	4.4536117
Olancha	143 17 21.9	4.6328137
Argus (5)	288 19 55.7	4.5637027
Back	108 33 28.0	

PILOT KNOB.
[Latitude, 35° 23′ 32″.1; longitude, 117° 13′ 49″.7; altitude, 5,525.]

San Antonio	17 37 18.9	5.1098432
Owens	118 48 04.8	4.9000873
Olancha	140 29 23.6	5.0988628
Maturango	163 20 57.0	4.9232490
Telescope	188 20 13.1	4.9375572
Grizzly	346 12 05.6	5.1695683

WEST BASE, WELDON.
[Latitude, 35° 39′ 14″.39; longitude, 118° 23′ 00″.53.]

Cooks Point	53 49 28.1	3.8157404
East Base	269 28 28.8	3.7135976

EAST BASE, WELDON.
[Latitude, 35° 39′ 15″.88; longitude, 118° 19′ 34″.93.]

Cooks Point	69 31 38.6	4.0476375
West Base	89 30 28.6	3.7135976
Sunday Peak	120 34 19.8	4.4390918
Owens Peak	253 05 30.7	4.4891280

COOKS POINT, SIERRA NEVADA.
[Latitude, 35° 37′ 09″.0; longitude, 118° 26′ 30″.4; altitude, 6,336.]

Sunday Peak	143 28 47.2	4.3469850
West Base (Weldon)	233 47 25.8	3.8157404
East Base (Weldon)	249 27 35.8	4.0476375
Camp near Weldon	249 30 05.3	4.1813911
Owens Peak	252 04 39.8	4.6230883
Nichols Point	271 08 20.4	4.1043342

TABLE I—Continued.

NICHOLS POINT (near Weldon), SIERRA NEVADA.

[Latitude, 35° 37′ 00″.5; longitude, 118° 18′ 05″.2; altitude, 6,233.]

To—	Azimuth.	Log. distance.
	° ′ ″	*Meters.*
Cooks Point	91 13 14.6	4.1043342
Sunday Peak	125 00 47.8	4.5003026
Camp near Weldon	195 14 49.7	3.7612589
Owens Peak	244 16 11.7	4.4807607

OLANCHA PEAK, SIERRA NEVADA.

[Latitude, 36° 15′ 43″.8; longitude, 118° 07′ 10″.2; altitude, 12,251.]

Pah-ute (5)	14 17 14.0	4.9535166
Back	194 08 38.4	
Tehachapai	17 05 49.6	5.1518033
Sunday	38 26 19.3	4.8334501
Thunder (5)	64 10 21.1	4.6615460
Back	243 54 07.0	
Fishermans Peak, or Mount Whitney	156 03 32.2	4.5808392
Corcoran (old Whitney)	159 23 15.6	4.4862551
Waucoba	186 49 52.6	4.9271953
Fossil	218 58 11.4	4.6389297
Cerro Gordo	224 33 13.9	4.6270863
Telescope	276 22 26.8	4.9690137
Maturango	286 00 48.6	4.7655330
Pilot Knob	319 58 10.1	5.0988628
Volcano	323 07 15.9	4.6328137
Owens	349 32 38.2	4.7744337

FOSSIL BUTTE, CERRO GORDO MOUNTAINS.

[Latitude, 36° 34′ 00″.8; longitude, 117° 48′ 48″.7.]

Olancha	39 09 05.3	4.6389297
Cerro Gordo	327 33 47.6	3.6380397

CERRO GORDO PEAK, CERRO GORDO MOUNTAINS.

[Latitude, 36° 32′ 01″.8; longitude, 117° 47′ 15″.0.]

Olancha	44 45 03.1	4.6270863
Fishermans Peak, or Mount Whitney	96 02 13.3	4.6572539
Fossil	147 34 43.4	3.6380397

MATURANGO PEAK, ARGUS MOUNTAINS.

[Latitude, 36° 06′ 56″.3; longitude, 117° 29′ 49″.9; altitude, 8,844.]

Owens	47 11 49.2	4.7924412
Olancha	106 22 51.4	4.7655330
North Base, Panamint Valley	250 55 13.1	4.3022202
Telescope	261 26 05.1	4.5678043
South Base, Panamint Valley	281 42 25.9	4.3207244
Pilot Knob	343 11 36.0	4.9232490

AZIMUTHS AND DISTANCES.

TABLE I—Continued.

NORTH BASE, PANAMINT VALLEY.

[Latitude, 36° 10′ 28″.32; longitude, 117° 17′ 11″.38; altitude, 1,684.]

To—	Azimuth.	Log. distance.
	° ′ ″	*Meters.*
Maturango	71 02 40.5	4.3022202
Telescope	273 32 17.2	4.2463077
South Base	352 00 48.0	4.0378738

SOUTH BASE, PANAMINT VALLEY.

[Latitude, 36° 04′ 37″.72; longitude, 117° 16′ 10″.79; altitude, 1,233.]

Maturango	101 50 28.5	4.3207244
North Base	172 01 23.7	4.0378738
Telescope	238 52 09.1	4.2739304

TELESCOPE PEAK, TELESCOPE RANGE.

[Latitude, 36° 09′ 52″.4; longitude, 117° 05′ 27″.2; altitude, 10,938.]

Pilot Knob	8 25 06.9	4.9375572
South Base, Panamint Valley (A)	58 58 28.5	4.2739304
Owens Peak	60 05 57.0	4.9771510
Maturango	81 40 27.7	4.5678043
North Base, Panamint Valley (B)	93 39 12.7	4.2463077
Olancha	96 58 54.6	4.9690137
Corcoran	111 17 39.6	5.0431416
Fishermans or Whitney	113 17 53.5	5.0683890
New York Butte	125 27 54.7	4.9655541
F (1875)	136 56 07.8	4.7633983
Waucoba	139 26 12.4	5.0978861
Wahguyhe	179 11 49.0	4.9315437
Tolicha	191 37 21.3	5.0947216
Base	203 56 39.7	4.9267081

NEW YORK BUTTE, INYO RANGE.

[Latitude, 36° 38′ 40″.8; longitude, 117° 55′ 56″.4; altitude, 10,675.]

Camp at Lone Pine (7)	69 45 38.9	4.1029282
Fishermans Peak, or Mount Whitney	76 45 28.9	4.5196726
Black Peak	116 03 21.8	4.6303932
Camp Independence (Flagstaff) (7)	129 07 24.7	4.5187043
Mount Hahn (7)	158 13 28.8	3.8513353
Back	338 12 25.4	
Telescope	304 57 56.9	4.9655541

FISHERMANS PEAK, OR MOUNT WHITNEY, SIERRA NEVADA.

[Latitude, 36° 34′ 33″.0; longitude, 118° 17′ 32″.0; altitude, 14,470.]

Sunday	16 51 55.5	4.9647619
Thunder Peak (5)	25 08 12.2	4.7823494
Back	204 58 02.8	

Table I—Continued.

FISHERMANS PEAK, OR MOUNT WHITNEY, SIERRA NEVADA—Continued.

[Latitude, 36° 34′ 33″.0; longitude, 118° 17′ 32″.0; altitude, 14,470.]

To—	Azimuth.	Log. distance.
	° ′ ″	*Meters.*
Black	166 38 32.3	4.4320388
Red Crater	179 31 53.2	4.7738870
White Mountain (approximate)	181 49 02.5	5.0685304
Camp Independence (Flagstaff) (5)	192 51 20.9	4.4648889
Back	12 53 57.4	
Waucoba	207 19 58.1	
Wahguyhe	249 05 12.6	5.0541378
New York Butte	256 32 36.2	4.5196726
Camp at Lone Pine (7)	260 50 56.2	4.3131535
Back	80 59 03.3	
Cerro Gordo	275 44 11.2	4.6572539
Telescope	292 35 08.8	5.0683890
Corcoran (5)	322 37 26.5	3.8873044
Olancha	335 57 23.1	4.5808392

BLACK MOUNTAIN, SIERRA NEVADA.

[Latitude, 36° 48′ 46″.5; longitude, 118° 21′ 44″.1.]

Waucoba	234 06 32.6	4.5919296
Inyo (7)	285 10 33.5	4.5430141
Back	105 24 06.5	
New York Butte	295 47 56.2	4.6303932
Fishermans Peak, or Mount Whitney	346 36 01.6	4.4320388

RED CRATER, SIERRA NEVADA.

[Latitude, 37° 06′ 40″.4; longitude, 118° 17′ 51″.7.]

Waucoba	291 40 41.4	4.4448896
Fishermans Peak, or Mount Whitney	359 31 41.5	4.7738870

WAUCOBA PEAK, INYO RANGE.

[Latitude, 37° 01′ 07″.8; longitude, 118° 00′ 23″.2; altitude, 11,267.]

Olancha	6 53 55.5	4.9271953
Fishermans (or Whitney)	27 30 14.3	
Tyndall (7)	36 06 21.9	4.6994774
Back	215 54 29.7	
Black	54 19 21.9	4.5919296
Red Crater	111 41 13.2	4.4448896
Wahguyhe	276 23 11.9	
Telescope	318 53 27.5	5.0978861
Inyo (7)	356 34 21.0	4.5066948
Back	176 35 07.4	

Table I—Continued.

WAHGUYHE PEAK.

[Latitude, 36° 36' 03''.5; longitude, 117° 06' 15''.6; altitude, 8,528.]

To—	Azimuth.	Log. distance.
	° ′ ″	Meters.
Fishermans Peak, or Mount Whitney	69 47 51.7	5.0541378
Gold Mountain	153 01 26.2	4.5913683
Tolicha	215 46 53.4	4.6521505
Base	283 00 55.0	4.5612862
Telescope	359 11 20.2	4.9315437

GOLD MOUNTAIN.

[Latitude, 37° 14' 51''.3; longitude, 117° 18' 14''.0.]

Tolicha	87 44 49.0	4.6432627
Wahguyhe	152 54 12.9	4.5913683

TOLICHA PEAK.

[Latitude, 37° 15' 43''.6; longitude, 116° 48' 30''.2; altitude, 7,022.]

Telescope	11 47 29.3	5.0947216
Wahguyhe	35 57 35.9	4.6521505
Gold	88 02 48.8	4.6432627
Base	348 29 12.2	4.6586164

BARE PEAK, BARE MOUNTAINS.

[Latitude, 36° 51' 35''.0; longitude, 116° 42' 23''.0; altitude, 6,039.]

Telescope	24 10 23.3	4.9267081
Wahguyhe	103 15 15.0	4.5612862
Tolicha	168 32 53.5	4.6586164

TABLE II.—AZIMUTHS AND DISTANCES BETWEEN PRIMARY STA-
TIONS IN NEVADA, CALIFORNIA, AND OREGON, DEPENDING UPON
THE SUTRO BASE, NEVADA, 1876.

NOTE.—The greater part of the triangulation executed in Western and Southwestern Nevada, Eastern and Northeastern California, and Southern Oregon is dependent upon a base measured and permanently marked along the comparatively level space between the town of Sutro, Nev., and the Carson River, and connected with the main astronomical monument on divide between Virginia City and Gold Hill, the mining centers of the Comstock region, the geographical co-ordinates of the latter having been determined in 1873. The extreme points of the scheme of triangulation resting on this base, as found reduced on the original triangulation plats, are: North—Warner Peak, Warner Range, latitude 42° 27′ 32″.6. South—Green Peak, Sierra Nevada, latitude 37° 15′ 43″.6. West—Lassens Butte, longitude 121° 30′ 09″.7. East—Bunker Hill, Toyabe Range, longitude 117° 07′ 17″.8. White Mountain Peak at the south is a point of connection with the net of triangulation extended from the Los Angeles base. The adopted length of the Sutro base, reduced to sea level, which was measured by a specially constructed twenty-foot rod, described on page 1219 of A. R. of 1877, is 23,416.387 feet, or approximates 4.435 miles. (See page 1223 A. R. 1877.)

G. M. W.

ENGINEER OFFICE
U. S. GEOGRAPHICAL SURVEYS.

ALPHABETICAL LIST.

	Page
(a) Base development, 1876	67–69
(b) Eastern development, 1876	69–72
(c) Northern development, 1876, '77, '78	72–77
(d) Southern development, 1877, '78, '79	77–83

(a) Base development:

Astronomical Monument	68
Davidson Peak	68
Emma Peak	67
McClellan Peak	67
Northeast Base Peak	69
Rawe Peak	67
Rocky Point	68
Sutro Base, east	67
Sutro Base, west	67
Tibbie Peak	69

(b) Eastern development:

Basalt Peak	70
Bunker Hill	71
Desatoya Peak	71
Fairview Peak	70
Grant Peak	70
Lyon Peak	69
Paradise Peak	71
Poston Peak	72
Tarogqna Peak	70
Tutib Peak	69

(c) Northern development:

Cedar Peak	76
Division Peak	75
Downieville Butte	72
Fredonyer Peak	73
Granite Peak	74
Hot Springs Peak	74
Ingalls Peak	73
Lassens Butte	74
Lolochowis Peak	77
Mahogany Peak	75
Observation Peak	74
Pinte, or Pah-nto Peak	76
Rose Peak	72
South Fork Peak	75
Sugarloaf Peak	76
Thompsons Peak	73
Tohakum Peak	73
Warner Peak	77
Warren Peak	76

(d) Southern development:

Alpine Peak	78
Castle Peak	77

1874 WH——5

(d) Southern development—Continued.

	Page.
Chiquito Peak	81
Clarks Peak	81
Conness Peak	80
Cory Peak	79
Dana Peak	80
Deadwood Peak	82
Devils Peak	82
Freels Peak	77
Green Mountain	83
Highland Peak	79
Hoffman Peak	82
Lyell Peak	81
McBride Peak	80
Mokelumne Peak	78
Morgan Peak	81
Oreana, or Silver Lake Peak	78
Pyramid Peak	77
Schultz Peak	83
Sonora Peak	79
Sweetwater Peak	79
White Mountain Peak	80

U. S. GEOGRAPHICAL SURVEYS. 67

TABLE II—Continued.

WEST BASE (SUTRO).

[Latitude, 39° 16' 24".86; longitude, 119° 34' 05".82.]

To—	Azimuth.	Log. distance.
	° ′ ″	*Meters.*
Emma	129 48 24.0	3.5548694
Rocky Point	180 34 30.7	3.9128355
Northeast Base Peak	266 05 58.1	4.3238320
East Base	232 30 42.0	3.8535524

EAST BASE (SUTRO).

[Latitude, 39° 18' 45".67; longitude, 119° 30' 09".38.]

West Base	52 33 11.7	3.8535524
Emma	76 22 42.6	3.9377776
Davidson	86 57 57.8	4.1342159
Rocky Point	124 32 58.3	3.8307947
Northeast Base	206 37 37.5	4.1591635
Rawe	350 23 43.0	4.1070376

RAWE PEAK, PINE NUT OR COMO RANGE (monument north end).

[Latitude, 39° 11' 56".5; longitude, 119° 28' 40".4; altitude, 8,404.]

McClellan	108 59 52.1	4.2993752
Davidson	127 05 56.5	4.2950499
Emma	135 03 57.3	4.1744083
Rocky Point	154 54 09.2	4.2594699
East Base	170 24 39.1	4.1070376
Northeast Base Peak	189 39 01.0	4.4129152

McCLELLAN PEAK, WASHOE MOUNTAINS.

[Latitude, 39° 15' 26".1; longitude, 119° 41' 46".2; altitude, 7,532.]

Genoa Peak (5)	33 18 52.8	4.4587050
Back	213 11 58.1	
Rose	116 29 30.6	4.3237979
Davidson	209 42 03.2	3.7952069
Astronomical Monument	223 44 38.2	3.7435791
Rocky Point	227 59 57.1	4.1744739
Tibbie	228 44 33.4	4.2750254
Northeast Base Peak	230 28 48.3	4.4769044
Emma	243 34 42.6	3.9657010
Rawe (north end)	288 51 35.1	4.2993752
Lyon	306 40 48.9	4.3869209

EMMA PEAK, WASHOE MOUNTAINS.

[Latitude, 39° 17' 39".3; longitude, 119° 36' 00".9; altitude, 6,439.]

McClellan	63 38 21.2	3.9657010
Astronomical Monument	88 39 26.9	3.6479254
Davidson	104 13 48.7	3.7280397

Table II—Continued.

EMMA PEAK, WASHOE MOUNTAINS—Continued.

[Latitude, 39° 17′ 39″.3; longitude, 119° 36′ 00″.9; altitude, 6,439.]

To—	Azimuth.	Log. distance.
	° ′ ″	Meters.
Rocky Point	205 43 59.3	3.8151044
Tibbie	215 22 06.9	4.0079058
Northeast Base Peak	224 50 31.1	4.3240573
East Base	256 19 00.0	3.9377776
West Base	309 47 11.2	3.5548694
Rawe (north end)	314 59 18.7	4.1744083

DAVIDSON PEAK, WASHOE MOUNTAINS.

[Latitude, 39° 18′ 21″.9; longitude, 119° 39′ 37″.2; altitude, 7,941.]

McClellan	29 43 24.9	3.7952069
Genoa (5)	32 41 35.4	4.5438765
Rose	100 18 01.3	4.3485643
Northeast Base Peak	235 44 25.2	4.3847454
Tibbie	237 42 27.5	4.1172029
Rocky	240 16 38.9	3.9651926
East Base	266 51 58.6	4.1342159
Emma	284 11 31.7	3.7280397
Rawe (north end)	306 59 00.9	4.2950499
Lyon	320 32 53.4	4.4130312
Astronomical Monument	332 28 48.8	3.2037768
Como (5)	332 44 36.0	4.5546140

ASTRONOMICAL MONUMENT, ON DIVIDE BETWEEN GOLD HILL AND VIRGINIA CITY.

[Latitude, 39° 17′ 35″.92; longitude, 119° 39′ 06″.35; altitude, 6,339.]

McClellan	43 46 19.4	3.7435791
Davidson	152 29 08.3	3.2037768
Rocky Point	230 31 36.3	3.9744011
Emma	268 37 29.4	3.6479254

ROCKY POINT, FLOWERY RIDGE, WASHOE MOUNTAINS.

[Latitude, 39° 20′ 50″.2; longitude, 119° 34′ 02″.4.]

West Base	00 34 31.8	3.9128355
Emma	25 45 14.3	3.8151044
McClellan	48 04 50.9	4.1744739
Astronomical Monument	50 34 48.9	3.9744011
Davidson	60 20 11.0	3.9651926
Tibbie	231 40 28.1	3.5909991
Northeast Base Peak	233 01 19.3	4.1780752
East Base	304 30 30.7	3.8307947
Rawe	334 50 45.3	4.2594699

U. S. GEOGRAPHICAL SURVEYS.

TABLE II—Continued.

TIBBIE PEAK, FLOWERY RIDGE, WASHOE MOUNTAINS.

[Latitude, 39° 22′ 08″.6; longitude, 119° 31′ 54″.6; altitude, 7,383.]

To—	Azimuth.	Log. distance.
	° ′ ″	*Meters.*
Emma	35 24 43.0	4.0079058
McClellan	48 50 48.3	4.2750254
Davidson	57 47 20.7	4.1172029
Rocky Point	63 52 52.2	3.5909991

NORTHEAST BASE PEAK.

[Latitude, 39° 25′ 43″.0; longitude, 119° 25′ 39″.0; altitude, 7,100.]

Lyon	6 15 00.7	4.5293107
Rawe (Monument, north end)	9 40 56.9	4.4129152
East Base	26 40 30.1	4.1591635
West Base	35 11 20.6	4.3238320
Emma	44 57 06.5	4.3240573
McClellan	50 39 01.4	4.4769044
Rocky Point	53 06 38.8	4.1780752
Davidson	55 53 16.9	4.3847454

LYON PEAK, PINE NUT (COMO) RANGE.

[Latitude, 39° 07′ 33″.2; longitude, 119° 28′ 12″.4; altitude, 8,794.]

Oreana or Silver Lake	1 00 37.4	4.4659001
Highland	20 47 52.0	4.8412370
Alpine	41 46 58.6	4.8387763
Freels	51 03 56.9	4.6782465
Pyramid	62 18 46.2	4.8271064
Rose	122 05 57.7	4.6558253
McClellan	126 49 23.1	4.3869209
Davidson	140 40 06.3	4.4130312
Northeast Base Peak	186 13 23.6	4.5293107
Tutib	201 55 56.0	4.8482444
Churchill Butte (5)	213 03 45.3	4.4486607
Back	33 10 30.2	
Tarogqua	244 16 32.0	5.0721815
Basalt	279 29 03.6	4.9594458
Cory	316 09 53.8	4.9337768

TUTIB PEAK, NATCHEZ MOUNTAINS.

[Latitude, 39° 41′ 52″.8; longitude, 119° 09′ 46″.6; altitude, 7,062.]

Churchill Butte	14 55 41.5	4.6363033
Lyon	22 07 38.2	4.8482444
Rose	57 36 29.9	4.8852059
Hot Springs	132 11 52.3	5.0396227
Tohakum	154 25 43.9	4.7562493
Tarogqua	280 13 11.5	4.9099982
Basalt	321 53 39.5	5.0105726

Table II—Continued.

BASALT PEAK.

[Latitude, 38° 59′ 09″.8; longitude, 118° 25′ 59″.0; altitude, 6,299.]

To—	Azimuth.	Log. distance.
	° ′ ″	Meters.
Cory	33 33 44.9	4.7473460
Lyon	100 08 15.8	4.9594458
Rose	107 36 08.3	5.1271390
Tutib	142 21 25.6	5.0105726
Tarogqua	194 40 16.0	4.8343683
Grant	215 55 31.1	4.8797241
Fairview	223 00 07.6	4.5562792
Desatoya	234 14 31.5	4.8572342
Bunker Hill	255 03 54.1	5.0687273
Poston (or Davies)	280 04 42.5	4.9804536
Paradise	290 39 53.0	4.7530595
McBride	356 51 24.3	5.1068251

TAROGQUA PEAK, PAH-UTE MOUNTAINS.

[Latitude, 39° 34′ 51″.7; longitude, 118° 13′ 54″.2; altitude, 8,772.]

Basalt	14 47 54.9	4.8343683
Lyon	65 03 38.9	5.0721815
Rose	80 08 39.7	5.1680897
Tutib	100 48 50.5	4.9099982
Grant	279 53 10.5	4.4406293
Bunker Hill	290 38 07.8	5.0102199
Desatoya	300 23 54.3	4.6776914
Poston (Davies)	317 15 56.8	5.0528758
Paradise	337 35 54.9	4.9692214
Fairview	349 46 49.7	4.6063330

FAIRVIEW PEAK, TOANO RANGE.

[Latitude, 39° 13′ 22″.4; longitude, 118° 08′ 55″.4; altitude, 8,412.]

Basalt	43 10 53.3	4.5562792
Tarogqua	169 49 59.4	4.6063330
Grant	209 47 29.4	4.6056317
Bunker Hill	267 40 53.6	4.9480266
Birchim (5)	277 54 30.4	4.7687535
Back	98 20 00.8	---
Paradise	328 37 39.6	4.7351603

GRANT PEAK.

[Latitude, 39° 32′ 16″.6; longitude, 117° 54′ 56″.2; altitude, 9,965.]

Fairview	29 56 21.8	4.6056317
Basalt	36 15 10.0	4.8797241
Tarogqua	100 05 15.3	4.4406293
Emigrant (5)	288 16 25.3	4.6783302
Back	108 36 28.3	---
Bunker Hill	294 44 44.5	4.8777077
Old Woman (5)	302 23 09.0	4.7483433
Back	122 44 01.7	---
D esatoya	324 31 58.9	4.3770196
Paradise	354 21 25.8	4.9128455

TABLE II—Continued.

PARADISE PEAK.

[Latitude, 38° 48' 15".9; longitude, 117° 49' 22".7; altitude, 8,662.]

To—	Azimuth.	Log. distance.
	° ′ ″	Meters.
Basalt	111 02 52.1	4.7530595
Fairview	148 49 57.7	4.7351603
Tarogqua	157 51 24.8	4.9692214
Grant	174 24 56.5	4.9128455
Birchim (5)	218 08 11.9	4.6864930
Back	38 21 17.8	
Cowles (5)	219 41 58.5	4.5569143
Back	39 52 00.3	
Bunker Hill	230 34 27.7	4.8941430

DESATOYA PEAK, DESATOYA RANGE.

[Latitude, 39° 21' 46".9; longitude, 117° 45' 18".7; altitude, 9,921.]

Basalt	54 40 13.0	4.8572342
Tarogqua	120 42 04.9	4.6776914
Grant	144 38 05.9	4.3770196
Prometheus (5)	256 31 35.0	4.8007880
Back	76 58 49.1	
Geneva (5)	270 23 22.4	4.7707700
Back	90 49 25.2	
Bunker Hill	282 39 24.9	4.7485431
Old Woman (5)	287 40 17.2	4.5455710
Birchim (5)	314 36 35.6	4.5303561
Poston (or Davies)	329 09 10.3	4.8375093

BUNKER HILL, TOYABE RANGE.

[Latitude, 39° 15' 02".9; longitude, 117° 07' 18".2; altitude, 11,404.]

Poston (or Davies)	22 56 22.9	4.7045301
Paradise	51 00 57.6	4.8941430
Birchim (5)	69 42 10.1	4.5138162
Back	249 28 44.0	
Basalt	75 53 32.9	5.0687273
Fairview	88 19 52.3	4.9480266
Old Woman	94 45 51.6	4.3280012
Back	274 36 31.7	
Desatoya	103 03 29.8	4.7485431
Tarogqua	111 20 25.3	5.0102199
Grant	115 14 58.7	4.8777077
Emigrant (5)	126 05 00.4	4.4562528
Back	305 54 48.3	
Geneva (5)	200 18 58.8	4.1015638
Back	20 20 54.9	

TABLE II—Continued.

POSTON PEAK (DAVIES), TOYABE RANGE.

[Latitude, 38° 49′ 48″.4 ; longitude, 117° 20′ 56″.0 ; altitude, 11,978.]

To—	Azimuth.	Log. distance.
	° ′ ″	Meters.
Cory	77 15 53.1	5.1090454
Basalt	100 45 33.7	4.9804536
Tarogqua	137 49 25.7	5.0528758
Desatoya	149 24 32.5	4.8375093
Bunker Hill	202 47 47.3	4.7045301

ROSE PEAK, LAKE TAHOE GROUP, SIERRA NEVADA.

[Latitude, 39° 20′ 30″.3 ; longitude, 119° 54′ 54″.07 ; altitude, 10,820.]

Pyramid Peak	20 38 03.7	4.7720233
Twin (5)	46 42 04.5	4.5728178
Back	226 30 08.0	
Needle (5)	64 27 19.1	4.5646618
Back	244 12 45.5	
Castle (Stanford)	93 51 03.4	4.5712746
Jackson (5)	102 00 56.7	4.7462964
Back	281 36 49.1	
Downieville	114 04 51.1	4.8363511
Lassens	133 37 52.8	5.2694161
Ingalls	140 06 25.4	4.9753645
Thompsons	151 56 09.0	5.0632623
Summit (5)	154 10 38.5	4.6468675
Back	334 02 02.5	
Fredonyer	158 57 04.4	5.2046435
Hot Springs	171 24 53.7	5.0639617
Peavine (5)	177 28 43.6	4.4322950
Back	357 28 11.9	
Tobakum	202 59 27.3	5.0040609
Tutib	237 07 46.7	4.8852059
Northeast Base Peak	256 52 53.9	4.6344267
Tarogqua	259 04 28.3	5.1680897
Davidson	280 08 20.3	4.3485643
Basalt	286 39 58.9	5.1271399
McClellan	296 21 11.6	4.3237979
Lyon	301 49 04.7	4.6558253
Como (5)	312 54 13.2	4.7204012
Back	133 11 03.8	
Genoa (5)	354 36 50.7	4.5259692
Back	174 38 13.5	
Freels	358 22 21.9	4.7326242

DOWNIEVILLE BUTTE (also called Sierra Butte), SIERRA NEVADA.

[Latitude, 39° 35′ 29″.8 ; longitude, 120° 38′ 39″.3 ; altitude, 8,541.]

Lassens Butte (1878)	143 52 54.0	5.0915334
Ingalls	182 09 10.8	4.6488166
Thompsons	185 51 27.3	4.8723861
Hot Springs	207 10 22.0	4.9900172
Rose	293 37 02.4	4.8363511

TABLE II—Continued.

TOHAKUM PEAK, VIRGINIA RANGE.

[Latitude, 40° 10' 40".2; longitude, 119° 27' 07".6; altitude, 8,174.]

To—	Azimuth.	Log. distance.
	° ′ ″	Meters.
Rose	23 17 13.2	5.0040609
Ingalls	78 45 21.8	5.0089656
Thompsons	95 52 23.0	4.9744707
Hot Springs	111 11 17.2	4.7832612
Fredonyer	120 34 02.4	5.0502187
Observation	137 37 55.4	4.9530350
Granite	181 34 39.3	4.8322101
Kumiva (7)	212 56 29.1	4.4772153
Back	33 03 56.6	
Tutib	334 14 35.6	4.7562493

INGALLS PEAK, SIERRA NEVADA.

[Latitude, 39° 59' 33".3; longitude, 120° 37' 28".8; altitude, 8,472.]

Downieville Butte	2 09 55.9	4.6488166
Lassens Butte	126 34 40.7	4.9670361
Fredonyer	181 49 17.8	4.8868878
Thompsons	191 20 05.2	4.4803382
Hot Springs	225 22 01.2	4.7808609
Tohakum	258 00 03.5	5.0089656
Rose	319 39 14.6	4.9753645

THOMPSONS PEAK, SIERRA NEVADA.

[Latitude, 40° 15' 34".1; longitude, 120° 33' 17".4; altitude, 7,752.]

Downieville Butte	5 54 53.9	4.8723861
Ingalls	11 22 47.2	4.4803382
Lassens Butte	107 42 53.1	4.9261048
Fredonyer	175 50 01.8	4.6769337
McDonald (5)	189 10 28.9	4.8837960
Back	9 16 08.3	
Observation (5)	209 44 22.6	4.8177507
Back	29 59 26.0	
Granite	237 56 12.0	5.0492923
Hot Springs	250 59 43.2	4.5929465
Tohakum	275 09 39.6	4.9744707
Rose	331 21 34.6	5.0632623

FREDONYER PEAK.

[Latitude, 40° 41' 12".0; longitude, 120° 35' 44".4; altitude, 7,995.]

Ingalls	1 50 25.2	4.8868878
Lassens Butte	74 11 37.9	4.9026154
South Fork	183 12 38.8	4.7160375
Cedar	194 58 38.0	5.0256770
Observation	254 57 34.8	4.5720771
Granite	262 58 47.1	4.9961650
Tohakum	299 49 34.2	5.0502187
Hot Springs	310 31 37.2	4.7266188
Rose	338 30 48.7	5.2046435
Thompsons	355 48 26.3	4.6769337

AZIMUTH AND DISTANCES.

TABLE II—Continued.

LASSENS BUTTE, SIERRA NEVADA.

[Latitude, 40° 29′ 12″.4; longitude, 121° 30′ 09″.7; altitude, 10,437.]

To—	Azimuth.	Log. distance.
	° ′ ″	*Meters.*
Shasta (7)	158 38 25.3	5.0707407
Back	330 11 16.9	
South Fork	226 41 23.4	5.0359158
Fredonyer	253 36 13.5	4.9026154
Hot Springs	275 39 44.0	5.0722346
Tohakum	280 28 21.9	5.2493861
Thompsons	287 06 02.7	4.9261048
Ingalls	306 00 38.7	4.9670361
Rose	312 36 45.1	5.2694161
Downieville Butte	323 19 45.9	5.0915334

HOT SPRINGS PEAK.

[Latitude, 40° 22′ 24″.8; longitude, 120° 07′ 07″.3; altitude, 7,692.]

Downieville Butte	27 30 37.7	4.9900172
Ingalls	45 41 36.5	4.7808609
Thompsons	71 16 39.1	4.5929465
Lassens Butte	96 33 35.2	5.0722346
Fredonyer	130 50 13.3	4.7266188
Observation	174 34 31.3	4.6487130
Granite	231 23 12.5	4.8715205
Tohakum	290 45 25.8	4.7832612
Tutib	311 34 58.6	5.0396227
Rose	351 17 03.4	5.0639617

OBSERVATION PEAK.

[Latitude, 40° 46′ 22″.2; longitude, 120° 10′ 06″.9; altitude, 8,009.]

Thompsons	29 59 26.0	4.8177507
Fredonyer	75 14 18.1	4.5720771
South Fork	142 09 38.1	4.7298456
Granite	268 02 53.2	4.7949908
Tohakum	317 10 01.1	4.9530350
Hot Springs	354 32 34.5	4.6487130

GRANITE PEAK, GRANITE MOUNTAINS.

[Latitude, 40° 47′ 22″.6; longitude, 119° 25′ 47″.7; altitude, 8,990.]

Tohakum	1 35 31.1	4.8322101
Hot Springs	51 50 05.5	4.8715205
Thompsons	58 40 03.4	5.0492923
Fredonyer	83 49 25.8	4.9961650
Observation	88 31 50.1	4.7949908
McDonald (5)	101 43 50.9	4.9257069
Back	281 05 22.6	
South Fork	113 23 53.9	5.0146480
Eagle (5)	130 31 54.7	4.9274031
Back	310 01 40.3	

TABLE II—Continued.

GRANITE PEAK, GRANITE MOUNTAINS—Continued.

[Latitude, 40° 47′ 22″.6; longitude, 119° 25′ 47″.7; altitude, 8,990.]

To—	Azimuth.	Log. distance.
	° ′ ″	*Meters.*
Warren	134 54 04.1	4.9679687
Cedar	142 37 32.6	5.0603123
Mahogany	158 00 16.5	4.4483821
Division	202 53 34.3	4.5677476
Piute (Pah-ute)	209 55 24.2	4.7974174
Kumiva (?)	341 20 27.7	4.6543715
Back	161 27 06.2	

SOUTH FORK PEAK, SIERRA NEVADA.

[Latitude, 41° 09′ 14″.3; longitude, 120° 33′ 39″.5; altitude, 7,409.]

Fredonyer	3 14 00.7	4.7160375
Lassens	47 18 19.6	5.0359158
Shasta (?)	102 13 07.5	5.1448445
Back	281 08 31.4	
Cedar	205 52 41.4	4.7496515
Warren	229 11 44.3	4.5804478
Eagle (5)	244 49 42.9	4.5267365
Back	65 04 04.8	
Granite	292 39 23.1	5.0146480
Observation	321 54 12.1	4.7298456

MAHOGANY PEAK, GRANITE RANGE.

[Latitude, 41° 01′ 26″.4; longitude, 119° 33′ 17″.9; altitude, 8,363.]

Warren	125 29 23.4	4.8322659
Cedar	137 41 52.2	4.9451702
Sugarloaf	161 48 19.2	5.1738987
Piute (Pah-ute)	235 47 50.8	4.7032642
Division	252 04 19.2	4.4175229
Granite	337 55 21.7	4.4483821

DIVISION PEAK, GRANITE MOUNTAINS.

[Latitude, 41° 05′ 46″.1; longitude, 119° 15′ 31″.5; altitude, 8,585.]

Granite	23 00 18.1	4.5677476
Mahogany	72 15 59.6	4.4175229
Warren	111 34 31.0	4.9352424
Cedar	124 21 17.1	5.0075777
Sugarloaf	152 04 13.3	5.1808086
Yellow Mesa (?)	159 52 04.8	4.9416407
Warner	165 26 36.4	5.1944989
Piute (Pah-ute)	219 53 30.4	4.4220690

AZIMUTHS AND DISTANCES.

Table II—Continued.

WARREN PEAK, WARNER MOUNTAINS.

[Latitude, 41° 22′ 38″.7; longitude, 120° 12′ 59″.6; 9,668.]

To—	Azimuth.	Log. distance.
	° ′ ″	*Meters.*
South Fork	49 25 22.0	4.5804478
Cedar	170 45 32.0	4.4156259
Sugarloaf	184 26 23.9	5.0115588
Piute, or Pah-ute	276 04 03.2	4.9900197
Division	290 56 38.2	4.9352424
Mahogany	305 03 14.7	4.8322659
Granite	314 23 03.1	4.9679688
Eagle (5)	351 27 42.1	4.0290143

CEDAR PEAK, WARNER MOUNTAINS.

[Latitude, 41° 36′ 31″.9; longitude, 120° 16′ 00″.2; altitude, 8,308.]

Fredonyer	15 11 37.3	5.0256770
South Fork	26 04 21.6	4.7496515
Lolochewis	159 01 37.4	4.9191694
Sugarloaf	188 57 21.5	4.8900950
Warner	204 44 19.3	5.0175099
Beatties Butte (5)	221 44 25.2	5.0648034
Back	42 22 06.1	
Yellow Mesa (5)	244 45 20.1	4.7729672
Back	65 11 07.0	
Piute, or Pah-ute	289 32 03.7	5.0317137
Division	303 41 19.6	5.0075777
Mahogany	317 13 40.5	4.9451702
Granite	322 04 28.3	5.0603123
Warren	350 43 32.3	4.4156259

PIUTE (or PAH-UTE) PEAK.

[Latitude, 41° 16′ 42″.8; longitude, 119° 03′ 23″.1; altitude, 8,618.]

Granite	30 10 07.0	4.7974174
Division	40 01 30.1	4.4220690
Mahogany	56 07 31.9	4.7032642
Warren	96 50 01.2	4.9900198
Cedar	110 20 07.6	5.0317137
Sugarloaf	142 24 14.2	5.1576370
Yellow Mesa (7)	142 51 36.7	4.8902622
Back	322 29 08.4	
Beatties Butte (5)	169 41 10.5	5.0966869
Back	349 30 18.2	

SUGARLOAF PEAK, WARNER MOUNTAINS.

[Latitude, 42° 17′ 57″.6; longitude, 120° 07′ 12″ 4; altitude, 8,416.]

Warren	4 30 15.4	5.0115588
Cedar	9 03 14.3	4.8900950
Lolochewis	91 13 35.4	4.6212609
Warner	240 31 28.7	4.5586785
Piute, or Pah-ute	321 41 42.3	5.1576370
Division	331 29 50.4	5.1808086
Mahogany	341 25 46.6	5.1738987

U. S. GEOGRAPHICAL SURVEYS.

Table II—Continued.

LOLOCHEWIS PEAK, DREWS VALLEY MOUNTAINS.

[Latitude, 42° 18′ 22″.6 ; longitude, 120° 37′ 37″.7 ; altitude, 7,957.]

To—	Azimuth.	Log. distance.
	° ′ ″	*Meters.*
Warner	256 39 54.9	4.8764328
Sugarloaf	270 53 06.9	4.6212609
Cedar	338 47 09.9	4.9191694

WARNER PEAK.

[Latitude, 42° 27′ 32″.6; longitude, 119° 44′ 13″.1.]

Cedar	25 05 36.3	5.0175099
Sugarloaf	60 46 58.5	4.5586785
Lolochewis	77 15 55.1	4.8764328
Division	345 07 29.3	5.1944989

CASTLE PEAK, SIERRA NEVADA.

[Latitude, 39° 21′ 48″.6; longitude, 120° 20′ 47″.30; altitude, 9,014.]

Jackson (5)	117 24 26.6	4.2922462
Back	297 16 42.6	
Rose	273 34 38.5	4.5712746
Freels	325 18 48.2	4.8356778
Pyramid	343 58 03.4	4.7790672

PYRAMID PEAK, SIERRA NEVADA.

[Latitude, 38° 50′ 32″.6; longitude, 120° 09′ 20″.6; altitude, 10,127.]

Castle (Stanford, 1877)	164 05 17.8	4.7790672
Needle (5)	162 36 54.7	4.6169682
Back	342 31 30.1	
Rose	200 28 58.5	4.7720233
Lyon	241 52 54.6	4.8271064
Freels	266 22 42.7	4.3506941
Oreana, or Silver Lake	267 39 02.7	4.7707547
Cory	284 03 25.0	5.0893289
Cary (5)	295 24 24.7	4.4390391
Back	115 35 08.6	
Sweetwater	301 08 10.8	4.9396130
Stevens (5)	308 52 39.6	4.2939022
Back	128 59 16.9	
Highland	313 34 58.9	4.6851623
Sonora	320 00 11.3	4.8516040
Alpine (or Woods)	325 51 36.8	4.3861024
Mokelumne	350 47 29.7	4.5381309

FREELS PEAK, LAKE TAHOE GROUP, SIERRA NEVADA.

[Latitude, 38° 51′ 18″.8; longitude, 119° 53′ 50″.43; altitude, 10,849.]

Alpine	22 12 07.1	4.3664394
Stevens (5)	27 19 14.8	4.1895171
Back	207 16 10.6	

78 AZIMUTHS AND DISTANCES.

Table II—Continued.

FREELS, LAKE TAHOE GROUP, SIERRA NEVADA—Continued.

[Latitude, 38° 51′ 18″.8; longitude, 119° 53′ 50″.4; altitude, 10,849.]

To—	Azimuth.	Log. distance.
	° ′ ″	*Meters.*
Pyramid	86 32 25.0	4.3506941
Castle (Stanford, 1877)	145 35 48.2	4.8356778
Rose	178 23 02.0	4.7326242
Lyon	230 47 49.1	4.6782465
Como (5)	243 40 52.3	4.6152849
Oreana	268 35 32.8	4.5631568
Cory	288 03 26.2	5.0073250
Sweetwater	311 51 14.2	4.8437164
Highland	340 06 21.3	4.5688444
Cary (5)	349 40 19.5	4.1281240

*ALPINE PEAK, SIERRA NEVADA.

[Latitude, 38° 39′ 40″.5; longitude, 119° 59′ 53″.9; altitude, 10,426.]

Mokelumne	30 20 09.5	4.2079163
Pyramid	145 57 30.3	4.3861024
Stevens (5)	192 09 19.7	3.9010324
Freels	202 08 19.6	4.3664394
Lyon	221 27 04.7	4.8387763
Cary (5)	233 20 14.7	4.1443607
Oreana, or Silver Lake	243 37 25.2	4.7040598
Sweetwater	292 19 39.3	4.8176548
Highland	301 50 08.5	4.4014112
Sonora	317 04 06.7	4.6713715

OREANA PEAK (or SILVER LAKE PEAK), PINE NUT RANGE.

[Latitude, 38° 51′ 45″.2; longitude, 119° 28′ 33″.8; altitude, 9,381.]

Sonora	13 33 32.2	4.7662589
Highland	34 05 31.3	4.6337256
Mokelumne	56 04 47.4	4.8108443
Alpine (or Woods)	63 57 02.3	4.7040598
Pyramid	88 04 36.4	4.7707547
Freels	88 51 24.3	4.5631568
Lyon	181 00 23.9	4.4659001
Sweetwater	342 16 17.1	4.6980668

MOKELUMNE PEAK, SIERRA NEVADA.

[Latitude, 38° 32′ 08″.5; longitude, 120° 05′ 30″.5; altitude, 9,385.]

Pyramid	170 49 52.3	4.5381309
Alpine (or Woods)	210 16 39.5	4.2079163
Oreana, or Silver Lake	235 41 41.4	4.8108443
Highland	268 42 22.6	4.4708279
Sonora	296 55 34.7	4.6533253

*Called "Woods Peak," by Whitney, and "Round Top," by U. S. Coast and Geodetic Survey.

TABLE II—Continued.

HIGHLAND PEAK, SILVER MOUNTAIN GROUP, SIERRA NEVADA.

[Latitude, 38° 32′ 28″.4; longitude, 119° 45′ 09″.7; altitude, 10,956.]

To—	Azimuth.	Log. distance.
	° ′ ″	*Meters.*
Mokelumne	88 55 03.2	4.4708279
Alpine	121 59 20.2	4.4014112
Pyramid	133 50 04.7	4.6851623
Freels	160 11 46.9	4.5688444
Lyon	200 37 14.0	4.8412370
Oreana, or Silver Lake	213 55 08.6	4.6337256
Cory	267 49 52.2	4.9250431
Sweetwater	286 39 49.1	4.6135320
McBride	302 08 41.7	5.1627133
Conness	329 10 31.7	4.8719881
Sonora	333 32 47.7	4.3721006

SONORA PEAK, SIERRA NEVADA.

[Latitude, 38° 21′ 04″.2; longitude, 119° 37′ 57″.5; altitude, 11,479.]

Mokelumne	117 12 42.5	4.6533253
Alpine (or Woods)	137 17 46.3	4.6713715
Pyramid	140 19 44.8	4.8516040
Highland	153 37 16.5	4.3721006
Oreana	193 27 40.5	4.7662589
Sweetwater	252 11 12.4	4.4816989

SWEETWATER PEAK, SWEETWATER RANGE.

[Latitude, 38° 26′ 03″.3; longitude, 119° 18′ 07″.2; altitude, 11,778.]

Sonora	72 23 31.7	4.4816989
Highland	106 56 38.8	4.6135320
Alpine (or Woods)	112 45 41.5	4.8176548
Pyramid	121 40 08.7	4.9396130
Freels	132 13 32.6	4.8437164
Oreana, or Silver Lake	162 22 48.4	4.6980668

CORY PEAK (called Mount Grant by U. S. Coast and Geodetic Survey), WALKER RIVER RANGE.

[Latitude, 38° 33′ 57″.4; longitude, 118° 47′ 15″.9; altitude, 11,326.]

Lyell Peak	24 44 57.3	5.0054302
Dana	27 02 30.9	4.9204222
Conness	34 58 32.6	4.9103091
Dunderberg, locally Castle (5)	37 14 20.8	4.8458256
Highland	88 25 57.3	4.9250430
Pyramid	104 54 43.3	5.0893289
Freels	108 45 04.4	5.0073250
Lyon	136 35 34.6	4.9337768
Basalt	213 20 25.5	4.7473460
Poston	256 21 54.5	5.1090454
McBride	334 43 52.5	4.9520255
Morgan	357 43 17.1	5.1115334

AZIMUTHS AND DISTANCES.

TABLE II—Continued.

McBRIDE PEAK, WHITE MOUNTAINS.

[Latitude, 37° 50′ 08″.0; longitude, 118° 21′ 12″.6; altitude, 13,415.]

To—	Azimuth.	Log. distance.
	° ′ ″	*Meters.*
Morgan	34 43 37.3	4.7668811
Lyell	82 30 25.4	4.9103895
Dana	95 23 18.9	4.8829661
Conness	99 50 54.2	4.9347399
Dunderberg (5)	107 35 14.6	4.9267679
Highland	123 00 36.1	5.1627133
Cory	154 59 59.3	4.9520255
Basalt	176 54 22.5	5.1068251
White Mountain	338 30 04.5	4.3873724

WHITE MOUNTAIN PEAK, WHITE MOUNTAINS.

[Latitude, 37° 37′ 51″.4; longitude, 118° 15′ 07″.9; altitude, 14,245.]

Morgan	59 05 51.3	4.6925568
Lyell	97 44 49.0	4.9566380
Dana	109 25 46.7	4.9546270
Conness	111 49 33.8	5.0039572
McBride	158 33 47.7	4.3873724

CONNESS PEAK, SIERRA NEVADA.

[Latitude, 37° 57′ 51″.2; longitude, 119° 19′ 06″.2; altitude, 12,552.]

Clarks	17 30 01.7	4.4983662
Echo (5)	24 07 09.3	4.2064240
Clouds Rest (5)	33 49 17.5	4.4252937
Devils	37 23 07.8	4.7858911
Hoffman	51 22 42.3	4.3292421
Moccasin (5)	78 50 33.2	4.9563355
Highland	149 26 39.7	4.8719881
Dunderberg (5)	200 51 08.0	4.0649526
Cory	214 38 49.5	4.9103091
McBride	279 15 20.3	4.9347399
White Mountain	291 10 21.3	5.0039572
Dana	310 12 40.7	4.0624314
Morgan	320 03 11.9	4.9094178
Lyell	350 10 17.1	4.4092379

DANA PEAK, SIERRA NEVADA.

[Latitude, 37° 53′ 49″.2; longitude, 119° 13′ 05″.3; altitude, 13,043.]

Lyell	14 02 17.3	4.2641566
Conness	130 16 22.5	4.0624314
Cory	206 46 32.0	4.9204222
McBride	274 51 28.2	4.8829661
White Mountain	288 50 17.1	4.9546270
Morgan	321 44 04.2	4.8440172

U. S. GEOGRAPHICAL SURVEYS. 81

TABLE II—Continued.

LYELL PEAK, SIERRA NEVADA.

[Latitude, 37° 44' 11".0; longitude, 119° 16' 07".3; altitude, 13,104.]

To—	Azimuth.	Log. distance.
	° ′ ″	*Meters.*
Chiquito	17 47 50.3	4.6575584
Merced (5)	43 09 27.8	4.2010060
Clarks	71 03 17.6	4.1658304
Clouds Rest (5)	99 23 03.8	4.2891099
Hoffman	119 37 51.9	4.3840797
Echo (5)	134 05 46.2	4.183079
Conness	170 12 06.9	4.4092379
Dana	194 00 25.7	4.2641566
Cory	204 27 07.7	5.0054302
McBride	261 56 46.7	4.9103895
White Mountain Peak	277 07 32.0	4.9566380
Morgan	307 46 11.6	4.7808090

MORGAN PEAK, SIERRA NEVADA.

[Latitude, 37° 24' 07".2; longitude, 118° 43' 46".9; altitude, 13,791.]

Chiquito	84 29 14.9	4.7919251
Merced (5)	113 45 24.9	4.8051582
Clarks	117 56 55.4	4.8419577
Lyell	128 05 54.8	4.7808090
Conness	140 24 47.6	4.9094178
Dana	142 01 58.4	4.8440172
Cory	177 45 25.8	5.1115334
McBride	214 29 50.7	4.7668811
White Mountain	238 48 24.5	4.6925568

CHIQUITO PEAK, SIERRA NEVADA.

[Latitude, 37° 20' 46".8; longitude, 119° 25' 31".8; altitude, 8,257.]

Green	79 34 10.8	4.7058520
Deadwood	80 07 42.1	4.3655189
Schultz	99 45 54.2	4.8086853
Devils	125 54 54.9	4.5327744
Hoffman	172 31 28.9	4.7459396
Clarks	179 57 30.7	4.5856991
Merced (5)	185 21 36.7	4.5028826
Lyell	197 42 06.3	4.6575584
Morgan	264 03 54.3	4.7919251

CLARKS PEAK (also called "Gothic," or the Obelisk), MERCED GROUP, SIERRA NEVADA.

[Latitude, 37° 41' 36".4; longitude, 119° 25' 33".0; altitude, 11,512.]

Devils	56 07 56.4	4.5215092
Schultz	66 28 35.0	4.8398363
Moccasin (5)	98 55 43.1	4.9043822
Wade (5)	119 02 39.0	4.5617799

1874 WH——6

Table II—Continued.

CLARKS PEAK (also called "Gothic," or the Obelisk), MERCED GROUP, SIERRA NEVADA—Continued.

[Latitude, 37° 41′ 36″.4; longitude, 119° 25′ 33″.0; altitude, 11,519.]

To—	Azimuth.	Log. distance.
	° ′ ″	Meters.
Clouds Rest (5)	145 56 06.4	3.9804878
Castle Rock	149 40 58.8	4.8516321
Hoffman	156 38 22.8	4.2602809
Echo (5)	190 37 39.0	4.1941379
Conness	197 26 04.5	4.4983662
Lyell	250 57 31.6	4.1658304
Morgan	297 31 28.1	4.8419577
Merced (5)	336 15 57.0	3.8726042
Chiquito	359 57 30.0	4.5856991

HOFFMAN PEAK, SIERRA NEVADA.

[Latitude, 37° 50′ 38″.5; longitude, 119° 30′ 28″.3; altitude, 10,747.]

Devils	29 59 04.1	4.6095769
Schultz	51 41 11.3	4.8546948
Wades (5)	92 14 00.6	4.3922018
Back	272 03 41.8	
Conness	231 15 43.3	4.3292421
Echo (5)	277 32 55.1	4.0082832
Back	86 58 26.4	
Lyell	299 29 04.3	4.3840797
Clarks	336 35 21.9	4.2602809
Chiquito	352 28 28.0	4.7459396

DEVILS PEAK, SOUTH FORK GROUP, SIERRA NEVADA.

[Latitude, 37° 31′ 34″.9; longitude, 119° 44′ 16″.8; altitude, 6,985.]

Green	37 13 48.1	4.5654480
Schultz	75 34 38.4	4.5676560
Moccasin (5)	120 44 38.0	4.7799268
Pilot (7)	146 24 25.5	4.4935560
Back	63 26 12.2	
Hoffman	209 50 37.6	4.6095769
Conness	217 07 43.1	4.7858911
Clarks	235 56 30.6	4.5215092
Chiquito	305 43 31.1	4.5327744
Deadwood	348 34 58.9	4.3882632

DEADWOOD PEAK, SIERRA NEVADA.

[Latitude, 37° 18′ 36″.7; longitude, 119° 41′ 00″.22; altitude, 4,451.]

Green	31 03 22.6	4.4408944
Schultz	58 36 59.7	4.6357549
Devils	91 21 20.8	4.3882632
Chiquito	178 58 18.0	4.3655189

TABLE II—Continued.

GREEN MOUNTAIN, FOOT-HILLS OF SIERRA NEVADA.

[Latitude, 37° 15' 43".6; longitude, 119° 59' 19".6; altitude, 1,352.]

To—	Azimuth.	Log. distance.
	° ′ ″	*Meters.*
Schultz	145 49 55.9	4.3840386
Devils	217 04 39.8	4.5654480
Deadwood	258 45 31.4	4.4408944
Chiquito	259 13 41.9	4.7058520

SCHULTZ PEAK.

[Latitude, 37° 26' 33".1; longitude, 120° 08' 32".9; altitude, 2,275.]

Hoffman	231 17 56.0	4.8546948
Clarks	246 02 22.4	4.8398363
Devils	255 19 52.3	4.5676560
Chiquito	279 19 46.7	4.8086853
Deadwood	289 43 16.4	4.6357549
Green	325 44 30.3	4.3840386

TABLE III.—AZIMUTHS AND DISTANCES BETWEEN PRIMARY TRIANGULATION STATIONS DEPENDING UPON THE OGDEN BASE, UTAH, 1877.

This base was measured in 1877, extending from the vicinity of North Ogden Village, along Main street in the city of Ogden, Utah, and its extremities permanently marked by iron rods incased in brick piers. It was measured four times, twice with a 20-foot wooden rod of special construction and twice with a 50-foot Stackpole compensated steel tape. The mean of the four determinations is 23,209.007 feet (about 4.395 miles), the direction being about N. 1° 1′ E. (see annual report 1878, p. 15).

Length in meters reduced to sea-level is given in the following tables.

The extremities of the base were connected by triangulation with the dome of the Ogden Observatory, the co-ordinates adopted for it being latitude 41° 13′ 08.″56, longitude, 111° 59′ 54″.47, the center of the dome being 0.″17 east of the east pier of the transit-room, the astronomical co-ordinates of which are deduced in Vol. II, Quarto Reports of the office, pp. 7–55.

Upon the Ogden base depends all the triangulation of Southern Idaho and Northern Utah, the principal elements of which are given in the following pages.

This triangulation extends approximately from latitude 39° 40′ to 43° 30′, and from longitude 111° 00′ to 114° 00′ west from Greenwich. It has not been connected with any of the other astronomical determinations by this office.

M. M. M.

ENGINEER OFFICE
U. S. GEOGRAPHICAL SURVEYS.

ALPHABETICAL LIST.

IDAHO.
	Page.
Bannock Peak	92
Big Butte	92
Black Pine Peak	90
Cache Peak	91
Deep Creek Peak	92
Elkhorn (northern point) Peak	91
Elkhorn (southern point) Peak	91
Meades Peak	92
Pillar Butte	93
Pisgah (Caribou) Peak	93
Putnam Peak	92

NEVADA.
Pilot Knob	96

UTAH.
Antelope Island Peak	94
Blue Springs Peak	90
Clear Creek Peak	95
Desert Peak	96
Grant Peak	89
Naomi Peak	90
Newfoundland Peak	95
North Base, Ogden	89
Observatory Peak	94
Ogden Observatory Dome	89
Ogden Peak	93
Promontory (or Benado) Peak	94
South Base, Ogden	89
Stansbury Island Peak	90
Tangent Peak	95

WYOMING.
Medicine Butte	94

TABLE III.

OGDEN OBSERVATORY DOME.

[Latitude, 41° 13′ 08″.56; longitude, 111° 59′ 54″.64; altitude, top of pier, 4,374.]

To—	Azimuth.	Log. distance.
	° ′ ″	*Meters.*
Antelope Island	33 06 12.0	4.5333586
Promontory	125 05 13.4	4.7197419
Ogden (formerly North Ogden)	190 02 54.7	4.2087428
North Base	203 01 16.4	3.7295424
Observatory Peak	283 10 03.2	3.9861495
South Base	317 13 54.3	3.4635227
Barton (5)	321 53 41.9	4.289168?
Back	141 59 20.5	
Twin Peaks (west) (7)	341 42 35.1	4.8625211
Back	161 53 12.0	

NORTH BASE, OGDEN, UTAH.

[Latitude, 41° 15′ 48″.62; longitude, 111° 58′ 24″.33; altitude, 4,300.]

South Base	1 01 05.9	3.8495994
Observatory Dome	23 02 15.8	3.7295424
Antelope Island Peak	31 45 19.6	4.5959426
Promontory	119 16 04.3	4.7126123
Ogden Peak (formerly North Ogden)	183 47 06.4	4.0417693
Observatory Peak	314 15 58.7	4.0102123

SOUTH BASE, OGDEN, UTAH.

[Latitude, 41° 11′ 59″.36; longitude, 111° 58′ 29″.73; altitude, 4,300.]

Antelope Island Peak	37 56 19.3	4.5257768
Promontory	125 44 11.0	4.7426887
Observatory Dome	137 14 50.1	3.4635227
North Base	181 01 02.3	3.8495994
Ogden Peak	182 42 07.0	4.2571372
Observatory Peak	270 34 09.0	3.8725924

GRANT PEAK.

[Latitude, 40° 27′ 31″.5; longitude, 112° 37′ 49″.0.]

Tangent	158 03 22.8	5.0881282
Stansbury Island Peak	194 00 45.9	4.6467210
Antelope Island Peak	211 43 06.4	4.8174641

TABLE III—Continued.

STANSBURY ISLAND PEAK, IN GREAT SALT LAKE.

[Latitude, 40° 50' 45".82; longitude, 112° 30' 10".7.]

To—	Azimuth.	Log. distance.
	° ' "	Meters.
Grant	14 05 44.5	4.6467210
Tangent	141 24 47.8	4.9563554
Antelope Island	241 41 43.1	4.4321919

BLUE SPRINGS PEAK (NORTH PROMONTORY), PROMONTORY RANGE.

[Latitude, 41° 47' 36".0; longitude, 112° 32' 54".4; altitude, 7,131.]

Tangent	56 43 27.31	4.7988251
Clear Creek	83 47 55.44	5.0010109
Cache	115 31 18.44	5.0095291
Black Pine	127 20 19.04	4.7774318
Elkhorn (south point)	196 30 53.24	4.7959421
North Ogden	314 19 07.89	4.8341416
Promontory	354 54 44.54	4.5300203

NAOMI PEAK, BEAR RIVER RANGE.

[Latitude, 41° 54' 38".9; longitude, 111° 40' 46".3; altitude, 9,951.]

Observatory Peak (Ogden)	12 21 45.3	4.9078858
North Ogden	21 24 31.9	4.8153735
Logan (Box Elder) (5)	42 44 24.8	4.6194475
Back	222 30 51.5	
Tangent	69 33 01.3	5.1257584
Elkhorn (north point)	131 13 34.5	4.8544983
South Putnam (not final)	161 37 50.2	5.0694142
Sedgwick (not final)	163 11 01.7	4.8959463
Sherman (not final)	189 44 10.5	4.7948462
Meades (not final)	208 27 10.3	4.8677418

BLACK PINE PEAK (1).

[Latitude, 42° 07' 08".5; longitude, 113° 07' 27".9; altitude, 9,386.]

Tangent	3 38 20.1	4.8514458
Cache	99 25 10.1	4.6559083
Big Butte	183 10 47.9	5.1521620
Badger	185 37 20.4	4.6824025
Back	5 39 39.6	
Cedar	188 20 55.9	4.5649407
Bannock	212 11 04.3	4.8030504
Back	32 27 44.8	
Putnam	219 57 56.5	5.0839251
Deep Creek	224 16 54.4	4.7375277
Back	44 35 38.4	
Elkhorn	249 46 13.7	4.8421161
Blue Spring Peak	306 57 12.8	4.7774318
North Ogden	310 40 18.0	5.1069389
Promontory	323 46 13.0	4.9368084

U. S. GEOGRAPHICAL SURVEYS.

TABLE III—Continued.

CACHE PEAK, RAFT RIVER RANGE.

[Latitude, 42° 11′ 04″.1; longitude, 113° 39′ 54″.8; altitude, 10,451.]

To—	Azimuth.	Log. distance.
	° ′ ″	*Meters.*
Clear Creek	6 56 17.7	4.7432236
Big Butte	200 59 51.6	5.1590841
Pillar Butte	205 08 32.8	4.9333630
Putnam	234 43 13.0	5.1746577
Badger	230 17 27.4	4.8052220
Back	50 41 38.6	
Cedar	239 35 22.0	4.7616604
Back	59 59 49.7	
Bannock	239 04 20.7	4.9599116
Deep Creek	248 41 11.4	4.9478375
Elkhorn (south point)	261 01 58.0	5.0459216
Black Pine	279 03 23.6	4.6559083
Blue Spring Peak (north promontory)	294 46 28.8	5.0095291
North Ogden	302 17 06.9	5.2260258
Promontory	308 29 36.6	5.0898373

ELKHORN PEAK (NORTHERN POINT).

[Latitude, 42° 20′ 00″.3; longitude, 113° 19′ 56″.6.]

Promontory	9 06 53.1	4.9773488
Tangent	36 49 37.5	5.0714104
Putnam	190 58 01.2	4.8457221
Naomi	310 47 18.2	4.8544983
Ogden	344 04 11.2	5.0488598
Box Elder (or Logan) (5)	341 22 08.0	4.9128013
Back	161 34 43.5	
Oxford (5)	290 34 52.6	4.3087692
Back	110 44 12.0	
Sedgwick (5)	238 44 09.9	4.5912997
Back	59 00 35.7	
Sherman (5)	257 01 16.5	4.8189895
Back	77 32 55.5	

ELKHORN PEAK (SOUTHERN POINT).

[Latitude, 42° 19′ 57″.8; longitude, 113° 19′ 58″.2.]

Promontory	9 06 00.4	4.9769869
Blue Springs	16 39 33.3	4.7959421
Tangent	36 50 04.1	5.0711115
Black Pine	70 18 08.8	4.8421161
Cache	81 55 43.6	5.0459216
Bannock	133 59 10.3	4.6358587
Putnam	190 58 01.2	4.8457222
Ogden	344 02 28.8	5.0492610
Deep Creek	119 38 32.6	4.4913227

Table III—Continued.

BANNOCK PEAK.

[Latitude, 42° 36′ 08″.8; longitude, 112° 42′ 43″.0; altitude, 8,359.]

To—	Azimuth.	Log. distance.
	° ′ ″	*Meters.*
Black Pine	32 27 44.8	4.8030504
Cedar Creek	58 49 17.8	4.5240654
Cache	59 42 54.5	4.9599116
Pillar Butte	127 01 54.2	4.7150914
Big Butte	163 49 55.3	4.9624460
Putnam	228 37 40.8	4.7708025
Elkhorn	313 43 48.8	4.6358587

BIG BUTTE.

[Latitude, 43° 23′ 42″.2; longitude, 113° 01′ 38″.0; altitude, 7,659.]

Black Pine	3 14 45.5	5.1521620
Pillar	15 24 03.8	4.7709609
Cache	21 25 51.9	5.1590841
Putnam	304 54 09.9	4.9311758
Bannock	343 37 01.3	4.9624460

DEEP CREEK PEAK.

[Latitude, 42° 28′ 13″.1; longitude, 112° 39′ 37″.7; altitude, 8,818.]

Black Pine	44 35 38.4	4.7375277
Cache	69 21 47.1	4.9478375
Cedar	85 27 42.1	4.5176717
Badger (5)	105 01 21.9	4.5386744
Bannock	163 56 31.7	4.1840306
Putnam	216 45 25.7	4.8257988
Sedgwick	265 02 26.6	4.7812665
Elkhorn (south point)	299 25 17.2	4.4913227
Blue Spring (north promontory)	352 56 27.9	4.8794100

MEADES PEAK.

[Latitude, 42° 29′ 41″.4; longitude, 111° 15′ 10″.7; altitude, 10,541.]

Naomi (not final)	28 44 27.1	4.8677408
Oxford (not final)	70 37 29.2	4.8708394
Elkhorn (not final)	79 02 08.3	4.9575013
Sherman	82 19 37.5	4.3962902
Sedgwick	92 32 27.3	4.7442857
Putnam	124 24 21.2	4.9572598
Pisgah	175 34 55.3	4.8236924

PUTNAM PEAK, PORT NEUF RANGE.

[Latitude, 42° 57′ 08″.0; longitude, 112° 10′ 09″.8; altitude, 8,905.]

Elkhorn (northern point)	11 04 39.8	4.8457221
Deep Creek (5)	37 05 24.9	4.8257988
Black Pine	40 36 40.9	5.0839251

U. S. GEOGRAPHICAL SURVEYS.

TABLE III—Continued.

PUTNAM PEAK, PORT NEUF RANGE—Continued.

[Latitude, 42° 57′ 08″.0; longitude, 112° 10′ 09″.8; altitude, 8,905.]

To—	Azimuth.	Log. distance.
	° ′ ″	Meters.
Bannock (5)	48 59 47.4	4.7708025
Back	228 37 40.8	
Cache	55 43 56.0	5.1746577
Pillar	85 12 31.8	4.9347186
Big Butte	125 29 22.9	4.9311758
Pisgah	257 02 37.6	4.8529898
Meades	303 47 02.9	4.9572598
Sherman	316 48 38.8	4.8695110
Sedgwick	337 45 03.7	4.7196637

PILLAR BUTTE.

[Latitude, 42° 52′ 57″.7; longitude, 113° 13′ 08″.7; altitude, 5,301.]

Cache	25 26 38.6	4.9333630
Big Butte	195 16 11.5	4.7709609
Putnam	264 29 38.5	4.9347186
Bannock	306 41 15.1	4.7150914

PISGAH (CARIBOU) PEAK.

[Latitude, 43° 05′ 34″.5; longitude, 111° 18′ 37″.7; altitude, 9,695.]

Sherman	15 36 44.2	4.8600265
Sedgwick	38 08 26.8	4.9105587
Putnam	77 37 33.6	4.8529898
Meades	355 32 21.1	4.8236924

OGDEN PEAK (FORMERLY NORTH OGDEN), WAHSATCH RANGE.

[Latitude, 41° 21′ 44″.8; longitude, 111° 57′ 53″.1; altitude, 9,696.]

South Base	2 42 31.2	4.2571372
North Base	3 47 27.1	4.0417693
Ogden Observatory Dome	10 04 14.9	4.2087428
Antelope	25 45 55.9	4.6940295
Tangent	97 46 43.2	5.0098430
Clear Creek	104 19 37.2	5.1846553
Promontory	107 17 57.1	4.6803459
Cache	123 25 05.4	5.2260258
Black Pine	131 26 37.6	5.1069389
Blue Springs (north promontory)	134 42 22.4	4.8341416
Box Elder or Logan (5)	171 33 09.4	4.4856974
Back	351 31 00.7	
Elkhorn (south point)	164 17 12.9	5.0492610
Elkhorn (north point)	164 18 54.2	5.0488598
Naomi	201 13 09.7	4.8153735
Observatory Peak	339 59 27.4	4.2854896
Twin Peaks (west) (7)	346 46 06.2	4.9416924
Back	166 55 24.4	

AZIMUTHS AND DISTANCES.

Table III—Continued.

OBSERVATORY (FORMERLY OGDEN) PEAK, WAHSATCH RANGE.

[Latitude, 41° 11′ 56″.8; longitude, 111° 53′ 09″.6; altitude, 9,589.]

To—	Azimuth.	Log. distance.
	° ′ ″	*Meters.*
Antelope Island Peak	46 50 35.2	4.5859248
South Base	90 37 39.8	3.8725924
Observatory Dome	103 14 29.9	3.9861495
Tangent	106 33 03.7	5.0515004
Promontory	121 47 34.4	4.7891700
North Base	134 19 26.1	4.0102123
North Ogden	160 02 34.4	4.2854896
Naomi	192 13 32.2	4.9078858
Medicine Butte	257 55 46.2	4.9185015
South Meridian Hill (5)	266 35 29.4	4.8818817
Back	87 11 21.7	
Porcupine (5)	287 01 17.3	4.8292973
Back	107 31 33.8	
Twin Peaks (west) (7)	348 43 50.2	4.8344967
Back	168 50 02.0	

MEDICINE BUTTE.

[Latitude, 41° 21′ 04″.1; longitude, 110° 55′ 02″.3.]

Twin Peaks (west)	39 23 53.6	5.03210068
Back	218 51 59.2	
Observatory Peak	78 34 06.8	4.9185015

ANTELOPE ISLAND PEAK, GREAT SALT LAKE.

[Latitude, 40° 57′ 40″.4; longitude, 112° 13′ 12″.1; altitude, 6,660.]

Grant Peak	31 59 09.7	4.8174641
Tangent	125 59 22.5	4.9952651
Promontory	157 24 36.4	4.8032445
North Ogden	205 35 51.0	4.6940295
North Base	211 35 35.9	4.5935426
Observatory Dome	212 57 27.8	4.5333586
South Base	217 46 39.6	4.5257768
Observatory Peak	226 37 25.0	4.5859244
Barton (5)	246 25 01.0	4.5239582
Back	66 39 22.2	
Twin Peaks (west point) (7)	314 12 04.2	4.7638398
Back	134 31 20.4	

PROMONTORY PEAK (ALSO BENADA), PROMONTORY RANGE.

[Latitude, 41° 29′ 21″.8; longitude, 112° 30′ 44″.9; altitude, 7,460.]

Tangent	89 13 37.4	4.7452160
Clear Creek	102 36 42.0	5.0219326
Cache	129 15 44.7	5.0898373
Black Pine	144 10 41.5	4.9368085
Blue Springs	174 56 10.6	4.5300204

U. S. GEOGRAPHICAL SURVEYS. 95

TABLE III—Continued.

PROMONTORY PEAK (ALSO BENADA), PROMONTORY RANGE—Continued.

[Latitude, 41° 29' 21".8; longitude, 112° 30' 44".9; altitude, 7,460.]

To—	Azimuth.	Log. distance.
	° ′ ″	*Meters.*
Elkhorn (southern point)	188 58 48.4	4.9769869
Elkhorn (northern point)	188 59 40.1	4.9773488
Logan (Box Elder) (5)	248 24 18.2	4.6458392
Back	68 43 57.5	
North Ogden	286 56 12.5	4.6803459
North Base	298 54 41.6	4.7126123
Ogden Peak (Observatory Peak)	301 22 44.6	4.7891700
Observatory Dome	304 44 50.8	4.7197419
South Base	305 22 52.6	4.7426887
Twin Peaks (west) (7)	326 08 45.0	5.0760657
Back	146 39 38.7	
Antelope Island Peak	337 13 02.6	4.8032445

TANGENT PEAK.

[Latitude, 41° 28' 50".6; longitude, 113° 10' 42".2.]

Newfoundland	26 20 42.4	4.5634607
Desert	41 25 26.2	4.8935024
Pilot Knob	56 13 46.0	4.9605333
Clear Creek	116 19 06.6	4.7215642
Black Pine	183 36 10.9	4.8514458
Elkhorn (northern point)	216 15 43.2	5.0714104
Elkhorn (southern point)	216 16 10.9	5.0711115
Blue Springs	236 18 20.5	4.7988251
Naomi	248 33 21.7	5.1257584
North Ogden	276 58 32.5	5.0098430
Promontory	268 47 09.3	4.7452160
Observatory	285 41 50.5	5.0515004
Antelope Island Peak	305 21 29.0	4.9952651
Stansbury Island Peak	320 58 07.3	4.9563556
Grant	337 41 49.0	5.0881282

CLEAR CREEK PEAK, RAFT RIVER RANGE.

[Latitude, 41° 41' 22".5; longitude, 113° 44' 44".0; altitude, 9,132.]

Pilot Knob	20 47 30.7	4.9002062
Cache	186 53 04.4	4.7432236
Blue Springs (north promontory)	263 00 06.2	5.0010109
Promontory	281 47 35.3	5.0219326
Ogden (formerly North Ogden)	283 08 46.8	5.1846553
Tangent	295 56 31.4	4.7215642
Newfoundland	330 44 42.6	4.8070136
Desert	362 48 34.7	4.9146336

NEWFOUNDLAND PEAK, DESERT RANGE.

[Latitude, 41° 11' 06".7; longitude, 113° 22' 19".2; altitude, 7,046.]

Desert	53 48 15.8	4.6430427
Pilot Knob	73 07 03.4	4.7945511
Clear Creek	150 59 32.5	4.8070136
Tangent	206 13 02.1	4.5634607

Table III—Continued.

DESERT PEAK, DESERT RANGE.

[Latitude, 40° 57′ 02″.4; longitude, 113° 47′ 36″.2; altitude, 8,175.]

To—	Azimuth.	Log. distance.
	° ′ ″	*Meters.*
Pilot Knob	107 45 39.3	4.4047847
Clear Creek	182 46 41.0	4.9146336
Tangent	221 01 07.4	4.8935024
Newfoundland	233 31 39.2	4.6430427

PILOT KNOB, GOSIUTE RANGE.

[Latitude, 41° 01′ 12″.2; longitude, 114° 04′ 51″.5; altitude, 10,758.]

Clear Creek	200 34 12.8	4.9002062
Tangent	235 38 03.5	4.9605333
Newfoundland	252 39 65.5	4.7945511
Desert	287 34 20.2	4.4047847

TABLE IV.—AZIMUTHS AND DISTANCES BETWEEN PRIMARY TRIANGULATION STATIONS SOUTH OF SANTA FE, N. MEX., DEPENDING UPON THE LINE TAYLOR-PLACER. 1877–'78.

The New Mexico triangulation south of Santa Fe, executed during the field seasons of 1877–'78, depends upon the position and azimuth of the line Taylor Placer, which, as herein given, depends upon the astronomical determination at Santa Fe. San Mateo Peak was separately determined from the Fort Bayard base, as shown under that heading. No adjustment was made between the two systems of triangulation, the connection between them not having been entirely completed. The points in each system are therefore affected with the station-error of their respective astronomical initial points.

M. M. M.

ENGINEER OFFICE,
    U. S. GEOGRAPHICAL SURVEYS.

ALPHABETICAL LIST.
NEW MEXICO.

	Page.
Capitan Peak	105
Cerro Colorado	104
Cerro Tecolote	103
Fra Cristobal Peak	104
Ladrones Peak	102
Magdalena Peak	102
Manzano Peak	103
Mosca Peak	101
Mount Taylor	101
Nogal Peak	105
Osha Peak	102
Pedernal Peak	101
Placer Peak	101
Rattlesnake Hill	102
Salinas Peak	104
San Mateo Peak	103
Sierra Blanca Peak (of New Mexico)	103

TABLE IV.

PLACER PEAK, PLACER MOUNTAINS.

[Latitude, 35° 20′ 03″.4; longitude, 106° 10′ 36″.0; altitude, 8,965.]

To—	Azimuth.	Log. distance.
	° ′ ″	*Meters.*
Mosca	20 08 06.5	4.7916872
Magdalena	32 18 32.4	5.2452435
Ladrones	40 11 25.3	5.1149147
Taylor	85 44 01.2	5.1182183
Pedernal	318 28 04.5	4.8602216

MOUNT TAYLOR, SAN MATEO RANGE.

[Latitude, 35° 14′ 15″.6; longitude, 107° 36′ 54″.8; altitude, 11,391.]

Placer	264 54 09.6	5.1182183
Pedernal	283 07 51.9	5.2658206
Mosca	292 58 21.2	5.0784640
Osha	301 39 25.1	5.1003384
Ladrones	331 36 58.2	5.0053693
Magdalena	344 17 40.0	5.1574674

MOSCA PEAK, MANZANO RANGE.

[Latitude, 34° 48′ 36″.5; longitude, 106° 24′ 34″.5; altitude, 9,723.]

Osha	9 39 35.7	4.2923698
Magdalena	38 37 41.7	5.0649042
Ladrones	56 27 00.2	4.8762324
Taylor	113 39 52.3	5.0784640
Placer	200 00 04.7	4.7916872
Pedernal	266 41 01.7	4.8418084
Rattlesnake Hill	296 31 19.4	4.7753947
Sierra Blanca	340 50 33.7	5.2265972

PEDERNAL PEAK.

[Latitude, 34° 50′ 38″.5; longitude, 105° 39′ 04″.2; altitude, 7,580.]

Sierra Blanca	5 21 09.0	5.2142819
Rattlesnake Hill	28 01 06.1	4.5387165
Magdalena	56 41 36.2	5.2319006
Manzano	69 14 12.4	4.8960614
Ladrones	71 23 09.8	5.1451211
Osha	72 37 01.3	4.8825486
Mosca	87 07 00.9	4.8418084
Taylor	104 15 31.9	5.2658206
Placer	138 46 12.0	4.8602216

AZIMUTHS AND DISTANCES.

Table IV—Continued.

MAGDALENA PEAK, MAGDALENA MOUNTAINS.
[Latitude, 33° 59′ 23″.2; longitude, 107° 11′ 39″.1; altitude, 10,798.]

To—	Azimuth.	Log. distance.
	° ′ ″	*Meters.*
San Mateo	25 16 33.7	4.7297314
Mount Taylor	164 32 01.1	5.1574674
Ladrones	190 50 58.0	4.7000279
Placer	211 43 48.9	5.2452435
Mosca	218 11 05.8	5.0649042
Osha	223 39 56.3	4.9974803
Manzano	225 29 11.2	4.9789883
Pedernal	235 49 16.3	5.2319006
Rattlesnake Hill	242 34 04.5	5.1498822
Cerro Tecolote	265 34 51.4	5.1421078
Cerro Colorado	289 16 02.1	4.6837603
Sierra Blanca	297 44 49.1	5.1612979

LADRONES PEAK, LADRONES MOUNTAINS.
[Latitude, 34° 26′ 01″.0; longitude, 107° 05′ 29″.5; altitude, 9,214.]

Magdalena	10 54 25.8	4.7000279
San Mateo	18 22 06.9	5.0127166
Taylor	151 54 55.1	5.0053693
Placer	219 40 01.6	5.1149147
Mosca	236 03 45.3	4.8762324
Osha	249 05 09.5	4.8021612
Manzano	253 20 24.3	4.7859500
Pedernal	250 34 02.3	5.1451211
Rattlesnake Hill	262 16 36.6	5.0681028
Cerro Tecolote	286 42 16.7	5.1287260
Sierra Blanca	314 31 55.4	5.2216644
Cerro Colorado	331 02 27.7	4.8722063

OSHA PEAK, MANZANO RANGE.
[Latitude, 34° 38′ 09″.3; longitude, 106° 26′ 43″.6; altitude, 10,023.]

Manzano	8 15 24.6	3.7135929
Magdalena	44 05 15.8	4.9974803
Ladrones	69 27 08.1	4.8021612
Taylor	122 19 36.8	5.1003384
Mosca	189 38 22.2	4.2923698
Pedernal	252 09 51.9	4.8825486
Rattlesnake Hill	277 19 14.0	4.7566643

RATTLESNAKE HILL, ANIMAS HILLS.
[Latitude, 34° 34′ 07″.5; longitude, 105° 49′ 41″.4; altitude, 6,617.]

Magdalena	63 20 13.4	5.1498822
Ladrones	82 59 32.8	5.0681028
Manzano	92 30 17.3	4.7590742
Osha	97 40 15.9	4.7566643
Mosca	116 51 10.9	4.7753947
Pedernal	207 55 03.3	4.5387165

TABLE IV—Continued.

MANZANO PEAK, MANZANO MOUNTAINS.

[Latitude, 34° 35' 23".2; longitude, 106° 27' 12".19; altitude, 10,086.]

To—	Azimuth.	Log. distance.
	° ′ ″	Meters.
Colorado	15 32 40.5	4.9329640
San Mateo	38 38 53.0	5.1667791
Magdalena	45 54 13.4	4.9789883
Ladrones	73 42 05.6	4.7859500
Osha	188 15 08.0	3.7135929
Pedernal	248 46 39.3	4.8960614
Rattlesnake Hill	272 08 59.6	4.7590742
Cerro Tecolote	308 59 05.9	4.9541816
Sierra Blanca	336 12 27.5	5.1680014

CERRO TECOLOTE.

[Latitude, 34° 04' 37".2; longitude, 105° 41' 44".2; altitude, 7,254.]

Sierra Blanca	8 07 02.4	4.8966034
Nogal	9 22 41.7	4.8145532
Salinas	42 18 23.1	5.0662442
San Mateo	70 40 00.6	5.2348846
Cerro Colorado	74 49 14.7	4.9843806
Magdalena	86 25 10.8	5.1421078
Ladrones	107 29 25.4	5.1287260
Manzano	129 24 44.9	4.9541816
Capitan	323 55 03.9	4.8242349

SAN MATEO PEAK, SAN MATEO RANGE.

[Latitude, 33° 33' 07".3; longitude, 107° 26' 04".9; altitude, 10,209.]

Ladrones	198 10 23.6	5.0127166
Magdalena	205 08 19.9	4.7297314
Manzano	218 05 41.4	5.1667791
Cerro Colorado	244 24 35.7	4.8799765
Cerro Tecolote	249 41 43.7	5.2348846
Sierra Blanca	277 00 51.9	5.1829988
Salinas	287 19 18.0	4.9475931
Fra Cristobal	294 54 00.7	4.5180002

SIERRA BLANCA PEAK, SIERRA BLANCA RANGE.

[Latitude, 33° 22' 24".3; longitude, 105° 48' 54".9; altitude, 11,892.]

Organ (?)	31 54 49.6	5.1273616
Back	211 30 18.7	
Salinas	83 03 00.9	4.8309648
Fra Cristobal	93 07 47.2	5.0844309
San Mateo	97 54 39.2	5.1829988
Magdalena	118 30 42.3	5.1612979
Cerro Colorado	122 41 59.5	4.9889390
Ladrones	135 14 38.5	5.2216644

Table IV—Continued.

SIERRA BLANCA PEAK, SIERRA BLANCA—Continued.

[Latitude, 33° 22′ 24″.3; longitude, 105° 48′ 54″.9; altitude, 11,892.]

To—	Azimuth.	Log. distance.
	° ′ ″	*Meters.*
Manzano	156 33 51.9	5.1680014
Mosca	161 10 51.7	5.2265972
Nogal	182 01 03.4	4.1354369
Pedernal	185 15 56.3	5.2142819
Tecolote	188 03 03.4	4.8966034
Capitan	244 22 57.9	4.7473050
Carrizo (7)	191 53 49.0	4.5569467
Back	11 56 28.5	
East Carrizo Cone (5)	210 21 29.8	4.5508554
Back	30 27 54.9	

CERRO COLORADO.

[Latitude, 33° 50′ 42″.5; longitude, 106° 42′ 06″.2; altitude, 5,654.]

Fra Cristobal	39 57 33.7	4.7816730
San Mateo	64 49 12.3	4.8799765
Magdalena	109 32 31.3	4.6837603
Ladrones	151 15 35.2	4.8722063
Manzano	195 24 18.2	4.9329640
Cerro Tecolote	254 15 31.3	4.9843806
Sierra Blanca	302 12 32.9	4.9889390
Salinas	345 51 57.4	4.7967848

FRA CRISTOBAL PEAK, FRA CRISTOBAL RANGE.

[Latitude, 33° 25′ 35″.0; longitude, 107° 04′ 10″.13; altitude, 6,646.]

San Mateo	115 04 39.3	4.5180002
Cerro Colorado	219 43 40.7	4.7816730
Sierra Blanca	272 24 42.4	5.0844309
Salinas	284 38 02.1	4.7483121

SALINAS PEAK, SAN ANDREAS RANGE.

[Latitude, 33° 17′ 50″.6; longitude, 106° 32′ 15″.0; altitude, 9,039.]

Organ (7)	1 34 09.2	5.0239673
Back	181 33 09.2	
Fra Cristobal	104 57 14.3	4.7483121
San Mateo	108 49 09.7	4.9475931
Colorado	165 57 24.4	4.7967848
Tecolote	221 50 22.0	5.0662442
Nogal	251 43 33.5	4.8523474
Capitan	254 13 24.0	5.0864418
Sierra Blanca	262 39 12.0	4.8309648

U. S. GEOGRAPHICAL SURVEYS.

TABLE IV—Continued.

NOGAL PEAK, SIERRA BLANCA.

[Latitude, 33° 29' 47''.5; longitude, 105° 48' 36''.2; altitude, 9,983.]

To—	Azimuth.	Log. distance.
	° ′ ″	*Meters.*
Sierra Blanca	2 01 13.7	4.1354369
Salinas	72 07 34.9	4.8523474
Cerro Tecolote	189 18 52.5	4.8145532
East Carrizo Cone (5)	225 46 07.5	4.3874986
Back	45 52 22.8	
Capitan	258 06 34.2	4.7076275

CAPITAN PEAK, CAPITAN RANGE.

[Latitude, 33° 35' 24''.4; longitude, 105° 16' 20''.3; altitude, 10,023.]

Sierra Blanca	64 40 56.2	4.7473050
Salinas	74 55 14.3	5.0864418
Nogal	78 24 23.9	4.7076275
Carrizo (7)	104 48 26.3	4.6471375
Back	284 33 03.3	
Cerro Tecolote	144 09 12.4	4.8242349

TABLE V.—AZIMUTHS AND DISTANCES BETWEEN PRIMARY TRIANGU-
LATION STATIONS DEPENDING UPON THE FORT BAYARD BASE, N.
MEX. 1878.

This line was laid out on the plain west of the Santa Rita Mountains, near the Warm Springs at Apache Tejo, about 10 miles south of Fort Bayard. It was measured with a 50-foot Stackpole compensated steel tape, the direction being about N. 17° 27′ E., the adopted length being 27,265.937 feet (5.164 miles), which, reduced to sea-level and converted into meters, is given in the following tables, with the principal elements of the triangulation depending upon it. The ends of the base were not permanently marked (see Annual Report 1879, p. 119 and p. 245).

The base was connected with the astronomical station (latitude 32° 47′ 40″.35, longitude 108° 09′ 08″.77) established by the survey at Fort Bayard, the discussion of the co-ordinates of which will be found in the Annual Report of this office for 1879, pp. 81–113.

The triangulation expanded from the Fort Bayard base has one main point in common (San Mateo Peak) with the triangulation running south-ward from the Santa Fe astronomical station, and depending upon the azimuth and distance of the line Placer–Taylor. For this triangulation see pp. 97–105 of this volume.

The co-ordinates of San Mateo, as determined from the two bases, are as follows:

From Fort Bayard, latitude 33° 33′ 07″.30, longitude 107° 26′ 04″.90.
From Santa Fe, latitude 33° 33′ 06″.94, longitude 107° 26′ 27″.56.

The difference, which is really all in longitude, is probably mainly due to a large station error at Santa Fe, the exact amount of which had not been accurately determined at the time of closing the field-work of the survey.

The two systems of triangulation are, therefore, independent of each other, and affected with the station errors of their respective astronomical points.

M. M. M.

ENGINEER OFFICE,
U. S. GEOGRAPHICAL SURVEYS.

ALPHABETICAL LIST.

NEW MEXICO.

	Page.
Astronomical monument	111
Station A	111
Station B	111
Station C	111
Station D	112
Station E	112
Station F	112
Bear Peak	112
Cookes Peak	113
Eagle Peak	114
Florida Peak	113
Hacheta Peak	114
San Mateo Peak	114
Thomas Peak	114

TABLE V.

ASTRONOMICAL MONUMENT, FORT BAYARD, N. MEX.

[Latitude, 32° 47′ 40″.35 ; longitude, 108° 09′ 08″.77; altitude, 6,097 feet.]

To—	Azimuths.	Log. distance.
	° ′ ″	*Meters.*
Station F	7 32 05.9	4.5877997
Station C	15 29 26.7	4.0373925
Bear Peak	102 39 56.8	4.2966608
Station D	319 41 36.7	3.8962539

STATION A, NORTH BASE, FORT BAYARD, N. MEX.

[Latitude, 32° 40′ 42″.13; longitude, 108° 07′ 16″.15.]

Station B (south base)	17 27 33.96	3.9194057
Station F	17 27 33.96	4.4268484
Station C	112 09 35.52	3.8000362
Station D	119 27 33.96	3.8577876
Station E	307 00 09.99	3.9727971

STATION B, SOUTH BASE, FORT BAYARD, N. MEX.

[Latitude, 32° 36′ 24″.88; longitude, 108° 08′ 56″.74.]

Station F	17 26 42.4	4.2651592
Station C	161 57 56.1	4.0348368
Station A (north base)	197 26 42.4	3.9194057
Station D	197 26 42.4	4.1907186
Station E	257 11 07.6	4.0106389
Cooks Peak	281 37 27.7	4.6009665

STATION C, FORT BAYARD, N. MEX.

[Latitude, 32° 41′ 59″.3; longitude, 108° 11′ 00″.5.]

Station F	4 25 29.3	4.4464502
Bear Peak	132 07 15.6	4.3448992
Astronomical monument, Fort Bayard, N. Mex	195 28 26.3	4.0373925
Station D	240 39 12.9	3.9629453
Station A	292 07 34.4	3.8000362
Cooks Peak	293 21 23.5	4.6649240
Station E	301 00 45.1	4.1924695
Station B	341 56 46.7	4.0348368

AZIMUTHS AND DISTANCES.

TABLE V—Continued.

STATION D, FORT BAYARD, N. MEX.

[Latitude, 32° 44′ 25″.34; longitude, 108° 05′ 53″.1.]

To—	Azimuth.	Log. distance.
	° ′ ″	*Meters.*
Station A	17 28 18.8	3.8577876
Station B	17 28 18.8	4.1907186
Station F	17 28 18.8	4.5305619
Station C	60 41 59.1	3.9629453
Bear Peak	112 59 54.7	4.4234811
Astronomical Monument, Fort Bayard, N. Mex	139 43 22.6	3.8962539
Flagstaff, Fort Bayard (7)	141 03 42.6	3.8927522
Back	321 02 00.5	
Cooks Peak	303 35 07.5	4.6161275
Station E	336 55 57.3	4.1341343

STATION E, FORT BAYARD, N. MEX.

[Latitude, 32° 37′ 38″.5; longitude, 108° 02′ 28″.4.]

Station F	38 04 45.13	4.4011288
Station B	77 14 34.30	4.0106389
Station C	121 05 21.43	4.1924695
Station A	127 02 45.27	3.9727971
Bear	127 36 40.82	4.5743861
Station D	156 57 47.87	4.1341343
Station 28 (5)	270 30 06.74	4.4883449
Back	90 40 43.48	
Cooks Peak	289 34 40.34	4.4894275

STATION F, FORT BAYARD, N. MEX.

[Latitude, 32° 26′ 54″.5; longitude, 108° 12′ 23″.1.]

Hacheta Point	11 25 35.1	4.9649568
Bear	161 31 52.0	4.6534708
Station C	184 24 44.8	4.4404502
Astronomical Monument, Fort Bayard	187 30 21.1	4.5877997
Station B	197 24 48.7	4.2651592
Station A	197 24 48.7	4.4268484
Station D	197 24 48.7	4.5305619
Station E	217 59 25.2	4.4011488
Cooks Peak	257 54 36.8	4.6590400
Florida Peak	303 11 33.7	4.8188555

BEAR PEAK, DIABLO RANGE.

[Latitude, 32° 50′ 00″.7; longitude, 108° 21′ 31″.6; altitude, 8,081.]

Hacheta	61 38 53.68	5.1244588
Graham (7)	84 26 00.69	5.1538899
Back	263 36 52.37	
Thomas	136 51 55.55	5.2147876
Eagle	167 43 08.83	4.9805775

U. S. GEOGRAPHICAL SURVEYS. 113

TABLE V—Continued.

BEAR PEAK, DIABLO RANGE—Continued.
[Latitude, 32° 50′ 00″.7; longitude, 108° 21′ 31″.6; altitude, 8,081.]

To—	Azimuth.	Log. distance.
	° ′ ″	*Meters.*
Black Peak (5)	245 54 09.97	4.3023279
Back	66 00 32.46	
Astronomical Monument	282 33 14.30	4.2966608
Station D	292 51 26.50	4.4234811
Cooks Peak	299 18 33.06	4.8296626
Station E	307 26 26.69	4.5743861
Station C	312 01 34.02	4.3448992
Florida Peak	318 32 13.29	5.0211712
Station F	341 26 56.14	4.6534708

COOKES PEAK, COOKE MOUNTAINS.
[Latitude, 32° 32′ 01″.4; longitude, 107° 43′ 53″.9; altitude, 8,330.]

Hacheta	32 25 22.68	5.0722534
Station F	78 09 54.91	4.6590400
Station B (south base)	101 40 53.98	4.6009665
Station E	109 44 40.44	4.4894275
Station C	113 36 00.21	4.6649240
Station A (north base)	113 47 40.25	4.6012082
Bear Peak	119 38 52.21	4.8296626
Station D	123 46 58.93	4.6161275
Black Peak	135 48 12.87	4.7625522
Back	315 34 13.44	
Eagle	148 16 34.74	5.1740003
Station 28 (5)	189 46 54.02	4.0092538
Back	9 47 29.87	
San Mateo	193 43 05.25	5.0655038
Station 6 (5)	204 35 35.48	4.4516945
Caballo Cone (5)	216 45 07.75	4.8953247
Back	37 01 36.61	
Sunday Cone (5)	250 20 57.51	4.4507381
Back	70 30 06.67	
Station 25 (5)	329 18 01.07	4.0459993
Back	149 56 16.06	
Florida	347 14 17.13	4.6705241

FLORIDA PEAK, FLORIDA MOUNTAINS.
[Latitude, 32° 07′ 18″.3; longitude, 107° 37′ 19″.2; altitude, 7,295.]

Hacheta	53 48 18.23	4.9606998
Lalacha (5)	68 29 30.47	4.9274505
Back	248 03 04.60	
Station F	123 30 17.43	4.8188555
Bear	138 55 57.54	5.0211712
Eagle	152 49 44.01	5.2881719
Cook	167 17 48.18	4.6705241
San Mateo	186 17 48.18	5.2029477
Sunday Cone (5)	196 27 54.05	4.7597313
Back	16 33 28.82	
Potrillo (7)	292 28 26.39	4.7574500
Back	112 46 13.54	
Boca Grande (7)	32 57 34.52	4.8121458
Back	212 45 47.08	

1874 WH——8

Table V—Continued.

HACHETA PEAK, HACHETA RANGE.

[Latitude, 31° 37' 58".2; longitude, 108° 23' 57".0; altitude, 8,352.]

To—	Azimuth.	Log. distance.
	° ′ ″	*Meters.*
Graham (7)	130 48 42.43	5.2610978
Back	310 01 39.55	
Lalacha (5)	167 16 24.48	4.3703351
Back	347 14 41.08	
Bear	181 37 36.15	5.1244588
Station F	191 19 46.96	4.9649568
Cooks	212 04 06.26	5.0722543
Florida	233 23 40.73	4.9606998
Boca Grande (7)	270 19 56.39	4.5845711
Back	90 32 41.08	

EAGLE PEAK, TULEROSA MOUNTAINS.

[Latitude, 33° 40' 33".2; longitude, 108° 34' 41".3; altitude, 9,791.]

Thomas	105 49 55.81	4.9797542
Station 25 (5)	165 06 48.37	4.6657812
Back	345 02 29.62	
Alamocita (5)	190 07 18.25	4.7709080
Back	10 11 04.40	
Horse Peak (5)	231 19 20.05	4.7294555
Back	51 34 28.20	
Round Peak (5)	270 03 01.33	4.6450596
Back	90 18 52.03	
San Mateo	277 03 37.81	5.0293257
Cooks	327 48 50.28	5.1740003
Florida	332 18 34.28	5.2871720
Bear	347 35 55.81	4.9805775
Hacheta	355 42 47.84	5.3563501

SAN MATEO PEAK, SAN MATEO RANGE.

[Latitude, 33° 33' 07".3; longitude, 107° 26' 04".9; altitude, 10,209.]

Florida	6 21 36.5	5.2029477
Cooks	13 52 48.2	5.0655038
Eagle	97 41 36.6	3.0293257

THOMAS PEAK.

[Latitude, 33° 54' 24".1; longitude, 109° 34' 16".0; altitude, 11,275.]

Alamocita Peak (5)	252 00 53.63	5.0295754
Back	72 38 03.41	
Station 25 (5)	256 14 16.19	4.9139827
Back	76 43 16.58	
Eagle Peak	285 16 47.67	4.9797542
Bear Peak	316 11 54.83	5.2147876

TABLE VI.—AZIMUTHS AND DISTANCES BETWEEN PRIMARY TRI-
ANGULATION STATIONS DEPENDING UPON THE FORT BLISS BASE,
TEXAS, 1878.

NOTE.—The Fort Bliss or El Paso Base was laid out in October, 1878, on the nearly level plain about five miles east of the village of El Paso (at one time called Franklin), El Paso County, Texas. This base was measured with a 50-foot Stackpole compensated steel tape, the adopted length reduced to sea-level being 8,048.960 feet (A. R., 1879, p. 226). When the base was measured the village was for the time also called Fort Bliss, the troops assigned to that post being quartered there.

The abandoned post lay between the village and the base-line, and its flagstaff was connected with and brought into the scheme of triangulation. Directly south of El Paso, Tex., and separated from it by the Rio Grande, is the old Mexican town of El Paso del Norte. The bell tower of its cathedral was observed upon and its position determined by connection with our astronomical determination of El Paso, Tex., made in September, 1878. The astronomical monument is situated in the public square of the Texas village, and all details regarding final determination of its co-ordinates are given in the annual report of this office for 1879, pp. 47–81.

The scheme of triangulation depending upon this base and astronomical determination has no direct connection with any of the previous or subsequent work of this office, but it is complete so far as it goes, and is important inasmuch as it gives a good connection between several points of the boundary between the United States and Mexico and the late astronomical determination made by this office at El Paso, Tex. The elements of the triangulation connecting the astronomical monument with the other points will be found in the following pages, the extreme occupied points being:

	Latitude.	Longitude.
	° ′ ″	° ′ ″
North Franklin Peak	31 54 06.80	106 29 23.4
Mexico Peak	31 43 13.42	106 34 53.30
East Base	31 47 11.43	106 24 40.72

The points on or near the boundary line connected with and located are as follows:

	Latitude.	Longitude.
	° ′ ″	° ′ ″
1. Boundary monument on right (west) bank of Rio Grande	31 46 58.28	106 31 33.49
2. Boundary monument in Mulera Mountains	31 46 58.29	106 32 00.50
3. Bell tower of El Paso Cathedral	31 44 14.88	106 28 59.24

A map in the Annual Report of this office for 1879, page 81, shows clearly the relative locations of the points referred to. In comparing these results with the work of the Mexican Boundary Commission some difficulty arises owing to errors and inconsistencies in the published results as given in Volume I, Mexican Boundary Report. If we take those results which the report shows to have been well and carefully established, and which can be identified beyond doubt, the agreement is good. Thus the boundary monuments connected with were known to have been located on the parallel 31° 47′ as nearly as possible by connection with J. H. Clark's astronomical station on the left bank of the Rio Grande, found by him to be in latitude 31° 46′ 51″.29.

Our latitude for these same monuments is 31° 46′ 58″.28 and 31° 46′ 58″.29, or about 1″.71 south of the boundary survey determinations. No entirely reliable data could be found showing beyond a doubt the connection between either of these monuments and the longitude stations at Frontera or San Elceario. Hence the only good comparison which can be made, so far as the monuments are concerned, is that in regard to latitude.

The Boundary Report, however, shows reliable data establishing the longitude of the bell tower of the El Paso (Mexico) church by direct connection between the carefully determined longitude station at El Paso and the tower, thus:

Final longitude of El Paso del Norte, Mexican Boundary Report, Volume I, page 192 .... } In time 7ʰ 5ᵐ 56ˢ.43
{ In arc ...... 106° 29′ 06″.45
Bell tower, 500 feet (5″.79) east of El Paso Observatory, }
Mexican Boundary Report, page 141 .... } .... 5″.79

Final longitude of bell tower .... 106° 29′ 00″.66

The longitude determined by this office for the same point (depending upon the telegraphic method) is 106° 28′ 59″.24, or 1″.42 east of the Mexican boundary determination, by the method of lunar culminations.

A final result for the latitude of El Paso del Norte does not seem to have been determined by Major Emory, although a result by Salazar is given in Table E, on page 244, Mexican Boundary Report, which makes the latitude of his observatory and the bell tower identical (31° 44′ 15″.7), although the observatory is stated to be 200 feet north of the tower at page 141.

For this reason the result of this office for latitude was compared with that assigned in said report to the boundary monuments.

ALPHABETICAL LIST.

TEXAS.

	Page.
Astronomical Monument	119
East Base, Ft. Bliss	119
Graveyard Hill	119
North Franklin Peak	120
South Franklin Peak	120
West Base, Ft. Bliss	119

NEW MEXICO.

Rodadero Peak	120

MEXICO.

Mexico Peak	120

Table VI.

ASTRONOMCIAL MONUMENT, FORT BLISS.

[Latitude, 31° 45′ 31″.14; longitude, 106° 29′ 05″.37; altitude (top of monument), 3,630.]

To—	Azimuth.	Log. distance.
	° ′ ″	*Meters.*
Graveyard Hill	124 38 32.20	3.0534606
South Franklin Peak	185 41 37.27	3.7039514
West Base	227 34 43.60	3.8317394
East Base	246 03 27.66	3.8817914

WEST BASE, FORT BLISS.

[Latitude, 31° 47′ 59″.78; longitude, 106° 25′ 54″.85.]

Astronomical Monument	47 36 23.93	3.8317394
Graveyard Hill	56 30 14.56	3.8529017
South Franklin Peak	95 46 26.24	3.6562810
East Base	307 21 35.51	3.3897721

EAST BASE, FORT BLISS.

[Latitude, 31° 47′ 11″.43; longitude, 106° 24′ 40″.72.]

El Paso Church Tower (7)	51 22 37.11	3.9399661
Back	231 20 21.03	
Astronomical Monument	66 05 47.01	3.8817914
Mexico Peak	65 35 33.20	4.2481784
Graveyard Hill	72 48 15.38	3.9171487
South Franklin Peak	106 46 01.76	3.8290079
West Base	127 22 14.57	3.3897721
North Franklin Peak	199 52 06.16	4.1700996

GRAVEYARD HILL.

[Latitude, 31° 45′ 52″.0; longitude, 106° 29′ 40″.7.]

Mexico Peak	59 19 26.13	3.9807724
North Franklin Peak	182 42 43.83	4.1831397
South Franklin Peak	198 03 53.08	3.6644121
West Base	236 28 15.59	3.8529017
East Base	252 45 37.39	3.9171487
Astronomical Monument	304 38 13.58	3.0534606
El Paso Church Tower (7)	339 56 58.79	3.5031626
Back	159 58 20.63	

AZIMUTHS AND DISTANCES.

TABLE VI—Continued.

MEXICO PEAK.

[Latitude, 31° 43′ 13″.42; longitude, 106° 34′ 53″.30.]

To—	Azimuth.	Log. distance.
	° ′ ″	*Meters.*
North Franklin Peak	203 17 58.45	4.3407117
Rodadero Peak	222 23 26.99	3.9134119
South Franklin Peak	226 07 55.69	4.1267475
Graveyard Hill	239 16 41.69	3.9807724
Old Fort Bliss (7)	244 45 44.90	4.1558544
Back	64 50 03.80	
East Base	245 30 10.82	4.2481784
El Paso Church (7)	258 29 58.61	3.9781664
Back	78 34 04.81	

SOUTH FRANKLIN PEAK.

[Latitude, 31° 48′ 14″.55; longitude, 106° 28′ 46″.29.]

Astronomical Monument	5 41 47.32	3.7039514
Graveyard Hill	18 04 21.76	3.6644121
Mexico Peak	46 11 08.88	4.1267475
Boundary Monument, right bank of Rio Grande (5)	61 54 18.49	3.6977412
Back	241 52 50.40	
Boundary Monument, on slope of Mulera Peak (5)	65 19 28.53	3.7499239
Back	145 17 46.21	
Rodadero Peak (5)	71 34 10.94	3.7959230
Back	251 32 12.16	
North Franklin Peak	174 51 55.34	4.0371287
West Base	275 45 01.90	3.6562810
East Base	286 43 52.37	3.8290079
Old Fort Bliss (flagstaff) (7)	313 57 31.14	3.6606005
Back	133 58 37.12	
El Paso Church Tower (7)	2 38 35.28	3.8686494
Back	182 39 28.46	

NORTH FRANKLIN PEAK, FRANKLIN RANGE.

[Latitude, 31° 54′ 06″.81; longitude, 106° 29′ 23″.40; altitude, 7,070.]

Graveyard Hill	1 42 52.97	4.1831397
Rodadero Peak	21 07 10.58	4.1382690
Mexico Peak	23 20 52.34	4.3407117
East Base	329 49 37.01	4.1700996
South Franklin Peak	354 51 35.75	4.0371287

RODADERO PEAK.

[Latitude, 31° 47′ 10″.33; longitude, 106° 30′ 31″.72.]

Mexico	27 03 41.65	3.9134119
North Franklin Peak	201 05 31.22	4.1382690
South Franklin Peak	251 32 12.16	3.7959230
Boundary Monument (5)	294 17 26.49	2.9547063
Back	114 17 42.94	
Graveyard Hill	298 11 14.01	3.7079320
El Paso Church Tower (7)	314 00 46.06	3.8907527
Back	134 03 37.91	

PART III.

BAROMETRIC ALTITUDES.

CERTAIN REFERENCE STATIONS.
TABLE I.—MILITARY POSTS.
II.—MOUNTAIN PEAKS.
III.—CITIES, TOWNS, AND SETTLEMENTS.
IV.—LAKES, SPRINGS, ETC.
V.—MOUNTAIN PASSES.

NOTE.—Where the minus sign appears, distances are in feet *below* sea-level.

NOTE.

The altitudes given in the following tables, with the few exceptions noted, are the results of cistern barometer observations, being usually adopted means after revision of the altitudes of initial reference stations. These have been selected from the many thousands of computed barometric altitudes that have contributed to the construction of the contours of the original plotting sheets, and are alone the best determined points, being those well known and easily identified, being but a fractional part of those actually observed and computed of prominent points, since revision of reference stations and determination of adopted means has not always been practicable for want of skilled assistance, while bringing finally to an end the multiple results of the survey, remaining incomplete when appropriations were suspended.

Mountain peaks with local names alone are given. The altitudes of many others ascended and barometrically measured will be found upon the published maps. Wherever altitudes herein are found to differ from results heretofore published the present figures are to be accepted.

Cistern barometer altitudes will be found in Vol. II (pp. 555 to 566 inc.), and in certain annual reports of this office, which appear as appendixes of the annual reports of the Chief of Engineers, U. S. Army

The above tables, in instances, contain altitudes not given herewith, for want, usually, of revision of altitudes of the reference stations upon which they depend.

G. M. W.

ENGINEER OFFICE,
U. S. GEOGRAPHICAL SURVEYS.

CERTAIN REFERENCE STATIONS USED IN COMPARISONS OF BAROMETRIC DIFFERENCE OF LEVEL.

NOTE.—The stations more or less regularly observed at, herewith given, situated within or in proximity to areas surveyed, have been availed of in making independent comparisons of barometric differences of level, in addition to the daily simultaneous observations and resulting level differences at points (selected at minimum distances horizontally and like differences in elevation, varying according to physical conformation and accessibility of the region) within the field occupied by a single party or those conjoining.

G. M. W.

Camp Douglas, Astronomical Monument, 4,905 feet; determined by level from Temple Pier, Salt Lake City, by Mr. Gilbert Thompson in 1872; also, sun dial, 4,904 feet; base of flag-staff, 4,902 feet.

Carson City, Nev., Friend's Observatory, Signal Office station, 4,660 feet; determined by three and one-half months' daily means (August 16 to November 30, 1876), referred to San Francisco and Salt Lake City. The two determinations differed by 11 feet, and the mean of the two has been adopted.

Colorado Springs, Signal Office, 6,030 feet; determined by mean of five months' observation (August to December, 1874), referred to Signal Office at Denver; astronomical monument, 6,010 feet, determined by observations from July 28 to August 10, 1873.

Corinne, Utah, Signal Office, 4,244 feet; barometer 11.4 feet above Central Pacific Railroad track at depot, leveled by Mr. Gilbert Thompson in 1873. Track is 4,233 feet, by Central Pacific Railroad levels.

Denver, Colo., Kansas Pacific Railroad, 5,196.6 feet is the deduced altitude by Mr. Gardner of the Kansas Pacific Railroad track at depot, published in 1873.

Denver, Colo., Signal Office, 5,263 feet. From latest information, November, 1877, the signal office is 66.1 feet above Kansas Pacific Railroad track—leveled by Mr. Cutshaw, city engineer. In 1872, '73, '74, and '75 the altitude of our reference station was 48 feet above the track = 5,244.6 feet. In 1876 the signal office was 13.5 feet higher = 5,258.1 feet. The altitudes of a number of points on the Denver and Rio Grande Railroad have been obtained from the profile of that road, and are inserted in the tables of altitudes. The determinations from the profile were all corrected by +54 feet, to bring the Denver and Rio Grande altitude of Denver up to that indicated above.

Fort Bayard, N. Mex., 6,068 feet; determined from daily means of our observations from September 25 to October 10, 1878, referred to Santa Fe and Silver City, N. Mex. The result of five days' observations in 1873 is also given weight.

Fort Bliss (*El Paso*), *Tex.*, 3,622.9 feet; determined from daily means of our observations extending from August 11 to September 18, 1878, and referred to Santa Fe and also to Silver City, N. Mex. This result is checked by the altitude of Frontera (15 miles above), determined in 1851 by Colonel Graham, United States Topographical Engineers, to be 3,870 feet. Frontera was found by our aneroid barometer to be about 250 feet higher than El Paso, which would make the latter 3,620 feet in altitude.

Fort Craig, New Mexico, 4,447.5 feet; determined from daily means of observations from July 10 to November 15, 1877, referred to Santa Fe.

Fort Mohave, Ariz. (bench-mark), 755.8 feet; determined from daily means observations July 8 to September 5, 1875, referred to Los Angeles, Cal.

Great Salt Lake, Utah, 4,210 feet, 22.6 feet below railroad track at Corinne (4,233 feet); leveled by Gilbert Thompson, 1872 and 1873.

Los Angeles, Cal., Signal Office, 320 feet; determined by levels of M. Kelliher, city surveyor, and the Southern Pacific Railroad. (Letter from Chief Signal Officer, January 30, 1879.) Rendezvous camp, 312 feet, determined (by level) by Frank Carpenter, from tide-guage at Wilmington (Cal.) Breakwater, 1875. Gartner's office, 1875, 326 feet. Lieutenant Bergland's office, 1875, 323 feet; these last two by level by Carpenter.

Ogden Observatory, astronomical monument, 4,374 feet; Great Salt Lake, 4,210.4 feet; Ogden (railroad junction) above lake, Kintner's levels, 1877, 89.2 feet; Ogden (railroad junction) above sea-level, 4,299.6 feet; Ogden (railroad junction) below astronomical monument, Kintner's levels, 1877, 74.4 feet; Ogden, astronomical monument above sea-level, 4,374 feet.

Prattville, Cal., 4,394.1 feet; camp near post-office determined from daily means observations October 4 to 12, 1878, referred to Red Bluff, Cal.

Red Bluff, Cal., Signal Office, 338 feet, by level; authority, General Cadwallader, engineer Central Pacific Railroad. (Extract letter from Signal Office, January 25, 1879.)

Sacramento, Signal Office, 76 feet; bench-mark above sea-level, 30 feet; ground above bench-mark, 2 feet; barometer above ground, 44.3 feet; barometer above sea-level, 76.3 feet. Authority for bench-mark, Central Pacific Railroad and John Prentin, engineer, Sacramento. (Letter from Signal Office, January 25, 1879.)

Salt Lake City, Utah, Temple Pier, 4,330 feet; Signal Office, 1877, 4,352 feet; Great Salt Lake, 4,210.4 feet; Temple Pier, above lake, Thompson levels, 1870 and 1873, 119.98 feet; Temple Pier, 4,330.4 feet; Signal Office barometer above pier, Lieutenant Young's levels, January, 1878, 21.5 feet=4,351.9 feet.

San Francisco, Signal Office, 60 feet; bench-mark above sea-level, 6.7 feet; ground above bench-mark, 6.3 feet; barometer above ground, 47 feet; barometer above sea-level, 60 feet. Authority for bench-mark, board of engineers and city surveyor (Mr. Richard Stretch). This bench-mark is used for grading all streets in the city. (Letter from Signal Office, February 15, 1878).

Santa Fe, N. Mex., Signal Office, 6,965 feet. The altitude of Santa Fe, determined from five months' barometric observations (July-November, 1874) and referred to Denver and also to Colorado Springs, gave 7,044.2 feet for each result. This altitude was used until February 12, 1878, when 6,965.2 feet was adopted, being the result of five months' observations in 1877, referred to Denver.

In 1875 a change was made in the error of the Signal Office barometer (No. 1860), the scale being lowered .070 inch; this error agrees well with the difference in altitude determined in 1874 by Lieutenant Marshall and by Lieutenant Tillman in 1877.

Silver City, N. Mex., Signal Office, 5,770.7 feet; determined from daily means of observations at Signal Office, August 20 to October 31, 1878, referred to Santa Fe.

Virginia City, Mont., Signal Office, 5,480 feet; bench-mark above sea-level, 5,482 feet; ground below bench-mark, 17.54 feet; barometer above ground, 15.5 feet; barometer above sea-level, 5,479.96 feet. Authority for bench-mark, city engineer. No change in location since 1873. (Letter from Signal Office, February 15, 1878.)

Winnemucca, Nev., Signal Office, 4,355 feet; determined from four months' barometric observations (July to October, 1877) daily means, referred to Salt Lake City. "No change has been made in elevation of barometer at Winnemucca." (Letter from Signal Office, January 25, 1879.)

U. S. GEOGRAPHICAL SURVEYS.   127

TABLE I.—MILITARY POSTS.

Name of post.	State or Territory.	Atlas sheet.	Altitude. in feet above sea.	Expeditionary year.
Apache, Fort	Arizona	83B	5,001	{ 1871 / 1873 / 1878
Bayard, Fort	New Mexico	84C	*6,068	1878
Bidwell, Fort	California	38B	4,647	{ 1877 / 1878
Bliss, Fort†	Texas	90B	3,630	1878
Bowie, Fort	Arizona	89B	4,872	1873
Burgwin, Camp‡	New Mexico	69D	7,277	1874
Cady, near Camp	California	73D	1,894	1875
Cameron, Fort, near	Utah	59A	6,058	1873
Churchill, Fort‡	Nevada	47D	a4,258	1876
Craig, Fort	New Mexico	84A	4,448	{ 1873 / 1874 / 1876 / 1877
Cummings, Fort‡	do	84C	4,840	1878
Curry, Camp†	Oregon	29B	4,273	1878
Defiance, Old Fort	Arizona	68D	7,042	1873
Defiance, Fort	Utah	67	4,052	1872
Douglas, Fort†	do	41D	l4,905	1873
Ellis, Fort†	Montana	15C	4,747	1877
Fillmore, Fort‡	New Mexico	90A	a3,720	1878
Floyd, Camp‡	Utah	50B	4,866	1872
Fred. Steele, Fort†	Wyoming	43A	l6,850	1873
Garland, Fort	Colorado	62C	l7,937	{ 1873 / 1875 / 1877
Goodwin, Old Camp‡	Arizona	83	2,816	1873
Grant, Fort	do	83C	4,833	{ 1873 / 1874
Grant, Old Camp‡	do	83	2,118	1871
Hall, Fort	Idaho	32D	4,752	1877
Halleck, Fort†	Nevada	40C	5,790	1869
Hualapais, Camp‡	Arizona	75	5,322	1871
Independence, Camp‡	California	65A	3,956	{ 1871 / 1875
Klamath, Fort	Oregon	29C	4,108	1878
Lewis, Fort§	Colorado	69A	7,057	{ 1873 / 1874
Lowell, Fort	Arizona	89A	2,538	1871
Lyon, Fort	Colorado	62D	3,910	{ 1876 / 1877
McPherson, Fort†	Nebraska	45	l2,789	1874
McRae, Fort‡	New Mexico	84A	4,395	{ 1877 / 1878
Marcy, Fort†	do	69D	6,965	{ 1874 / 1875 / 1877
Mohave, Fort	Arizona	74B	756	{ 1871 / 1875
North Platte Station	Nebraska	45D	2,789	1874

* Astronomical monument 29 feet higher.   ‡ Abandoned.
† Astronomical monument.   § Pagosa Hot Springs.

BAROMETRIC ALTITUDES

TABLE I.—MILITARY POSTS—Continued

Name of post.	State or Territory.			
Polk, Camp	Oregon			
Rawlins, Camp*	Utah	50B	4,567	{ 1872 / 1873
Ruby, Camp*†	Nevada	49A	6,153	1869
Russell, Fort D. A. †	Wyoming	44C	6,041	1872
San Carlos, Camp	Arizona	83A	a2,559	1874
Sanders, Fort†	Wyoming	43D	7,168	1873
Selden, Fort*	New Mexico	84C	3,900	1878
Sherman, Camp	do	84A	6,927	1878
Sidney, Fort†	Nebraska	44D	4,106	1874
Stanton, Fort	New Mexico	84B	6,152	{ 1877 / 1878
Tejon, Fort*	California	73A	3,245	1875
Tulerosa, Fort*	New Mexico	83B	6,740	1873
Union, Fort †	do	70C	6,744	{ 1874 / 1875 / 1876
Verde, Fort	Arizona	75D	3,160	1877
Vincent, Camp*	New Mexico	84A	6,188	1871
Walla Walla, Fort†	Washington	12C	1,034	1878
Warner, Camp*	Oregon	29D	5,730	{ 1877 / 1878
Whipple, Fort†	Arizona	75C	5,318	1871
Wingate, Fort‡	New Mexico	76B	7,038	{ 1873 / 1875
Wingate, Old Fort*	do	77A	6,507	{ 1873 / 1875
Yuma, Fort	California	81D	205	1876

*Abandoned.   †Astronomical monument.   ‡Flagstaff.

TABLE II.—MOUNTAIN PEAKS.

Locality and name of peak.	Atlas sheet.	Range or group.	Altitude in feet above sea.	Expeditionary year.
ARIZONA.				
Carrizo	68B	Carrizo	9,330	1874
Escudilla	83B	Datil	10,691	1873
Graham	83C	Pinaleño	a10,516	1874
Greens	76D		10,093	1873
Humphreys	75A	San Francisco	12,562	1871
Humphreys (Timber Line)	75A		11,468	1871
Ord	83B	White Mountain	10,266	1873
San Francisco Mountains, crater edge.	75A		10,122	1871
Signal	68B	Carrizo	9,390	1874
Thomas	83B	White Mountain	f11,275	1878
Tipton	74D	Cerbat	7,364	1875
CALIFORNIA.				
Abbot	56D	Sierra Nevada	f13,582	1879
Adams	47B	do	8,432	1876
Agua Caliente	80B	San Jacinto	a7,034	1876
Alder Hill	56B	Sierra Nevada	7,731	1877
Alturas Hill	38D		4,459	1877
Alpine (or Woods), called Round Top by U. S. Coast and Geodetic Survey.	56B	Sierra Nevada	10,426	1877
Argus	65D	Argus	f6,333	1875
Arnot	56B	Sierra Nevada	10,068	1877
Bald Mountain, on Sonora Road.	56B	Foot-hills of Sierra Nevada	5,830	1878
Bare Point	56D	Spur of Sierra Nevada	f7,804	1879
Bear	56D	Bear Mountains	a2,984	1879
Bidwell	38B	Warner	8,551	1877
Big Hill (75)	56D		f1,518	1879
Black Mountain	65A	Sierra Nevada	13,009	1875
Black Mountain (southern point)	56D	do	f10,481	1879
Blue Mountain	56B	Foot-hills of Sierra Nevada	6,076	1879
Breckenridge	73A	Spurs of Sierra Nevada	7,418	1875
Browns	65D	Panamint	5,392	1875
Buckeye	56B	Sierra Nevada	f11,755	1879
Buckhorn Ranch, peak 2 miles south of.	73C		2,981	1875
Buckingham	56D		f4,622	1879
Buena Vista	56D	Sierra Nevada	f9,707	1879
Bullion Knob	56D	Mount Bullion	f4,292	1879
Burrows Mountain	64B		4,267	1878
Butt Mountain	47A	Sierra Nevada	7,831	1878
Cary	56B	Hope Valley Group, Sierra Nevada.	9,970	1877
Castle (Stanford)	47D	Sierra Nevada	9,014	{ 1876 1877
Castle Rock	56B	do	9,872	{ 1878 1879
Castro	73C		a3,046	1878
Cathedral (637)	56D	Yosemite Group, Sierra Nevada.	f10,920	1879
Cedar	38B	Warner	8,308	1877

BAROMETRIC ALTITUDES.

Table II.—MOUNTAIN PEAKS—Continued.

Locality and name of peak.	Atlas sheet.	Range or group.	Altitude in feet above sea.	Expeditionary year.
CALIFORNIA—Continued.				
Chamisal	56D	Foot-hills of Sierra Nevada	t3, 238	1879
Chiquito	56D	Sierra Nevada	t8, 257	{ 1878 / 1879 }
Cinder Cone	47A	do	a6, 906	1878
Cinder Cone, foot of slope	47A	do	a6, 512	1878
Cisco Butte	47D	do	6, 665	1877
Claremont Hill, south of Quincy	47A	do	6, 999	1878
Clarks (Gothic, also The Obelisk)	56D	Merced Group, Sierra Nevada	t11, 512	{ 1878 / 1879 }
Cloud Rest	56D	Yosemite group, Sierra Nevada	t9, 912	{ 1878 / 1879 }
Coahuila	80B	San Jacinto	a5, 606	1876
Cone, near Hickmans Ranch	47A	Foot-hills of Sierra Nevada	a3, 127	1878
Cone, near Shingletown	47A		2, 654	1878
Conejo	73C		a3, 311	1878
Conglomerate	56B	Sierra Nevada	9, 626	1877
Conness	56D	do	t12, 552	{ 1878 / 1879 }
Cook Point	73A	Spurs of Sierra Nevada	t6, 336	1875
Corcoran (Mt. Whitney No. 1)	65A	Sierra Nevada	14, 094	1875
Coso	65D	Coso Mountains	t8, 425	1875
Cottonwood	56D	Sierra Nevada	t7, 633	1879
Cowles	56B	do	10, 085	1877
Cucamonga	73D	San Bernardino	8, 529	1875
Dana	57C	Sierra Nevada	t13, 043	1879
Dardanelle Cone	56B	do	10, 829	1877
Deadwood	64B	do	t4, 451	{ 1878 / 1879 }
Denels	65A	do	13, 376	1875
Desert Creek	56B	Sweetwater	9, 053	1877
Devils	56D	{ South Fork Group, Sierra Nevada. }	t6, 985	{ 1878 / 1879 }
Devils Nose	56D	do	t6, 435	1879
Double Head	65D	Argus	t7, 411	1875
Double Point (1)	56D	Moccasin	t2, 518	1879
Double Point (2)	56D	do	t2, 556	1879
Downieville Butte	47C	Sierra Nevada	8, 541	1876
Duncan	47D	do	t7, 268	1877
Dunderberg (locally Castle)	56D	do	12, 289	1878
Dyer	47A	do	7, 369	1878
Eagle	38D	Warner	9, 934	1877
Eagle Peak	56D	Yosemite Group, Sierra Nevada	t7, 751	{ 1878 / 1879 }
Echo	56D	Cathedral Group, Sierra Nevada	t11, 184	{ 1878 / 1879 }
Ellis	47D	Sierra Nevada	8, 675	1876
Fairview Dome (Tuolumne Meadows).	56D	do	9, 707	1878
Fandango	38B	Warner	7, 848	1877
Fish Valley	56B		10, 749	1877
Fowlers	64B		1, 760	1878
Fredonyer	38D		7, 995	1877
Freels	56B	{ Lake Tahoe Group, Sierra Nevada. }	10, 849	{ 1876 / 1877 }
Glacier Point (jutting rock)	56D	Yosemite Group, Sierra Nevada	t7, 211	1879

TABLE II.—MOUNTAIN PEAKS—Continued.

Locality and name of peak.	Atlas sheet.	Range or group.	Altitude in feet above sea.	Expeditionary year.
CALIFORNIA—Continued.				
Gleasons	73C		6,493	1875
Gray (Mount Florence)	56D	Merced Group, Sierra Nevada	*11,554	1879
Great West	56D	Foot-hills of Sierra Nevada	*5,798	1879
Green Mountain	64B	do	1,352	1878
Grizzly	56B	Sierra Nevada	10,369	{ 1878 / 1879 }
Grizzly	73D	do	11,723	1875
Grizzly Hill	47A		*5,709	1878
Guide	47D	Sierra Nevada	*8,028	1877
Hahn	65A	Inyo	*11,030	1876
Harkness	47A	Sierra Nevada	*8,875	1878
Haskells	47D	do	8,126	1876
Hat	38D	Warner	7,676	1877
Haystack	56D	Sierra Nevada	*9,867	1879
Hazelton	64B	Foot-hills of Sierra Nevada	2,960	1878
Hazelton, foot of	64B	do	479	1878
Highland	56B	Silver Mountain Group, Sierra Nevada.	10,956	1877
Hoffman	56D	Sierra Nevada	*10,747	{ 1878 / 1879 }
Hot Springs	47B	do	7,692	1877
Houghs Mountain	47A	do	*7,391	1878
Ingalls	{47A / 47B}	do	8,472	1876
Inyo	65A	Inyo	*10,972	1875
Jackson	47D	Sierra Nevada	8,390	1877
Joes	65C		9,712	1875
Kettle Rock	47A	Sierra Nevada	7,843	1878
La Joya	73C		1,562	1875
Lassens Butte	47A	Sierra Nevada	10,437	1878
Liberty Cap	56D	Yosemite Group, Sierra Nevada	*7,062	1879
Lookout Hill	65D		*4,214	1875
Lookout Mountain	56B	Sierra Nevada	9,732	1877
Lookout Mountain	65A		9,670	1878
Los Cerritos	80A		357	1875
Lyell	56D	Sierra Nevada	*13,104	1878
McBride	57C	White Mountain	*13,415	1878
McClure	56D	Sierra Nevada	*12,974	1878
McDonald	38D		7,954	1877
McGill	73C		9,214	1875
McKesicks	47B	Sierra Nevada	7,083	1876
McKinstry	47D	do	*8,040	1877
Markleeville	56B	do	9,431	1877
Matterhorn	56D	do	*12,260	1878
Maturango	65D	Argus	*8,844	1875
Meadow Mountain	65C	Sierra Nevada	a11,734	1875
Merced	56D	Merced Group, Sierra Nevada	*11,442	{ 1878 / 1879 }
Minarets	57C	Sierra Nevada	*12,266	1879
Moccasin	56D	Moccasin	3,003	{ 1878 / 1879 }
Mokelumne	56B	Sierra Nevada	9,385	1877
Morgan	57C	White Mountain	*13,791	1879
Morrow	64B		2,065	1878
Mount Bullion	56D	Mount Bullion	*4,227	1878

BAROMETRIC ALTITUDES.

Table II.—MOUNTAIN PEAKS—Continued.

Locality and name of peak.	Atlas sheet.	Range or group.	Altitude in feet above sea.	Expeditionary year.
CALIFORNIA—Continued.				
Mount Washington	73D		a10,802	1875
Needle	47D	Sierra Nevada	8,833	1877
Needle	65D	Panamint	17,086	1875
New York Butte	65A	Inyo	110,675	1875
Nichols Point	73A	Spurs of Sierra Nevada	a6,233	1875
Observation	38D		8,009	1877
Olancha	65C	Sierra Nevada	12,251	1875
Old Bony Mountain	73C	Coast	1,892	1875
Omjumi	47B	Sierra Nevada	8,293	1876
Ophir	65D		16,063	1875
Oreana (Silver Lake Peak)	56B	Sierra Nevada	9,381	1877
Ostranders Rocks (North Point)	56D	Yosemite Group, Sierra Nevada	18,142	1878
Ostranders Rocks (South Point)	56D	do	18,157	1878
Pah-ute	73A	Sierra Nevada	8,342	1875
Pah-ute Monument (bottom)		Inyo	8,279	1875
Pah-ute Monument (top)		do	8,344	1875
Paleta	72B	Coast	4,508	1875
Palisades, N. W	65A	Sierra Nevada	14,275	1878
Palisades, S. E	65A	do	14,200	1878
Pilot	56D	Foot-hills of Sierra Nevada	16,024	1879
Pilot Knob	73B	Mohave Desert	5,525	1875
Pino Blanco	56D	Moccasin	12,951	1879
Pinto (Calico)	65D	Pinto	17,267	1875
Pyramid	56B	Sierra Nevada	10,127	1877
Pyramid	65D	Amagosa	16,754	1875
Raymond (Alpine County, California)	56B	Sierra Nevada	8,693	1877
Raymond (Mariposa County, California)	56D	do	18,374	1879
Red (west of Lake Tahoe)	47D	do	16,844	1877
Red	56D	Merced Group, Sierra Nevada	111,686	1878
Red Lake (north of Carson Pass)	56B	Sierra Nevada	10,120	1877
Red Slate	57C	do	113,067	1879
Ritter	57C	do	113,130	{ 1878 1879
Robbs	56B	do	6,746	1877
Round Top	56B	do	9,424	1877
Rush Creek, peak head of	47B		6,274	1877
Saddle (Malaga)	73C		2,897	1875
San Antonio	73D	Sierra Nevada	10,120	{ 1875 1878
San Fernando	73C	Coast	3,793	1875
San Gabriel	73C		6,232	{ 1875 1878
San Jacinto	80B	San Jacinto	10,987	1876
San Pedro Hill	80A		1,462	1875
Santiago (or Temescal) Peak	80B		5,730	1873
Schafier	47B	Sierra Nevada	6,864	1877
Schultz	56D		2,275	1878
Sentinel Dome	56D	Yosemite Group, Sierra Nevada	18,122	1879
Shinns	38D		7,628	1877
Signal (Red)	47D		7,857	1877
Silver Mountain	56B	Sierra Nevada	10,841	1877
Sixteen-Mile (Richardsons) Peak.	56D	do	19,794	1878
Smiths	80B	San Jacinto	a6,852	1876

U. S. GEOGRAPHICAL SURVEYS.

TABLE II.—MOUNTAIN PEAKS—Continued.

Locality and name of peak.	Atlas sheet.	Range or group.	Altitude in feet above sea.	Expeditionary year.
CALIFORNIA—Continued.				
Smoke Creek, peak head of	47B		6,283	1877
Sonora	56B	Sierra Nevada	11,479	1877
South Dome (Lip)	56D	Yosemite Group, Sierra Nevada	t8,823	1879
South Fork	38D		7,409	1877
Stanislaus	56B	Sierra Nevada	11,123	1877
Starr King	56D	Yosemite Group, Sierra Nevada	t9,080	1879
Stevens	56B	Sierra Nevada	10,011	1877
Stokes Mountain	65A		2,069	1878
Sugar Loaf	73A		3,643	1878
Summit	47D	Sierra Nevada	8,311	1876
Sunday	65C	do	8,335	1875
Sweetwater	56B	Sweetwater	11,778	1877
—Tehachapai	73A	Tehachapai	8,056	1875
—Tehachapai Double	73A	do	8,263	1875
Telescope	65D	Telescope	t10,938	1875
Tells	56B	Tells Peak Group, Sierra Nevada.	9,042	1877
"The Needle"	47D	Sierra Nevada	8,833	1877
Thomas	80B	San Jacinto	6,748	1876
Thompsons	47B	Sierra Nevada	7,752	{ 1876 1877
Thunder	65C	do	9,122	1875
Tower	56D	do	t11,719	1879
Tres Cerritos (1)	56D	Foot-hills of Sierra Nevada	t1,142	1879
Tres Cerritos (2)	56D	do	t1,125	1879
Tres Cerritos (3)	56D	do	t1,034	1879
Tuledad	38D		7,397	1877
Twin (west of Lake Tahoe)	47D	Sierra Nevada	8,824	1876
Union Point	56D	Yosemite Group, Sierra Nevada.	t6,290	1879
Volcano No. 2	80B	San Jacinto	a6,191	1876
Volcano (crater)	65D		5,434	1875
Wade's	56D	Sierra Nevada	7,154	1878
Wahguyhe	65B		t8,528	1875
Wamelo	56D	Sierra Nevada	t7,501	1879
Warren	56B	do	12,264	1878
Warren	38D	Warner	9,668	1877
Waucoba	65A	Inyo	t11,267	1875
Wellington	47B	Sierra Nevada	7,665	1876
White Granite	73C		7,069	1875
White Mountain	57C	White Mountain	t14,245	{ 1878 1879
Fishermans Peak, or Mt. Whitney	65A	Sierra Nevada	t14,470	1875
Williamson	65A	do	t14,360	1875
Workmans Hill	73C		1,364	1875
COLORADO.				
Æolus	61C	San Juan	t14,211	1875
Agency Knob (Popes Nose)	61B	Sierra Madre	12,273	1874
Altar	61C		13,254	1874
Antelope Butte	62C	Wet Mountains	9,287	1876
Antoro	61B	Sierra Madre	13,497	1875
Banded	69D	Navajo Mountains, San Juan	12,824	1875
Basaltic	61B		11,565	1873
Belleville	61C	Pagosa Mountains	8,383	1874
Bellevue	61D	Del Norte Mountains	12,673	1874

BAROMETRIC ALTITUDES.

TABLE II.—MOUNTAIN PEAKS—Continued.

Locality and name of peak.	Atlas sheet.	Range or group.	Altitude in feet above sea.	Expeditionary year.
COLORADO—Continued.				
Blaine	61C	Unaweep	*14,249	1875
Boulder	61C	Pagosa Mountains	12,417	1874
Bristol Head	61C	San Juan	a12,638	1875
Bross	52D	Park	*14,280	1878
Buffalo	53C	Kenosha	*11,326	1873
Buffalo	61B	Park	13,329	1873
Buffalo (Hunchback)	61C	San Juan	13,755	1874
Canby	61C	Del Norte Mountains	13,356	1874
Cap Butte	62A	Front	9,317	1876
Carbon	61A	West Elk	12,078	1877
Cathedral	61A	do	*11,169	1877
Cerro Blanco	62C	Sangre de Cristo	14,270	{ 1874 1875 1876
Chalk	61B	Saguache	14,041	1873
Chama	69B	Navajo Mountains, San Juan	12,248	1874
Cheops Pyramid (Signal Butte)	53C	Front	9,487	1876
Christ	53C	do	9,689	1876
Cochetopa Dome	61B		*11,673	1873
Conejos	69B	San Juan	13,347	1874
Conejos, peak southeast of	69B	do	12,596	1874
Craig	53C	Kenosha	a10,261	1873
Crested Butte	61A	West Elk	*11,944	1877
Cuerno Verde	62C	Wet Mountains	12,305	{ 1874 1876
Cuerno Verde, timber line	62C		12,074	1876
Culebra	70A	Culebra	14,049	{ 1874 1875
Del Norte Hill	61D	Del Norte Mountains	8,218	1874
Del Norte	61D	do	13,084	1874
Del Norte, foot of	61D	do	11,111	1874
Deer	53C	Kenosha	10,716	1876
Deer	62C	Wet Mountains	11,537	1876
Dome	62C	do	*10,125	1876
Dunns	61C	San Miguel Mountains	13,502	1875
Elbert	52D	Saguache	14,101	1879
Eighteen-Mile (locally Castle)	61C	San Juan	12,278	1874
Engineer	61C	do	13,277	1874
Evans	52D	Front	14,321	1873
Evans Plateau, timber line	52D		11,723	1873
Farnum	53C	Kenosha	12,264	1875
Fishers	70A	Raton Mountains	9,639	1874
Fourth of July Hill	61A		9,656	1876
Frustum	61C	San Juan	*13,893	1875
Frustum	61D	Sangre de Cristo	14,173	1873
Gibson	61D	do	13,729	1873
Glacier	61C	San Miguel Mountains	14,243	1874
Gothic	61A	West Elk	*12,491	1877
Grays	52D	Front	14,411	1873
Gunnison	61A	West Elk	12,242	1877
Gunnison, foot of	61A	do	8,207	1877
Handie	61C	Lake Fork Mountains	14,149	1875
Harvard	61B	Sierra Madre	14,152	1873
Horn	61D	Sangre de Cristo	13,447	1873
Horsefly	61A	Uncompahgre Plateau	10,504	1877
Horsefly, southwest of	61A	do	9,944	1877

U. S. GEOGRAPHICAL SURVEYS.   135

TABLE II.—MOUNTAIN PEAKS—Continued.

Locality and name of peak.	Atlas sheet.	Range or group.	Altitude in feet above sea.	Expeditionary year.
COLORADO—Continued.				
Humboldt	61D	Sangre de Cristo	14,041	1876
Humboldt, timber line	61D		11,810	1876
Hunchback (Buffalo)	61C	Florida Crags	13,755	1875
Hunts	61B	Sierra Madre	14,055	1874
Hurricane	61C	San Juan	13,565	1874
Kendall	61C	do	ƒ13,542	1874
Lands-end	61A	West Elk	ƒ10,772	1877
La Plata	61C	La Plata	13,316	1875
Las Tapiacitas	69A		8,810	1874
Leon	52C	Grand Mesa	11,218	1877
Lincoln	52D	Park	ƒ14,456	1873
Little Crestones	61D	Sangre de Cristo	13,190	1876
Little Crestones, timber line	61D		12,107	1876
Lone Butte	62C		ƒ8,666	1876
McClellan	52D	Front	13,842	1873
Macomb	61C	Pagosa Mountains	aƒ13,154	1875
Marcellina	61A	West Elk	11,319	1877
Mears	61C	San Miguel	13,009	1875
Meigs (Summit)	61D	San Juan	13,393	1875
Murderers Mesa (Cannibal Plateau).	61C	do	12,310	1874
Music	62C	Sangre de Cristo	ƒ13,291	1876
Needle	62A	Front	9,463	1876
Ohio	61A	West Elk	ƒ12,292	1877
Owens	61D	Sangre de Cristo	13,309	1875
Pagosa	61C	Pagosa Mountains	12,676	1875
Pass	61C	Front	13,092	1874
Peak 16 miles northeast of Rosita.	62C	Wet Mountain	10,142	1874
Peak between Forks of Hardscrabble Creek.	62C	do	ƒ10,284	1876
Peak south of Music Pass	62C	Sangre de Cristo	ƒ12,385	1876
Pikes (altitude from Signal Service, U. S. A.).	62A	Front	ƒ14,147	1876
Pilate	62A	do	ƒ12,420	1876
Pisgah	62A	do	10,487	1876
Pisgah, Little	62A	do	10,027	1876
Pole Creek	61C	San Juan	ƒ13,804	1875
Princeton	61B	Saguache	14,041	1873
Prospect	69B		9,909	1874
Pyramid	62A	Front	9,750	1876
Quadrate	62A	do	10,873	1876
Red Bluffs	62C	Wet Mountains	10,980	1876
Red Cloud	61C	Lake Fork Mountains	14,093	1875
Red Mountain	61B	Saguache	13,323	1873
Red Mountain (Timberline)	61B		11,746	1873
Red	61A		12,611	1877
Red	61C	Unaweep	ƒ11,123	1875
Red	70A	Culebra	11,625	1874
Rito Alto	61B	Sangre de Cristo	13,561	1876
Rito Alto (Timber line)	61B		11,817	1876
Rocky Butte	61B		8,508	1877
Rosa	62A	Front	ƒ11,572	1876
Rosalie	52D	Park	14,236	1873
St. Charles	62C	Wet Mountains	ƒ11,746	1876

BAROMETRIC ALTITUDES.

TABLE II.—MOUNTAIN PEAKS—Continued.

Locality and name of peak.	Atlas sheet.	Range or group.	Altitude in feet above sea.	Expeditionary year.
COLORADO—Continued.				
Saw-tooth	61A	Tongue Mesa	*11,372	1877
Silesia	61D	Sangre de Cristo	13,599	1876
Silesia, Timber line	61D		11,940	1876
Simpsons Pyramid	61C	San Juan	14,056	1874
Slate	61A	Elk	*12,857	1877
Spanish (Eastern)	62C	Sangre de Cristo	12,790	1875
Spanish (Western)	62C	....do	13,718	1874
Stewart	61C	San Juan	14,032	1874
Sultan	61C	....do	*13,501	1875
Teocalli	61A	Elk	*12,949	1877
Three-point Block	61A	West Elk	12,190	1877
Three Tetons	61D	Sangre de Cristo	14,198	1873
Torrey	52D	Park	14,380	1873
Trinchera	70A	Culebra	13,611	{ 1874 / 1875 }
Tumichi Dome	61B	Saguache	*11,389	1873
Tyndall	62C	Wet Mountain	9,482	1876
Uncompahgre	61C	San Juan	14,408	{ 1874 / 1875 / 1877 }
Veta	62C	Veta Mountains	11,654	1874
Vulcan Crest	61D	San Juan	13,977	1875
West Elk	61A	West Elk	13,102	1877
West Point	60D	San Miguel	*12,635	1875
White	61D	Sangre de Cristo	13,156	1873
White Rock	61A	Elk	*13,361	1877
Wilson	61C	San Juan	14,309	1875
Wulsten	61D	Sangre de Cristo	13,659	1873
Wetterhorn	61C	San Juan	*14,062	1875
Yale	61B	Saguache	14,121	1873
Yellow	61C		13,618	1874
IDAHO.				
Antelope	41A	Wahsatch	7,282	1877
Badger	32C		6,389	1877
Bannock	32C		8,359	1877
Basin Point	32C		5,791	1877
Black Pine	41A		9,386	1877
Bloomington	41B	Bear River	9,354	1877
Bonneville	32D	Port Neuf	a9,200	1877
Big Butte	32A		7,659	1877
Cache	41A	Raft River	10,451	1877
Castle Rock	41B	Bear River	9,611	1877
Cedar Creek	32C		7,586	1877
Cone Butte, three-fourths mile west of Franklin.	41B		5,215	1877
Deep Creek	32C		8,818	1877
Eyrie	41A		9,458	1877
Fountain (north side)	32D	Port Neuf	a8,900	1877
Lane Butte	32D		a7,822	1877
Meades	32D		a10,541	1877
Montpelier	41B		a8,438	1877
Ogden, No. 2	41A		9,343	1877
Oxford	41B	Port Neuf	9,386	1877
Pillar Butte	32C		5,301	1877
Pisgah	32D		a9,695	1877
Putnam	32D	Port Neuf	8,905	1877

U. S. GEOGRAPHICAL SURVEYS. 137

TABLE II.—MOUNTAIN PEAKS—Continued.

Locality and name of peak.	Atlas sheet.	Range or group.	Altitude in feet above sea.	Expeditionary year.
IDAHO—Continued.				
Sedgwick	32D	Port Neuf	9,207	1877
Sherman	32D	Bear River	9,572	1877
"The Capitol"	41A		7,877	1877
NEVADA.				
Abbie	47D	Washoe Mountains	7,440	1876
American Flat	47D	do	6,659	1877
Badger Flat	48C		7,038	1876
Bare	65B	Bare Mountain	6,039	1875
Basalt	57A		6,599	1876
Basalt Hill	47D	Washoe Mountains	6,180	1877
Birchim	48D	Reese River	10,408	{ 1876 1878
Bismarck	47D	Pine Nut	t7,604	1876
Black Rock (Railroad Peak)	47D	Washoe Mountains	5,436	1877
Borax Flat, peak northeast of	57A		6,651	1876
Brown Knob	48C		6,202	1876
Bull Run	40C		9,041	1871
Bunker Hill	48D	Toyabe	11,404	1876
Butler	47D	Washoe Mountains	7,525	1877
Caledonia Hill	47D	do	5,860	1877
Cedar Hill (highest point)	47D	do	7,304	1876
Chalk Wells	48D		7,604	1876
Charleston	66C	Spring Mountain	10,874	1869
Churchill Butte	47D		6,009	1876
Cleaver	48C		a6,682	1876
Como	47D	Pine Nut	9,017	{ 1876 1877
Cory	57A	Walker River	11,326	1878
Cowles	48D		9,980	1876
Davidson	47D	Davidson	7,941	1876
Desatoya	48D	Desatoya	9,921	1876
Division	38D	Granite	8,585	1877
East McClellan	47D	Washoe Mountains	6,181	1877
Emigrant Pass	48D		7,876	1876
Emma	47D	Flowery Ridge	6,439	1876
Emma Point, northwest of	47D	do	6,225	1876
Fairview	48C	Toano	8,412	1876
Flowery	47D	Flowery Ridge	6,650	1876
"Forty-nine"	38B		7,498	1877
Frenchs	48D	Toyabe	10,779	1876
Gass	66D	Las Vegas	6,200	1869
Genoa	47D	Lake Tahoe	9,156	1876
Geneva	48D	Toyabe	10,708	{ 1876 1878
Grafton	58B	Schell Creek	10,964	1869
Granite	38D	Granite	8,990	1877
Grant	48C		9,965	1876
Grape Vine	65B	Grape Vine Mountains	8,528	1875
Justice Hill	47D	Washoe Mountains	5,770	1877
Kate	47D	Flowery Ridge	6,141	1877
Lodi	57A		6,486	1876
Lone Butte, north of Carson Lake.	48C		a4,201	1876
Lyon	47D	Pine Nut	8,794	{ 1876 1877

TABLE II.—MOUNTAIN PEAKS—Continued.

Locality and name of peak.	Atlas sheet.	Range or group.	Altitude in feet above sea.	Expeditionary year.
NEVADA—Continued.				
McClellan	47D	Washoe Mountains	7,532	1876
McClellan Cone	47D		5,892	1876
Mahogany (formerly North Granite).	38D	Granite	8,363	1877
Marlette	47D	Lake Tahoe	8,631	1876
Monument Hill	38D		6,734	1877
Mount Airy Mesa	48D		a7,590	1876
Newberry	74B		a3,395	1875
Northeast Base Peak	47D	Flowery	7,100	1876
Olcott	66C	Spring Mountain	7,974	1869
Ophir Hill	47D	Washoe Mountains	7,861	1877
Painted Mesa	4CC		6,027	1876
Paradise	57B		8,662	1876
Park	57B		8,670	1876
Peavine	47D	Sierra Nevada	8,281	1876
Pilot Knob	40D	Gosiute	10,758	1878
Piute or Pah-ute	39C		8,618	1877
Poston (Davies)	57B	Toyabe	11,978	{ 1876 1878 }
Prometheus	48D	...do	8,144	{ 1876 1878 }
Quartz	58C	Pahranagat	8,700	1869
Rawe	47D	Pine Nut	8,404	1876
Rose (Mount Rose)	47D	Lake Tahoe	10,820	1876
Rose	47D	Flowery Ridge	6,314	1877
Rose Knob	47D	Tahoe	9,492	1876
Sharp Point	47D		7,186	1876
Silver City	47D	Washoe Mountains	6,739	1877
Sinkwater	48C		7,511	1876
Slate	48C	Fairview	7,115	1876
Spanish	47D	Virginia	7,402	1876
State Line	47B	Sierra Nevada	8,405	1876
Sugar-loaf	47D	Flowery Ridge	6,346	1876
Sugar-loaf, bare peak west of	47D	...do	5,975	1876
Sugar-loaf, rocky peak west of	47D	...do	5,933	1876
Tarogqua	48C	Pahute	8,772	1876
Tibbie	47D	Flowery Ridge	7,383	1876
Tolicha	65B		7,022	1875
Tohakum	47B	Lake	8,174	1877
Toyabe	48D	Toyabe	10,144	1876
Tutib	48C	Natchez	7,062	1876
Union, formerly Wheeler	58B	Snake	13,063	1869
Worthington	58C	Worthington Mountains	8,400	1869
NEW MEXICO.				
Abiquiu	69D	Valles	11,241	1874
Agua Azul, peak southwest of	77A		9,347	1873
Agua Fria	70C	Cimarron	/10,965	
Animas	84C	Mimbres	6,106	1878
Baldy (Elizabethtown)	70A	Costilla	12,491	1874
Baldy (Santa Fe)	69D	Santa Fe	12,661	1874
Bear	83D	Diablo	8,081	1873
Bernal Hill	78A		7,029	1875
Black	70C	Cimarron	10,900	1874
Black	84C	Mimbres	8,910	1878
Block Hill	84C		7,217	1878

U. S. GEOGRAPHICAL SURVEYS. 139

TABLE II.—MOUNTAIN PEAKS—Continued.

Locality and name of peak.	Atlas sheet.	Range or group.	Altitude in feet above sea.	Expeditionary year.
NEW MEXICO—Continued.				
Brazos	69B	San Juan	11,212	1874
Caballo Cone (1)	84C	Sierra de los Caballos	t7,751	1877
Caballo Cone (2)	84C	do	6,057	1878
Cabezon	77A		t7,897	1874
Capitan	85A	Capitan	10,023	1877
Cerro Alesna	77A		t7,372	1874
Cerro Colorado	84B		5,654	1877
Cerro Escobas	77B	Santa Fe	8,278	1874
Cerro Orejas	69B		7,707	1874
Cerro Pelon	77B	Placer Mountains	6,939	1875
Cerro Roblado	84C		t5,798	1878
Cerro Tecolote	77D		7,254	1877
Chasco Knoll	68D		8,803	1873
Cibolo Hill	77D		6,472	1876
Compass	69B		10,460	1874
Cone	69D	Santa Fe	a12,690	1875
Cone "B," east of San Ysidro	77B		7,031	1873
Cookes	84C	Cookes	a8,330	1878
Costilla	70A	Cimarron	12,615	1875
Costilla, first high point north of	70A		a12,062	1875
Costilla, second high point north of.	70A		a11,822	1875
Cow Spring Pyramid	84C	Antelope Plains	5,768	1878
Cubero Butte	77A		6,820	1873
Cuervo	78A		5,462	1875
Cuervito Hill	78A		5,128	1875
Culebra	77C		6,992	1876
Eagle	83B	Tulerosa	9,791	1873
East Carrizo Cone	84B	Carrizo	7,976	1877
Fairview Hill	84C		6,589	1878
Florida	90A		7,295	1878
Fort Wingate (old), peak south of.	77A		8,544	1873
Fra Cristobal	84A	Fra Cristobal	6,646	1877
Gallinas	69D	Gallinas	9,798	1874
Garcia	77C		9,920	1876
Goodsight	84C		6,061	1878
Hanover	84C		7,396	1878
Hacheta	89B		8,352	1878
Hendricks	84C	Mimbres	7,574	1878
Hillsboro	84C	do	10,061	1873
Horse	84A	Sierra Hacheta	9,434	1878
Hurricane Rock	84C		6,479	1878
Hosta Butte	77A		8,815	1873
Jacks	84B	Jicarilla	a7,530	1877
Jemez	77B	Nacimiento	8,569	1874
Kneeling Jesus Bluff	84C	Santa Rita Mountains	a7,903	1873
Ladrones	77C	Ladrones	9,214	1876
Lake	69D	Santa Fe	12,405	1873
La Lacha	89B	Las Animas	6,527	1878
Las Cuatas	77A		t7,079	1874
Las Truchas	69D	Santa Fe	t13,150	1874
Laughlins	70A		8,950	1875
Little Crater, west of Rio Grande	77B		6,215	1873
Lone Mountain	84C		5,986	1878
Magdalena	84A	Magdalena	10,798	1876
Manzano Cone	77D	Manzano	8,828	1876

TABLE II.—MOUNTAIN PEAKS—Continued.

Locality and name of peak.	Atlas sheet.	Range or group.	Altitude in feet above sea.	Expeditionary year.
NEW MEXICO—Continued.				
Manzano	77D	Manzano	a10,086	1876
Mesa Agua Segura	78A		5,998	1875
Mesa Chupaines, south end	78A		6,598	1876
Mesa Cueva	78A		5,982	1875
Mesa Martinez	78A		6,820	1875
Mesa Pina, west end	78A		5,715	1875
Mimbres Head	84C	Mimbres	9,823	1878
Mogollon	83B	Mogollon	9,725	1873
Mora	70C	Mora	12,020	1874
Mosca	77D	Manzano	9,723	1876
Needle Point, south	68D		6,341	1874
Niblack	68D		9,436	1875
Niggerhead	90A		5,207	1878
Nogal	84B	Sierra Blanca	9,983	1877
Ocate Crater	70C		8,903	1874
Organ	84D	Organ	t9,108	1878
Oscuro	84B	Oscuro	8,732	1877
Osha	77D	Manzaño	10,023	1876
Pedernal	69D	Gallinas	9,799	1874
Pedernal	77B		7,580	1876
Pelado	69D	Jemez	11,260	1874
Picacho	90A		4,824	1878
Pinos Altos	84C		8,128	1878
Placer	77B	Placer	8,965	1876
Polvadera	77C		7,325	1876
Pyramid Hill	77D		6,628	1876
Rattlesnake Hill	77D	Animas Hills	6,617	1876
Salinas	84B	San Andreas	9,039	1877
San Antonio	69B		10,912	1874
San Mateo	84A	San Mateo	10,209	1877
Sandia	77B	Sandia	10,609	1873
Santa Clara	69D	Valles	t11,507	{ 1874 / 1875 }
Sierra Blanca	84B	Sierra Blanca	11,892	1877
Socorro	77C		7,281	1876
Solitario	70C	Las Vegas	10,258	1874
South Florida	90A		7,261	1878
South Oscuro	84B	Oscuro	8,732	1877
South Sandia	77B	Sandia	8,567	1876
Sunday Cone	84C		6,030	1873
Taos	70A	Taos	13,099	{ 1874 / 1875 }
Taos, cone east of	70A		13,052	1874
Taylor	77A	San Mateo	11,391	{ 1873 / 1874 / 1875 }
Tetilla	77B		7,060	1873
Tres Hermanos	77C		7,151	1873
Truchas Peak	69D	Santa Fe	t13,150	1875
Tunicha Mesa	68D		5,510	1874
United States Mountain	69D		10,734	1874
Ute	69B		10,152	1874
West Gallinas	77D	Turkey	8,464	1877
West Jicarilla Cone	84B	Jicarilla	7,727	1877

TABLE II.—MOUNTAIN PEAKS—Continued.

Locality and name of peak.	Atlas sheet.	Range or group.	Altitude in feet above sea.	Expeditionary year.
OREGON.				
Crooks	29D	Warner	7,898	1877
Dalles Hill	20A	Cascade	1,210	1878
Diamond	28B	do	8,807	1878
Klikatat Hill	11C	Klikatat Mountains	3,070	1878
Lolochewis	38B	Drew's Valley Mountains	7,957	1877
Mesa Summit, West Warner Valley.	29D		4,894	1877
Mutton	20A		5,792	1878
North end	38B	Warner	8,472	1877
Pauline	29A	Pauline Mountains	7,387	1878
Pitt	28D	Cascade	9,818	1878
Scott	28D	do	9,016	1878
Sugarloaf	38B	Warner	8,416	1877
Timber Mountain	29C	Rim Rock Mountains	7,519	1878
Union	28D	Cascade	7,298	1878
Warner	29D		5,730	1877
TEXAS.				
North Franklin	90B	Franklin	7,070	1878
UTAH.				
Antelope Island Peak	41D	Promontory	6,660	1877
Baldy	58	Beaver	11,730	1872
Barton	41D	Wahsatch	9,854	1877
Belknap	59	Beaver	11,894	1872
Blue Springs, formerly North Promontory.	41A	Promontory	7,131	1877
Box Elder, formerly Logan	41B	Wahsatch	9,542	1877
Citadel	40B	Raft River	7,784	1878
Clear Creek	41A	do	9,132	1877
Conner, formerly T	50B	Oquirrh	9,997	1877
Deer	40B	Raft River	7,630	1878
Desert	40D	Desert	8,175	1878
Detour Mountain	59	Sevier	10,359	1872
Hansel	41A		6,266	1877
Kelton	41A	Clear Creek	10,045	1877
Kimballs (Nub)	41B	Fair River	7,778	1877
Lake Butte, near Laketown	41B		a6,346	1877
Little Promontory	41C	Promontory	4,914	1878
Monte Cristo	41D	Wahsatch	9,217	1877
Naomi	41B	Fair River	9,951	1877
Nebo	50B	Wahsatch	11,999	1872
Newfoundland	41C	Desert	7,046	1878
Newfoundland, peak east of	41C	do	6,845	1878
Observatory, formerly South Ogden.	41D	Wahsatch	9,589	1877
Ogden No. 2 (formerly North Ogden No. 2; also Willard).	41D	do	4,276	1877
Ogden, formerly North Ogden	41D	do	9,696	1877
Pilot	40D	Ombe	10,900	
Promontory, formerly South Promontory.	41C	Promontory	7,460	1877
Provo Mountains, north side	50B	Wahsatch	11,044	1873
Provo Mountains, south side	50B	do	11,066	1873
South Promontory	41C	Promontory	7,075	1878
Thousand Lake Mountain	59B		11,125	1872

TABLE III.—CITIES, TOWNS, SETTLEMENTS, ETC.

Locality and name.	Atlas sheet.	Altitude in feet above sea.	Expeditionary year.
ARIZONA.			
Anvil Rock	75	5,354	1871
Bowers Ranch, near Prescott	75	4,412	1871
Bushs Ranches (San Francisco River)	83B	a7,663	1878
Bushs Ranch (No. 3), San Francisco River	83B	a7,704	1878
Chloride	74B	4,201	1875
Chriswells Ranch (Salt Springs on Rio Colorado Chiquito)	76D	a5,772	1878
Cienega Amarilla	76D	a7,179	1878
Colorado Chiquito Bridge	83D	a5,600	1878
Colorado River (Southern Pacific Railroad crossing)	74D	671	1875
Cooleys Ranch	83	5,367	1873
Cosniño Caves (Colorado Chiquito Plateau)	75	6,244	1873
Desert Station	82	2,135	1871
Fort Apache and Springerville Trail, divide	76D	a9,036	1878
Jacobs Well	76	6,065	
Jaycocks Ranch	75	6,814	1873
La Pilla	76D	a5,850	1878
Liverpool Landing	74D	606	1875
Milligans Ranch, near Springerville	76D	a7,018	1878
Nobmans Ranch (Quail Spring)	74D	3,735	1875
Nutrioso Creek and San Francisco River, divide	83B	a8,262	1878
Oraybe, three-quarters of a mile east of	68C	a4,757	18/3
Painted Cañon, entrance to	74B	746	18/1
Paria Cañon, mouth of	67B	3,018	1873
Picacho Station	82	1,750	1871
Picket Post	83	2,667	1871
Pipe Springs (Ast. Mon't)	67A	5,397	1872
Prescott	75	5,319	1871
Prieto Crossing, Salt River	83	5,333	1873
Pueblo Viejo (Safford post-office)	83	a2,712	1873
Ruggs Ranch (Cienega)	76D	a7,476	1878
Saint Johns	76D	a5,650	1878
San Carlos Indian Agency	83A	a2,559	1874
Shungo-pah-we	68C	6,032	1873
Sunset Crossing (Rio Colorado Chiquito)	76	4,892	{ 1871 / 1873 }
Spears Ranch	74B	681	1875
Springerville (Beckers store)	76D	a6,759	1878
Tegua (Moquis Town)	68C	6,299	1873
Tucson	89A	2,538	1871
Vigils Ranch	76D	a6,034	1878
Walls Ranch	76D	a8,127	1878
Whitlocks Cienega	83D	3,580	1873
Williams Ranch (Nutriosa Creek)	83B	a7,487	1878
CALIFORNIA.			
Adobe Station, near Bakersfield	73A	284	1875
Agua Caliente	80B	725	{ 1875 / 1876 }
Alamo Station (S. P. R. R.)	81C	l 54	1876
Algodones	81D	l 114	1876
Alturas	38D	4,365	1877
Anaheim	81A	a 125	1876

U. S. GEOGRAPHICAL SURVEYS. 143

TABLE III.—CITIES, TOWNS, SETTLEMENTS, ETC.—Continued.

Locality and Name.	Atlas sheet.	Altitude in feet above sea.	Expeditionary year.
CALIFORNIA—Continued.			
Andrews (Southern Pacific Railroad)	73C	*1,264*	1878
Antelope Ranch	72B	359	1875
Arlington Bridge	47A	*a*3,376	1878
Armstrongs Ranch	56B	5,083	{ 1876 / 1877
Azusa	73C	594	1878
Bacons Ranch	47B	4,076	1877
Bagley and Slinkard Valleys, divide between	56B	8,277	1877
Bakersfield, near Southern Pacific Railroad	73A	432	{ 1875 / 1878
Bald Rock	65A	7,825	1878
Bares Ranch (Surprise Valley)	38D	4,679	1877
Barkers Ranch	73A	594	1878
Battle Creek Meadows (toll-gate)	47A	4,700	1878
Baxters Station (Sonora road)	56D	4,114	1878
Bear Valley (Bloods toll-house)	56B	6,979	{ 1877 / 1878
Bear Valley (post-office)	56D	*a*2,088	1878
Bear Valley (Town Hotel)	73D	6,592	1878
Beaver Creek and North Fork Stanislaus, divide between, trail to to South Grove	56B	4,562	1878
Beaver Creek Crossing, trail to South Grove	56B	4,417	1878
Beckworth Store (post-office)	47D	4,887	1876
Bee Ranch	80B	*a*1,701	1876
Belle Mill	47A	*a*3,681	1878
Bergman Station	80B	1,807	1876
Berhings Store	64B	4,974	1878
Bidwells Bar (South Fork Feather River)	47C	342	1878
Big Meadows (toll-gate)	56D	4,234	1878
Big Meadows Creek (Big Tree road)	56D	6,464	1878
Big Meadows Ranch	56B	6,838	1878
Big Trees of Calaveras (Hotel)	56B	4,730	{ 1877 / 1878
Big Trees of Calaveras (Cabin in South Grove)	56B	4,820	1878
Big Trees of Mariposa, "Grizzly Giant"	56D	5,838	1878
Big Tree Tunnel (Oak Flat Road)	56D	5,794	1878
Blacks Ranch (Bull Creek)	56D	2,621	1879
Blackmores Ranch	56D	*a*2,230	1879
Blackwood Creek, mouth of (Lake Tahoe)	47D	6,202	1876
Blodgetts (Old Morley Ranch)	56D	216	1879
Blue Mountain City (abandoned)	56B	4,613	1879
Bobbie Store (Mariposa road)	56D	3,778	1879
Boca (Central Pacific Railroad)	47D	5,530	1876
Bolds Ranch	80A	141	1875
Boundary Stone Mon't, between California and Nevada, near Pine Station, Reno and Susanville Road	47D	5,133	1876
Boundary Stone Mon't, between California and Nevada, near Verdi	47D	4,918	1876
Bower Cave House, North Fork Merced River	56D	*a*2,360	1879
Boyds Ranch	65A	622	1878
Bridgeport (post-office)	57A	6,424	{ 1877 / 1878
Bridgeport	56D	*a*1,357	1878
Bronco (Central Pacific Railroad)	47D	5,310	1876
Brooks, head of Jess Valley	38D	5,274	1877
Browns Flat	56D	1,964	1878
Browns Ranch	73C	1,758	1878

144   BAROMETRIC ALTITUDES.

TABLE III.—CITIES, TOWNS, SETTLEMENTS, ETC.—Continued.

Name and locality.	Atlas sheet.	Altitude in feet above sea.	Expeditionary year.
CALIFORNIA—Continued.			
Buckeye Ranch (Stage Station)	47C	a4,938	1878
Bucks (post-office)	47A	a5,112	1878
Buena Vista	56C	323	1879
Buntingville, near Honey Lake	47B	a4,278	1877
Burst Rock	56B	9,157	1878
Butte Creek Bridge	47A	4,692	1878
Butte Creek Toll-gate	47A	5,427	1878
Butte Creek House	47A	5,758	1878
Butte Creek House and Longville, divide on road between	47A	6,706	1878
Caliente (Southern Pacific Railroad)	73A	1,314	{ 1875 1878
Camulos Ranch	73C	799	1875
Canebrake Ranch	65C	3,904	1878
Caples Ranch	56B	7,780	1877
Caribou Bridge (North Fork Feather River)	47A	2,843	1878
Caribou Bridge and Kingsbury Ranch, divide on trail	47A	4,628	1878
Carrizo Creek, ruins on	81C	466	1876
Carthage Landing (Owens Lake)	65C	3,589	1875
Cascade Creek (Sonora road)	56B	6,272	1878
Cattle Cañon, mouth of	73D	1,934	1878
Cattle Ranch, Painter Flat	38D	a5,715	1877
Cattle and San Antonio Cañons, divide between	73D	4,470	1878
Cedarville (Surprise Valley)	38B	4,674	1877
Centreville	47C	502	1878
Cerro Gordo Landing (Owens Lake)	65D	3,656	1875
Chaparral House	47A	a5,076	1878
Chapman Ranch, Sierra Valley	47D	4,992	1878
Charity Valley	56B	7,844	1877
Chico, Central Pacific Railroad, Oregon Division	47C	h193	{ 1878 1879
Chico (post-office)	47C	177	1877
Chico, camp at	47C	175	1878
Chinese Camp (post-office)	56D	a1,299	1879
Chiquito Meadows	56D	6,690	1879
Chuckawalla	81A	2,095	{ 1875 1876
Cisco, site of old village	47D	5,654	1877
Clarks (Big Tree Station)	56D	3,925	{ 1878 1879
Clarks Ranch, near Honey Lake	47B	a4,028	1877
Cohens Ranch	46B	281	1878
Colbys Ranch	47A	4,990	1878
Colbys Ranch and Butte Creek Toll-house, divide on road	47A	6,619	1878
Cold Spring Ranch	47C	564	1878
Cold Spring Station	56D	3,126	1878
Coldwater Cañon, mouth of	80B	1,320	1876
Coles Ranch	64B	1,221	1878
Coleville	56B	5,190	1877
Colton	73D	808	1878
Columbia (post-office)	56B	2,157	1878
Concow Valley Reservoir	47C	2,022	1878
Conejo Ranch	73C	579	1878
Conejo and Triunfo Creeks, divide between	73C	887	1878
Coombs Station (Southern Pacific Railroad)	73A	2,885	1875
Coopers Ranch, near Castle Rock Peak	56B	8,406	1878
Copperopolis (Dutch Harrys Ranch)	56C	1,015	1878
Coso	65D	5,884	1875

U. S. GEOGRAPHICAL SURVEYS. 145

TABLE III.—CITIES, TOWNS, SETTLEMENTS, ETC.—Continued.

Locality and name.	Atlas sheet.	Altitude in feet above sea.	Expeditionary year.
CALIFORNIA—Continued.			
Cottonwood Ranch	73D	2,397	1875
Cottonwood Station (Mohave River)	73D	2,488	1875
Coulterville	56D	1,665	1878
Cow Creek Ranch (Sonora road)	56B	5,905	1878
Cow and Herring Creeks, divide between	56B	6,729	1878
Coxs Cabin	73D	5,329	1878
Coyote Hole (Stage Station)	73A	3,368	1878
Crane Flat	56D	6,054	1878
Crane Valley, lower end	64B	3,185	1878
Crescent City	47A	a3,306	1878
Cress Ranch	47A	5,157	1878
Crimea House	56D	1,222	1879
Crows Ranch (Red Clover Valley)	47B	5,464	1876
Cucamonga	73D	1,248	1875
Cuddys Ranch	73C	5,278	1875
Camulos Ranch	73C	799	1875
Cunninghams Ranch	56D	a387	1879
Darwin City	65D	4,840	1875
Davis Ranch	56D	284	1879
Death Valley, greatest depression measured	65D	—110	1875
Densers Station (Amador road)	56B	2,922	1878
Diamond Valley (Thompsons Ranch)	56B	5,482	1877
Doons Saw-mill	47A	3,420	1878
Dos Palmas	81A	103	{ 1875 1876
Dry Well Station	81B	625	1876
Dunnings Ranch (Reno and Susanville road)	47B	4,571	1871
Dumonts Meadows (Carson River, East Fork)	56B	6,817	1877
Dusys Ranch on Dinky Creek	65A	5,542	1878
Dutch Henrys Ranch	73C	1,195	1875
Dutch Hill Mining Camp, near Prattville	47A	4,692	1878
Dutch Valley (Gallanars Ranch)	56B	5,277	1877
Eagle Meadows	56D	7,071	1879
Eagleville	38D	4,632	1877
East Walker River, west branch, Sonora road crossing	56B	7,019	1877
Ehrenberg, Colorado River, opposite	81B	408	{ 1875 1876
Eisen Vineyard	64B	358	1878
Eleven-mile Station (Mariposa road)	56D	5,567	1878
Elizabeth Lake (post-office)	73C	3,317	1876
Elliott Ranch (Henness Pass road)	47D	6,298	1876
El Paso Mines Tunnel	73B	4,113	1875
Encino Ranch	73C	772	{ 1875 1878
Encino and Sepulveda Cañon, divide between	73C	1,310	1878
Essex (Central Pacific Railroad)	47D	l4,938	1876
Eureka Valley (Hays Station)	56B	5,958	1877
Fears Station (Cajon Cañon)	73D	3,278	{ 1875 1878
Fish Valley	56B	8,191	1877
Fish Valley and Silver Creek, divide between	56B	9,966	1877
Fitzhugh Creek, crossing of road	38B	4,431	1877
Five-mile House	73C	429	1875
Flea Valley	47A	3,655	1878
Fletcher's Ranch	38B	4,819	1877
Flints Ranch (Sierra Valley)	47D	4,812	1876
Fords Ranch (Indian Valley)	47A	3,518	1878

1874 WH——10

BAROMETRIC ALTITUDES.

TABLE III.—CITIES, TOWNS, SETTLEMENTS, ETC.—Continued.

Locality and name.	Atlas sheet.	Altitude in feet above sea.	Expeditionary year.
CALIFORNIA—Continued.			
Fornis Ranch (Pilot Creek)	56B	4,225	1877
Forest Ranch	47A	2,217	1878
Forsees Ranch	73D	3,587	1878
Fosters Ranch	56B	2,881	1878
Fosters Station (Amador road)	56B	3,265	1878
French Gulch	56D	1,812	1878
Frenchmans Cove	47B	5,565	1876
Frenchmans Cove and Dixie Creek, divide between	47B	6,209	1876
French Meadows	47D	5,081	1877
Fresno (Astronomical Monument)	64B	314	1878
Fresno Flat, near	56D	2,202	1879
Fresno Flat (post-office)	64B	2,192	1878
Fulsom and Halls Ranch	56B	4,282	1878
Furnace Creek, camp at	65D	405	{ 1871 1875
General Stonemans House	73C	645	1878
Georgetown Junction	56B	a5,440	{ 1877 1878
Glendale	65C	9,924	1875
Glenville	65C	3,094	1875
Gold Spring (Jollys) Ranch	56D	2,014	{ 1878 1879
Goodrichs Ranch	47A	4,883	1878
Gorman Ranch	73C	3,838	1875
Granite Station	73A	1,744	1878
Grapevine Ranch	73D	2,247	1875
Grays Ranch	47A	3,388	1878
Grays Ranch	56D	307	1879
Greenville (post-office)	47A	3,544	1878
Grenos Ranch (Upper Long Valley)	47B	4,187	1877
Greys Ranch	73C	1,387	1875
Halfway House (Big Tree road)	56B	3,358	1878
Hams Station (Amador road)	56B	5,439	1878
Hanlons Ferry (Colorado River)	81D	l120	1875
Harts Ranch	47A	1,100	1878
Havilah	73A	3,150	1878
Hazel Green	56D	5,550	{ 1878 1879
Hazel Valley Settlement	56B	3,404	1877
Hennessys Bridge (South Fork Merced River)	56D	1,822	1879
Hermit Valley	56B	7,039	{ 1877 1878
Hetch-Hetchy Valley	56D	3,469	{ 1878 1879
Hickmans Ranch, near Georgetown	47A	1,907	1878
Highland Lakes, divide between	56B	8,646	1877
Hites Cove Mining Village	56D	a1,601	1879
Hite Mine	56D	a2,022	1879
Hodgdons Meadows (Bronsons Meadows, by Whitney)	56D	4,506	1878
Honey Lake and Indian Valley, divide between	47A	6,428	1878
Hornitos	56D	a847	1878
Horns Ranch, near Observation Peak	38D	a5,410	1877
Horsleys Camp (Amador road)	56B	3,860	1878
Hotchkiss Ranch	56A	a2,931	1877
Hot Springs (Lake Tahoe)	47D	6,237	1876

TABLE III.—CITIES, TOWNS, SETTLEMENTS, ETC.—Continued.

Locality and name.	Atlas sheet.	Altitude in feet above sea.	Expeditionary year.
CALIFORNIA—Continued.			
Hot Springs (Stage Station)	73A	a2,398	1875
Hughes Ranch	73C	3,222	1878
Humbug Ranch (Little Humbug Valley)	47A	4,847	1878
Hunters Ranch	65B	6,275	1875
Huntington (Mohave River)	73D	2,899	1875
Hupps Saw-mill	47A	a2,667	1878
Husselkus Ranch (Genesee Valley)	47A	a3,635	1878
Hydes Union Saw-mill	65A	5,288	1878
Illinois Ranch	56B	1,759	1877
Indian Gulch (post-office)	56D	a951	1879
Indian Settlement, near Tejon Reservation	73A	2,137	1875
Indian Valley	56B	8,034	1877
Indian Wells	65C, 65D, 73A, 73B	2,608	1875
Inskip Toll-gate (post-office)	47A	4,808	1878
Ivanpah	74A	4,238	1871, 1875
Jackson Ruins (Henness Pass road)	47D	5,980	1876
Jacksonville Hotel	56D	a602	1879
Janesville	47B	a4,386	1877
Jellies Ranch	46B	360	1878
Jewetts Ranch, near Breckenridge Mountain	73A	5,693	1878
Johnsons Ranch	65A	3,700	1875
Johnsons Ranch	80A	44	1875
Johnsons Ranch, on Gold Run	47A	4,379	1878
Johnsons Ranch (Prosser Creek)	47D	5,643	1876
Johnsons Ranch, near Sentinel Peak	65D	5,015	1875
Jordan Mine (Panamint Range)	65D	l5,225	1875
Junction House, near Bidwells Bar	47C	3,562	1878
Junction House, near Beckworth Pass	47D	4,639	1876
Kelso Valley, ranch in	73A	4,033	1875
Kernville	65C	2,550	1875
Keystone House	56D	a1,093	1879
Kimshew Settlement	47A	4,992	1878
Kincaids Ranch	73D	1,771	1875
Kingsburys Mining Claim, orchard near	47A	2,678	1878
Kirkwoods Ranch	56B	a7,677	1877
La Bayonne	80A	16	1875
La Grange (post-office)	56D	a222	1879
Laguna Ranch	73C	129	1875
Lake City	38B	4,624	1877
La Motte Ranch	65C	6,461	1875
Lanes Upper Crossing (Mohave River)	73D	2,819	1875
Lankershim Ranch	73C	568	1878
Lassens Grave (Honey-Lake Valley)	47A	4,281	1878
Last Chance Creek and Milford, divide between	47B	5,999	1876
Las Posas Ranch	73C	258	1878
Lauers Ranch (Parker Creek)	38D	a5,964	1877
Laughton and Sierra Valleys, divide between	47D	7,075	1876
Leachs Point (Astronomical monument)	73B	3,619	1871, 1875
Lewis Ranch	64B	966	1878
Liebre Ranch	73C	3,756	1878

BAROMETRIC ALTITUDES.

TABLE III.—CITIES, TOWNS, SETTLEMENTS, ETC.—Continued.

Locality and name.	Atlas sheet.	Altitude in fect above sea.	Expeditionary year.
CALIFORNIA—Continued.			
Lillies Ranch	56B	3,647	1878
Lions Head	73C	1,693	1878
Lomo	47A	3,848	1878
Lone Pine	65A	3,810	1875
Longville (Humbug Valley)	47A	a4,309	1878
Longville and Miller's, divide on road	47A	5,092	1878
Loomis Ranch	47A	4,356	1878
Lopez Ranch	73C	3,248	1875
Los Angeles, curb at No. 79 Main street	73C	305	1875
Los Angeles (Southern Pacific Railroad)	73C	l290	1880
Los Angeles (Rendezvous Camp)	73C	l312	1875
Los Toros	81A	203	1875
Lots Diggings	47A	6,310	1878
Loyalton (Lewis Ranch)	47D	4,949	1876
Loyalton and Truckee Road Toll-gate	47D	5,415	1876
Lusks Ranch (Lake Tahoe)	47D	6,212	1876
Lyons Ranch	73C	1,397	1875
Lyons Station	73C	1,507	1875
Lyell Creek, mouth of	56D	8,575	1878
Lytle Creek Cañon, mouth of	73D	1,891	1878
Lytle and San Gabriel Creeks, divide between	73D	8,311	1878
McConnahas Station (three-quarters mile east of), Placerville and Virginia road	56B	3,981	1877
McDonald Ranch (Madeline Plains)	38D	5,297	1877
McFaddens Ranch	47B	4,420	1876
McGills Meadows	56D	5,004	1879
McGills Ranch	73C	5,594	1875
McKennies Ranch	73A	3,715	1878
McKesicks Ranch (Secret Valley)	47B	4,469	1877
McKinneys (Lake Tahoe)	47D	6,232	1876
Madera Flume and Trading Company, mills of	56D	4,499	1878
Malaga Ranch	73C	4	1875
Mapes Ranch	47B	5,039	1876
Mariposa	56D	1,962	1878
Markleeville (Johnsons Hotel)	56B	5,525	1877
Mark Mood Meadows	65A	5,928	1878
Marshalls Flat	56D	1,927	1879
Martins Ranch	47A	4,484	1878
Martins Ranch	73D	2,055	1875
Mathews Ranch	73D	6,294	1878
Merced (Central Pacific Railroad, Visalia Division)	64B	l171	1878
Merced Falls Village	56D	a360	1879
Miles Ranch	56B	a3,291	1877
Milford	47B	a4,204	1877
Mill Creek (Sonora road)	56B	6,467	1878
Millers Ranch	47A	4,055	1878
Milton	47D	5,845	1876
Milton	56C	376	1878
Mitchells Ranch	47A	4,285	1878
Mogul (abandoned)	56B	7,273	1877
Mokelumne River, Middle Fork Bridge	56B	2,436	1878
Mokelumne River, Middle and Licking Forks, divide between	56B	2,834	1878
Mokelumne River, Licking Fork, West Point, and Railroad Flat road	56B	2,196	1878
Mokelumne and Stanislaus River, divide between	56B	8,157	1878
Mokelumne River Suspension Bridge	56B	2,092	1878

TABLE III.—CITIES, TOWNS, SETTLEMENTS, ETC.—Continued.

Locality and name.	Atlas sheet.	Altitude in feet above sea.	Expeditionary year.
CALIFORNIA—Continued.			
Mokelumne River and Wolf Creek, divide between	56B	8,729	1878
Moonlight Valley	47A	5,433	1878
Moores Station (Toll-house)	56B	a3,207	1877
Morans Ranch (Big Tree road)	56B	3,984	1878
Morrows Ranch, near	64B	475	1878
Moseman Stage Station	73A	3,157	1875
Mountain House (Carson and Aurora road)	56B	5,641	1877
Murphys Camp	56D	2,195	1878
Murphys Cabin (Lake Tenaya)	56D	7,971	1878
Mutaus Flat	73C	4,745	1875
Myers Station (formerly Thorps), (Amador road)	56B	3,759	1878
Nashs Ranch, near Mount Dyer	47A	4,431	1878
Newbury Park	73C	830	1878
Newhall Ranch	73C	974	1878
Newhall (Southern Pacific Railroad)	73C	h,151	1878
Newhall and Culbertson Vineyard	56D	980	1878
Newtons Ranch, near Honey Lake	47B	4,079	1877
New York Tent	56D	a1,143	1879
Niagara Creek, Sonora road	56B	6,690	1878
Nimshew	47C	2,451	1878
Nordhoff	73C	818	1875
Northrups	56D	4,519	{ 1877 1878
Nulls Ranch	56D	1,299	1879
Oakdale	56C	148	1879
Oak Grove Station	80B	2,702	1876
Ogburns Ranch	47A	2,270	1878
Old Saw Mill	72D	5,324	1878
Owens River Bridge, near Owens Lake	65A	3,618	1871
Owens River, near Eclipse Mill	65A	3,666	1875
Oroville Toll Bridge	47C	a188	1878
Pacific Ocean and Triunfo Creek, divide between	73C	1,773	1878
Pacific Station (Placerville and Virginia road), (post-office)	56B	3,451	1877
Pacific Valley	56B	7,505	1877
Pah-ute Mines	73A	6,608	1875
Paleta Ranch	72B	3,624	1875
Palmers Ranch	73A	2,346	1878
Pampa (Southern Pacific Railroad)	7 A	871	1878
Panamint	65D	6,605	1875
Parkers Ranch	47A	4,136	1878
Parrotts (formerly Pendola) Ferry	56D	834	1878
Peavine Ranch	47C	a3,924	1878
Peddlers Ranch (Amador road)	56B	6,831	1878
Peñon Blanco (Haighs Ranch)	56D	1,807	{ 1878 1879
Perdues Cabin	73D	5,551	1875
Perrins Ranch	56B	a3,828	1877
Phillips Ranch (Sacramento Valley)	47A	242	1878
Phillips Station (Carson and Placerville road)	56B	6,871	1876
Picacho Mill (Colorado River)	81D	173	1876
Pinto Rock	73D	3,903	1878
Placerville Court House	56A	1,893	1877
Places Ranch	80B	4,907	1876
Pleasant Valley	56B	2,405	1877
Point of Rocks	73D	2,542	1875

TABLE III.—CITIES, TOWNS, SETTLEMENTS, ETC.—Continued.

Locality and name.	Atlas sheet.	Altitude in feet above sea.	Expeditionary year.
CALIFORNIA—Continued.			
Poison Valley	56B	8,029	1877
Porcupine Flat	56D	7,748	1878
Potatoe Ranch	73D	4,176	1875
Potrero	73C	1,028	1878
Powelton Hotel (post-office)	47A	a3,631	1878
Prattville (post-office)	47A	4,394	1878
Probascos Ranch	64B	972	1878
Quincy	47A	a3,381	1878
Quincy and Taylorville, divide between	47A	5,958	1878
Quincy and Taylorville, old toll-house between	47A	5,510	1878
Railroad Flat	56B	2,606	1878
Ravenna (Southern Pacific Railroad)	73C	l2,357	1878
Red Bluff (Central Pacific Railroad, Oregon Division)	46B	l308	1878
Red Bluff (Signal Office)	46B	l338	1879
Redmans Ranch	56D	a1,181	1878
Red Rock Cañon, freight station	73A	2,394	1875
Red Rock Ranch (Madeline Plains)	38D	5,339	1877
Richardsons Cabin (Cherry Valley)	56D	4,615	1879
Rileys store	73C	1,478	1875
Ritgers Ranch	65A	4,345	1875
Riverside, church at	80D	892	1878
Roberts Ferry (Tuolumne River)	56C	a184	1879
Roberts, mouth of San Gabriel Cañon	73C	730	1878
Rock Creek Meadows	73D	3,826	1875
Rock and San Gabriel creeks, divide between	73D	6,703	1878
Rose Ranch (Poso Creek)	73A	683	1875
Roses Store	73A	1,334	1875
Rowlands (Lake Tahoe)	56B	6,222	1876
Rubicon Point (Lake Tahoe)	56B	6,202	1876
Rush Creek, ranch on	47B	4,437	1877
Saint Clairs (Southern Pacific Railroad)	80B	1,961	1875
Saint John Mine (Kelso Valley)	73A	5,083	1875
San Andreas	56B	1,033	1877
San Antonio Creek, mouth of	73D	1,841	1878
San Antonio Creek, West Point road crossing	56B	3,848	{ 1877 1878 }
San Antonio and North Fork Stanislaus creeks, divide between	56B	1,935	1878
San Bernardino	73D	980	{ 1875 1876 1878 }
San Diego (Signal Office)	80D	l62	1875
San Emigdio Store	73A	788	1875
San Felipe	80D	2,538	1876
San Fernando Mission	73C	1,013	{ 1875 1878 }
San Fernando Plain and Simi Valley, divide on stage road	73C	1,627	1878
San Fernando (Southern Pacific Railroad)	73C	l1,065	1878
San Fernando Tunnel, south end Southern Pacific Railroad	73C	l1,400	1878
San Francisco (Signal Office)	55D	l60	1878
San Gabriel Mine	73D	1,702	1878
San Gabriel Mission, near	73C	357	1878
San Gabriel (Southern Pacific Railroad)	73C	l416	{ 1875 1876 1878 }
San Jacinto Valley, ranch in	80B	1,634	1876

U. S. GEOGRAPHICAL SURVEYS. 151

TABLE III.—CITIES, TOWNS, SETTLEMENTS, ETC.—Continued.

Locality and name.	Atlas sheet.	Altitude in feet above sea.	Expeditionary year.
CALIFORNIA—Continued.			
Santa Ana Hotel	80B	141	1878
Santa Clara Valley and San Fernando Plains, divide between	73C	1,951	1878
Santa Monica	73C	82	1875
Santa Paula	73C	384	1875
Savannah (Lexington), (Southern Pacific Railroad)	73C	*l*300	1878
Saw Mill (Little Bear Valley)	73D	4,885	1878
Sawyers Ranch	56B	7,551	1877
Schaffers Station	47B	4,026	1877
Schulers Ranch	46B	a1,075	1878
Scodie Ranch	65C	2,716	1878
Secret Valley and Smoke Creek, divide between	47B	5,698	1877
Sesma	46B	260	1878
Sheep Ranch, near Sacramento Valley	47A	1,094	1878
Sheep Ranch School House	56B	2,466	1879
Sheep Ranch (Snow Storm Valley)	47B	5,058	1877
Shinus Ranch	38D	5,040	1877
Shoo-Fly Toll-gate	47A	a3,205	1878
Shumways Ranch, near Horse Lake	38D	5,067	1877
Sierra City	47C	4,202	1876
Sierra Valley and South Fork Yuba River, divide between	47D	6,700	1876
Sierraville (post-office)	47D	4,880	1876
Sierra and Sardine Valleys, divide between	47D	6,346	1876
Silver Lake Hotel	56B	7,174	1877
Silver Mountain City	56B	6,446	1877
Simi Ranch	73C	674	1878
Simi Valley, head of	73C	1,118	1878
Slinkards Valley, lower end of	56B	6,256	1878
Slinkards Valley, upper end of	56B	6,688	1877
Snake Cañon Summit	47D	7,249	1877
Snelling post-office	56D	a252	1879
Snows Hotel, near foot Nevada Fall	56D	5,217	1878
Soda Springs and French Meadows Creek, divide between	47D	5,779	1877
Soledad City, Ravenna Station, Southern Pacific Railroad	73C	2,513	1875
Sonora, McQuaid Ranch	56D	1,888	{ 1878 1879
Sonora (post-office)	56D	1,816	1878
Spadra	73D	802	1875
Springville	73C	48	1878
Stanislaus River, South and Middle Forks, divide between	56B	6,352	1878
Stanislaus River, South and Middle Forks, divide between	56B	8,843	1878
Stanislaus and Tuolumne Rivers, divide between	56B	9,617	1878
Stevens Ranch (Hope Valley)	56B	7,382	1877
Stockton's Cabin	73D	5,877	1878
Stockton Mill	47A	4,639	1878
Strawberry, lower reservoir, ¼ mile east of	56B	5,582	1878
Strawberry Toll-house (Virginia and Placerville road)	56B	5,695	1878
Strawberry Stage Station (Sonora and Mono road)	56D	5,238	{ 1877 1878
Sugar Pine Point, (Lake Tahoe)	47D	6,202	1876
Sulphur Spring Hotel (Wash post-office)	47D	4,466	1876
Summit Post-office (Sierra Valley)	47D	4,875	1876
Summit Station (Central Pacific Railroad)	47D	6,983	{ 1876 1877
Summit Valley (Relief Trail)	56B	9,585	1878
Summit Valley (Sonora road)	56B	9,462	1877
Susanville and Eagle Lake, first divide	47A	5,363	1878

152 BAROMETRIC ALTITUDES.

Table III.—CITIES, TOWNS, SETTLEMENTS, ETC.—Continued.

Locality and name.	Atlas sheet.	Altitude in feet above sea.	Expeditionary year.
CALIFORNIA—Continued.			
Susanville and Eagle Lake, second divide	47A	5,774	1878
Susanville and Eagle Lake, main divide	47A	6,245	1878
Susanville (post-office)	47A	4,195	1877
Susanville and Taylorville, divide on road	47A	6,428	1878
Sycamore Grove	73C	447	1878
Swizzers Ranch (Sierra Valley)	47B	4,910	1876
Tahoe City	47D	6,252	1876
Tamarack Flat	56D	6,234	{ 1878 1879
Tannery	73D	4,400	1878
Tapo Ranch	73C	1,373	1878
Taylorville (post-office)	47A	a3,479	1878
Tehachapai	73A	3,831	1875
Tejon Reservation	73A	1,450	1878
Tejon Reservation, house near	73A	1,275	1875
Tells Ranch	56B	6,766	1877
Temecula, near	80B	1,088	1876
Ten-mile House	80A	a108	1876
The Narrows	73D	2,507	1878
Thomas Ranch	73C	3,772	1875
Thomas Ranch	80B	4,438	1876
Thompsons Ferry (Tuolumne River)	56D	a107	1879
Tilleys Ranch	65C	2,609	1878
Tin Mine (Temescal Range)	80B	1,250	1876
Truckee (Central Pacific Railroad)	47D	5,795	1876
Truckee and Lake Tahoe, divide between	47D	7,236	1876
Truckee and Sierra Valley, divide between	47D	6,894	1876
Tuledad Ranch	38D	a5,046	1877
Tule Marsh	38D	5,376	1877
Tuolumne River, Middle Fork, on trail to Hog Ranch	56D	4,158	1878
Tuolumne and Walker Rivers, divide between	56B	9,805	1878
Turners Ranch (Sierra Valley)	47D	4,904	1876
Tuttletown Mining Village	56D	a1,321	1878
Tylers Ranch	47A	a4,802	1878
Uhls Ranch	65C	2,662	1875
Vallecito post-office	56D	1,748	1878
Vallecito Station	81C	1,574	1876
Vida (Sepulveda), (Southern Pacific Railroad)	73C	460	1878
Virginia House, between Truckee and Loyalton	47D	a5,689	1876
Virgin Tears Cliff, foot of Yosemite Valley	56D	5,311	1878
Volcano	56B	2,075	1878
Wades Meadows	56D	4,567	1878
Warner Valley	80B	2,784	1876
Warrens Station (Buckhorn Ranch)	73C	693	1875
Waterloo Hotel	56D	215	1879
Watermans	73D	1,908	1878
Weldon (post-office)	73A	2,668	1878
Wellington Station	56B	4,796	1877
West Point	56B	2,774	1878
Wests Ranch (Colorado River)	74D	596	1875
West Walker River, West Fork, Sonora road crossing	56B	6,728	{ 1877 1878
Whiskey Johnnys	73D	5,186	1878
White Water Station	80B	1,304	{ 1875 1876
Whitney Meadows, near Fishermans Peak or Mt. Whitney	65C	9,371	1875

U. S. GEOGRAPHICAL SURVEYS. 153

TABLE III.—CITIES, TOWNS, SETTLEMENTS, ETC.—Continued.

Locality and name.	Atlas sheet.	Altitude in feet above sea.	Expeditionary year.
CALIFORNIA—Continued.			
Wileys Station (Amador road)	55B	5,027	1878
Williams Ranch (Amador road)	56B	7,757	1877
Willow Ranch (Long Valley)	47B	4,275	1877
Willow Tree Spring Station	73B	2,500	1875
Winters Mine, one-half mile northwest of Oreana Peak	56B	8,599	1877
Wilsons Ranch	46B	a1,114	1878
Wiltons Bridge (American River)	47C	1,408	1877
Woodford	56B	5,676	1877
Workmans Ranch	73C	361	1875
Yanks Landing (Lake Tahoe, Tallac Post-Office)	56B	6,202	1876
Yarnells (Cold Spring) Ranch	47C	564	1878
York Gulch, head of	56D	1,705	1879
Yosemite Valley, Lower Iron Bridge or El Capitan Bridge, Merced River.	} 56D	3,925 {	1878 1879
Yosemite Valley, Upper Iron Bridge at Barnards, Merced River	56D	3,934 {	1878 1879
COLORADO.			
Acequia (Denver and Rio Grande Railroad)	53C	l5,551	1877
Alamosa (Denver and Rio Grande Railroad)	61D	l7,492	1879
Aldens Junction	61C	8,904	1877
Andersons Ranch	62D	4,248	1877
Animas City	61C	6,662	1874
Anthracite and Coal Creeks, junction of	61A	6,153	1877
Anthracite and Ohio Creeks, divide between	61A	10,151	1877
Anton Smiths Ranch	62A	4,748 {	1874 1875
Apishpa (Denver and Rio Grande Railroad)	62C	l6,195	1878
Badito	62C	6,386 {	1874 1875
Bakerville (Georgetown and Grays Peak and Leadville Road)	52D	l9,875	1880
Beaver Creek Station (Denver and Rio Grande Railroad)	62A	l5,000	1878
Big Graneros Creek, crossing of, near junction Little Graneros	62C	6,012	1874
Bismarck (post-office)	61D	7,736	1876
Boists (Denver and Rio Grande Railroad)	53C	l6,865	1877
Box Elder (Kansas Pacific Railroad)	53C	l5,546	1877
Bradfords	62C	8,105	1874
Breckenridge, near	52D	9,794	1873
Butte Valley (post-office)	62C	5,894	1875
Byers Station (Bijou, Kansas Pacific Railroad)	53C	l5,221	1877
Camp Monarch	61B	a10,272	1879
Cañon City (Denver and Rio Grande Railroad)	62A	l5,341 {	1873 1876
Capitol	61C	9,430	1874
Carbonateville	52D	a11,125	1879
Carlisle Springs Station (Denver and Rio Grande Railroad)	62A	l4,969	1878
Carrs Cabin (Antelope Park)	61C	9,999	1873
Castle Rock (Denver and Rio Grande Railroad)	53C	l6,211	1877
Cement and Eureka Creeks, divide between	61C	12,786	1874
Centreville (post-office)	61B	a7,727	1879
Chama and Navajo Creeks, divide between	69B	8,784	1874
Clear Creek and Platte River, divide between	52D	11,416	1873
Coal Mines, near Cañon City	62A	5,441	1873
Colfax	62C	8,599	1873
Colonas Ferry (Rio Grande)	69B	7,443	1875

BAROMETRIC ALTITUDES.

Table III.—CITIES, TOWNS, SETTLEMENTS, ETC.—Continued.

Locality and name.	Atlas sheet.	Altitude in feet above sea.	Expeditionary year.
COLORADO—Continued.			
Colonas Ferry and San Antonio Creek, divide between	69B	7,865	1874
Colorado Springs (Astronomical Monument)	62A	6,010	1873
Colorado Springs (signal office)	62A	6,030	1874
Conejos Ferry	69B	7,835	1874
Costilla	69B	7,751	1874
Costilla	62D	7,792	1877
Costilla Ferry (Colonas, Valdez, or Myers Ferry)	69B	7,434	{ 1875 1878
Cottonwood (Wet Mountain Valley)	62C	8,323	1879
Cowles Ranch (Wet Mountain Valley)	62C	8,035	1874
Cuchara (Denver and Rio Grande Railroad)	62C	/5,949	1878
Cucharas and Trinchera Creeks, divide between	62C	10,955	1874
Culebra Church	69B	8,010	1874
Del Norte	61D	7,743	{ 1874 1875 1877
Denver (Kansas Pacific Railroad)	53C	/5,197	1873
Denver (signal office)	53C	/5,263	1877
Deserted Ranch (South Park)	52D	9,632	1873
Dillon Junction (Georgetown, Grays Peak and Leadville Railroad)	52D	/8,690	1880
Divide (Denver and Rio Grande Railroad)	53C	6,919	1877
Dotsons Ranch (South Fork and Saint Charles Creek)	62C	6,379	1874
Douglass (Denver and Rio Grande Railroad)	53C	/6,331	1877
Doyles Ranch	62C	4,714	1875
Dudley	52D	/10,600	1879
Edgerton (Denver and Rio Grande Railroad)	62A	/6,393	1878
Eighteen-mile Ranch (Currant Creek)	62A	7,180	1876
Fairplay (center of town)	52D	10,026	{ 1873 1879
Florissant (post-office)	62A	a8,149	1876
Florissant, near	62A	8,184	1876
Fosters (Apishpa Creek)	62C	6,328	1875
Fountain (Denver and Rio Grande Railroad)	62A	/5,626	1878
Gardners (post-office)	62C	6,956	1874
Georgetown (Astronomical Monument)	52D	8,588	1873
Georgetown Depot (Colorado Central Railroad)	52D	/8,419	1880
Golden (Colorado Central Railroad)	53C	/5,668	1880
Goodnight (Denver and Rio Grande Railroad)	62A	/4,731	1878
Graneros (Denver and Rio Grande Railroad)	62C	/5,949	1878
Grant (post-office)	52D	8,497	1873
Granite (Denver and Rio Grande Railroad)	52D	/8,986	1880
Grape Creek 1½ miles west Silver Cliff	62C	7,727	1879
Grayback Gulch settlement	62C	8,609	1879
Greenhorn (Denver and Rio Grande Railroad)	62C	/5,109	1878
Greenhorn Creek, crossing of	62C	5,860	1874
Greenhorn River (post-office)	62C	6,926	1874
Greenland (Denver and Rio Grande Railroad)	53C	/6,690	1877
Greenwood post-office, near, on Hardscrabble Creek	62A	6,205	1874
Gunnison post-office (Kellys store)	61A	7,428	1877
Half-way House	62A	6,028	1874
Halls Gulch, mouth of	52D	9,099	1873
Halls Gulch, summit of	52D	12,671	1873
Halls smelting works	52D	9,917	1873
Hamilton Ranch	62C	7,227	1874

U. S. GEOGRAPHICAL SURVEYS.

TABLE III.—CITIES, TOWNS, SETTLEMENTS, ETC.—Continued.

Locality and name.	Atlas sheet.	Altitude in feet above sea.	Expeditionary year.
COLORADO—Continued.			
Hartzels Ranch	52D	8,885	1873
Heads Cattle Ranch, near San Luis Lakes	61D	7,535	1875
Hermosa (Johnson Ranch)	61C	6,618	1875
Hillerton	61B	a9,851	1879
Hog-back	62D	5,467	{ 1876 / 1877 }
Hot Spring, forks of road near	61C	6,988	1877
Howardville	61C	9,545	1873
Hughes (Astronomical Monument)	53A	5,022	1873
Huerfano (Denver and Rio Grande Railroad)	62C	l5,652	1878
Huerfano and mountains of Wet Mountain Valley, divide between	62C	9,534	1875
Husted (Denver and Rio Grande Railroad)	53C	l6,599	1877
Idaho Springs	52D	7,284	1873
Jefferson (Denver, South Park and Pacific Railroad)	52D	l9,516	1877
Jefferson, near	52D	9,862	1873
Johnsons Ford (Uncompahgre River)	61A	5,702	1877
Julesburg (Astronomical Monument)	45C	l3,500	1874
Junction (Denver Pacific Railroad)	53C	l5,212	1877
Kennys Ranch (Chatillon Creek)	61D	7,830	1876
Kiowa (Kansas Pacific Railroad)	53C	l5,514	1877
Kokomo (Georgetown, Grays Peak and Leadville Railroad)	52D	l10,550	1880
Labran (Astronomical Monument)	62A	5,218	{ 1873 / 1874 / 1875 }
Lake City	61C	8,753	{ 1875 / 1877 }
Lake City and Antelope Park, divide between	61C	11,777	{ 1875 / 1877 }
Lake Fork of Gunnison, crossing second bridge	61C	a7,941	1875
Lake House, slope of Pikes Peak	62A	10,108	1876
La Junta	62D	4,094	1876
Lamberts Ranch	61C	6,561	1875
Lanes Ranch (Kerber Creek)	61B	8,380	1874
Larkspur (Denver and Rio Grande Railroad)	53C	l6,516	1877
Leadville (Post-office)	52D	a10,250	1879
Little Buttes (Denver and Rio Grande Railroad)	62A	l5,375	1878
Littleton (Denver and Rio Grande Railroad)	53C	l5,372	1877
Lockwoods Ranch	62D	4,997	{ 1876 / 1877 }
Los Pinos Agency, new	61A	6,400	1877
Los Pinos Agency, old	61B	9,088	{ 1873 / 1874 }
Los Pinos and Rio Grande, divide between	61C	10,737	1875
Lowes Ranch (Four-mile Creek)	52D	a10,022	1879
McClures Ranch	62A	5,318	1873
McLaughlin Ranch	52D	9,672	1873
McLaughlins (Tarryall Creek)	53C	8,226	1876
Malta, California Gulch (Denver and Rio Grande Railroad)	52D	l9,613	1880
Mineral City	61C	11,474	1874
Mosquito Town	52D	10,446	1873
Monument (Denver and Rio Grande Railroad)	53C	l7,240	1877
Nine-Mile Ranch	52D	a9,468	1879
Olivers Ranch (Tarryall Creek)	52D	a8,873	1879
Ouray	61C	7,766	1877
Park Gulch, near Lilienthals Ranch	52D	a9,515	1879
Parrott City	61C	a8,674	1875

TABLE III.—CITIES, TOWNS, SETTLEMENTS, ETC.—Continued.

Locality and name.	Atlas sheet.	Altitude in feet above sea.	Expeditionary year.
COLORADO—Continued.			
Pass Creek, divide at head of	62C	9,494	1874
Petersburg (Denver and Rio Grande Railroad)	53C	*5,328	1877
Piñon (Denver and Rio Grande Railroad)	62A	*5,037	1878
Plum (Denver and Rio Grande Railroad)	53C	*5,850	1877
Pueblo (Denver and Rio Grande Railroad)	62A	4,713	1878
Pueblo (Astronomical Monument)	62A	4,732	1876
Purgatory River and Vermejo Creek, divide between	70A	9,173	{ 1874 1875
Quartzville	52D	a11,706	1876
Red Creek Ranch	62A	5,466	1874
Red Rock Cañon	61A	7,432	1877
Rito Alto (Post-office)	61D	8,169	1876
Riverside Post-office (Leonard's Ranch), Arkansas River	61B	8,335	1873
Rock Cliff (Post-office)	61D	8,271	1875
Rosita	62C	8,736	{ 1874 1875 1876
Round Mountain (Post-office)		a8,732	1876
Saguache	61D	7,620	{ 1875 1877
Salt Creek (Denver and Rio Grande Railroad)	62C	*5,484	1878
San Carlos (Denver and Rio Grande Railroad)	62C	*4,925	1878
San Francisco, south fork of Purgatory River	70A	8,082	1875
San Juan City	61C	8,901	1875
San Luis	70A	7,596	1874
Santa Clara (Denver and Rio Grande Railroad)	62C	*6,172	1878
Saint Marys	62C	6,167	1874
Silver Cliff	62C	7,919	1879
Silverton	61C	a9,201	1875
Sizers Ranch	62D	4,035	{ 1876 1877
Slate and Iron Creeks, divide between	61A	12,287	1877
Slater Ranch	52D	9,257	1873
South Pueblo (Denver and Rio Grande Railroad)	62A	4,669	1876
South Pueblo (Astronomical Monument)	62A	4,732	1874
Star Ranch	61D	7,327	{ 1877 1879
Sternes Store	62C	9,068	1874
Stiles Ranch	52D	a10,734	1879
Summit Mines, north fork Alamosa Creek	61D	11,089	1874
Summit Station (Denver and Rio Grande Railroad)	52D	9,981	1873
Swallows	62A	4,868	1878
Tabor	52D	a10,623	1879
Tellurium	61C	10,878	1875
Ten-Mile and Eagle Creeks, divide between	52D	10,756	1873
Trinchera	69B	7,535	{ 1874 1878
Trinidad (Astronomical Monument)	70A	5,990	{ 1873 1874
Twelve-Mile Bridge (Arkansas River)	62A	a5,772	1879
Twelve-Mile Ranch (Somerville)	62A	a6,205	1879
Twin Lakes (formerly Dayton)	52D	9,333	1873
Ula	61B	7,727	1877
Uncompahgre River and Cimarron Creek, divide between	61A	11,557	1877
Union Park	61B	9,655	1873

U. S. GEOGRAPHICAL SURVEYS. 157

TABLE III.—CITIES, TOWNS, SETTLEMENTS, ETC.—Continued.

Locality and name.	Atlas sheet.	Altitude in feet above sea.	Expeditionary year.
COLORADO—Continued.			
Ute Creek, seven miles above Fort Garland	62C	8,671	1879
Varnums Post-Office, on Indian Creek	61A	a7,990	1877
Venables Ranch (Rio Grande)	61D	7,628	1875
Veta (Denver and Rio Grande Railroad)	62C	b7,024	1878
Vigil (Apishpa River)	70A	7,233	1875
Vogels Ranch	62D	4,205	1876
Walsens (Denver and Rio Grande Railroad)	62C	b6,188	1878
Websters	62A	5,507	1874
Wet Mountain Valley and Muddy Creek, divide between	62C	8,890	1875
White Earth Creek (post-office)	61A	8,163	1877
Whites Ranch (Huerfano Park)	62C	7,469	1875
White River Agency, crossing of trail to	61A	5,018	1877
Wideheld (Denver and Rio Grande Railroad)	62A	b5,715	1878
Wilcox Ranch (Antelope Park)	61C	a9,000	1875
Zapato	61D	7,562	1877
IDAHO.			
Andersons Ranch	32C	a4,491	1877
Barrys Ranch, on Black Pine Creek	41A	5,114	1877
Black Rock (stage station)	32D	a4,589	1877
Bennington	32D	a6,150	1877
Bloomington	41B	6,076	1877
Burtons Ford (Bear River, Gentile Valley)	32D	4,916	1877
City of Rocks	41A	6,078	1877
Clifton Post-Office	41B	a4,926	1877
Devils Corral	31D	3,601	1877
Elkhorn	41A	4,950	1877
Elkhorn Mail Station	32D	4,998	1877
Fish Haven	41B	a5,964	1877
Franklin (Websters shop)	41B	4,585	1877
Georgetown	32D	a6,022	1877
Harkness Toll-Gate	32D	a4,802	1877
Heads Ranch	41B	4,947	1877
Hildreths Ranch	31D	4,308	1877
Hitchings Ranch	41A	5,205	1877
Howells Ranch	32C	a5,041	1877
Keenan City	32D	a6,641	1877
Lands Lower Ranch (Goose Creek)	31D	4,357	1877
Landers Crossing, Taylor Bridge road	32D	a6,381	1877
Lanes Fork, crossing	32D	6,635	1877
Lanes Ranch (Marsh Lake)	32C	4,323	1877
Liberty	41B	6,105	1877
Malade City (Post-office)	41B	4,663	1877
McCreas Ranch	32C	4,331	1877
Mink Creek Bridge	41B	a5,023	1877
Montpelier (co-operative store)	41B	5,936	1877
Mormon Salt Works	32D	a6,734	1877
Nine-Mile Settlement	32D	a5,013	1877
Oneida Salt Works	32D	6,341	1877
Oxford	41B	a4,875	1877
Packers Bridge (Bear River)	41B	4,486	1877
Paris	41B	a6,019	1877
Pocatillo Stage Station	32C	a4,620	1877
Raft River Stage Station	41A	5,041	1877
Rices Ferry (Snake River)	31D	4,192	1877
Rices Ranch, on Cache Creek	41A	4,722	1877

158 BAROMETRIC ALTITUDES.

TABLE III.—CITIES, TOWNS, SETTLEMENTS, ETC.—Continued.

Locality and name.	Atlas sheet.	Altitude in feet above sea.	Expeditionary year.
IDAHO—Continued.			
Richardsons Ranch	41A	5,268	1877
Robbins Ford (Bear River)	41B	4,621	1877
Ross Fork (Indian Agency)	32C	4,545	1877
Samaria	41B	4,560	1877
Soda Springs	32D	5,778	1877
St. Charles	41B	6,057	1877
Summit Stage Station	40B	5,945	1877
Sweetzers Ranch	41A	4,509	1877
Toponce Ranch	32C	5,072	1877
Warren (Blackfoot Stage Station)	32C	4,447	1877
Weston	41B	5,011	1877
MONTANA.			
Bozeman (Astronomical Monument)	14D	4,839	1873
NEBRASKA.			
North Platte (Union Pacific Railroad) (Astronomical Monument)	45D	2,789	1874
NEVADA.			
Adobe Meadows	57C	6,594	1878
Alta Mine	47D	5,558	1877
Antoines Ranch, Smith Creek	48D	6,517	1876
Atlantic Mine, Gold Cañon, on road	47D	5,136	1877
Aurora	57A	7,449	1878
Austin (Astronomical Monument)	48D	7,521	1871
Austin, base line, north end of	48D	5,774	1878
Austin, base line, south end of	48D	5,799	1878
Austin, camp at	48D	6,594	1876
Bacon Mill Point	47D	5,327	1877
Baltimore Mine	47D	5,729	1877
Baltimore Mine Boarding House, near	47D	5,784	1877
Barretts Ranch	47D	4,369	1877
Base Line (Carson River)	47D	4,306	1876
Battle Mountain (Astronomical Monument)	48B	4,508	1871
Belcher Mine	47D	5,979	1877
Belmont, near	57B	8,092	1871
Best and Belcher and Gould and Curry, joint shafts	47D	5,965	1877
Birchims Ranch (Reese River)	48D	5,743	1876
Brassfield Cañon, head of	48D	9,658	1876
Buckeye Mine, junction of roads	47D	5,163	1877
Buckeye Mine	47D	5,221	1877
Bucklands Ranch (Carson River Toll Bridge)	48C	4,151	1876
Buffalo Salt Works (Murphys)	47B	3,845	1877
Bull Run, near White Rock Creek	40C	6,114	1871
Bullion City	49	6,386	1871
Bullion Mine	47D	6,306	1877
Caledonia Mine	47D	5,676	1877
Callville	66	945	1875
Carlin (Astronomical Monument)	40C	4,908	1871
Carlin, near	40C	4,849	1871
Camp Rock	47D	5,628	1877
Captain John Thomas Ranch	48D	5,887	1876
Carson, Capitol	47D	4,634	1876
Carson City (Friends Observatory)	47D	4,660	1876
Carson City (Rendezvous Camp)	47D	4,700	1876

U. S. GEOGRAPHICAL SURVEYS. 159

TABLE III.—CITIES, TOWNS, SETTLEMENTS, ETC.—Continued.

Locality and name.	Atlas sheet.	Altitude in feet above sea.	Expeditionary year.
NEVADA—Continued.			
Carson States Prison	47D	a4,542	1876
Cedar Ravine, Summit Head of	47D	7,179	1876
Centre Station (American Flat)	47D	5,541	1877
Chalk Wells	48D	5,755	1876
Chapman Ranch (Dry Valley)	47B	4,932	1878
Childs Ranch	47D	4,779	1876
Chollar Potosi Mining Company, office of	47D	6,242	1877
Chollar Potosi Mine, shaft	47D	l6,225	1877
Clarks Ranch	38D	4,677	1877
Clarks Ranch (Truckee River)	47D	4,221	1876
Cleavers Ranch (Masons Valley)	48C	4,338	1876
Coal Mines in El Dorado Cañon	47D	5,880	1876
Combination Mine, shaft	47D	l6,132	1877
Consolidated Virginia Mine	47D	l6,155	1877
Cottage Camp	40C	6,437	1871
Cottonwood Cañon, mouth of	38D	6,066	1877
Cottonwood Cañon, head of	48D	10,849	1876
Cottonwood Island, north end	74B	800	1875
Cottonwood Island, south end	74B	794	1875
Coxs Station	48C	a4,379	1876
Cradlebaughs Bridge (Carson River)	47D	a4,614	1877
Crow Point Mine	47D	l5,925	1877
Crystal Peak (village)	47D	4,918	1876
Dayton	47D	4,369	1876
Dead Horse Wells	57A	4,117	1876
Deep Hole (Old Emigrant Road through Squaw Valley)	38D	3,922	1877
Deep Hollow Station	48C	5,244	1876
Derby Mine	47D	4,885	1877
Desert Station (Central Pacific Railroad)	48C	4,014	1876
Deveringhams Ranch	57B	6,497	1878
Devils Gate Toll-House, near Silver City	47D	5,148	1877
Dyers Ranch	48D	6,037	1876
East Gate, Lookout Mountains, Captain Simpsons wagon route	48D	5,291	1876
El Dorado Mill	66	863	1875
Elkhorn Ranch	48D	6,123	1876
Elko (Astronomical Monument)	40C	5,148	1869
Ellsworth	57B	6,871	1876
Emma Peak and peak northwest of Rose, divide between	47D	6,072	1876
Empire City	47D	4,593	1876
Erie Consolidated Mine	47D	5,265	1877
Eureka	49	5,906	1871
Europa Mine	47D	5,978	1877
Five-mile House (Geiger Grade)	47D	6,368	1876
Franktown	47D	5,054	1876
Frenchs Mill, at creek	47D	4,875	1877
Galena	48	5,650	1871
Gates Ranch (Carson River)	48C	4,154	1876
Geiger Grade, toll-gate	47D	6,479	1876
Geiger Grade, first summit	47D	6,651	1876
Geiger Grade, second summit	47D	6,733	1876
Geigers Ranch (Walker River)	48C	a4,352	1876
Genoa	47D	4,802	1876
Gila Mina Post, near Succor Mine	47D	5,452	1877
Glenbrook, camp at (Lake Tahoe)	47D	6,282	1876
Glendale	47D	4,453	1876
Globe Consolidated Mine	47D	5,781	1877
Gold Hill Mine	47D	6,373	1877

BAROMETRIC ALTITUDES.

TABLE III.—CITIES, TOWNS, SETTLEMENTS, ETC.—Continued.

Locality and name.	Atlas sheet.	Altitude in feet above sea.	Expeditionary year.
NEVADA—Continued.			
Gould and Curry Mine	47D	6,193	1877
Haines, foot of Kingsbury Grade	56B	a4,733	1876
Hale and Norcross Mine	47D	6,155	1876
Half-way House (Devils Gate Toll-house)	47D	5,006	1876
Hamilton (Astronomical Monument)	49C	7,601	1869
Hieroglyphic Rocks (Central Pacific Railroad)	47D	4,351	1876
High Rock and Yellow Rock Cañons, junction of	38D	5,121	1877
Hill and Grimes Ranch (New River)	48C	3,944	1876
Home Station	48B	4,816	1878
Homer (Cedar Valley)	58D	5,821	1869
Houstons Well	48C	4,148	1876
Imperial Mine	47D	6,159	1877
Ione	57B	6,844	1876
Italian Joes	47D	4,437	1876
Jacks Valley	47D	5,043	1876
Jews Ranch, McLarnahans road	47D	a5,882	1877
Jones Milk Ranch	47D	5,736	1877
Julia Mine	47D	6,116	1877
Justice Mine	47D	5,458	1877
Kentuck Mine	47D	5,944	1877
Knickerbocker Mine	47D	5,876	1877
Lake Tahoe and Little Valley, divide between	47D	7,960	1876
Lake View, divide between Carson and Washoe Valley	47D	5,134	1876
La Plata (deserted)	48C	6,043	1876
Las Vegas	66	2,018	{ 1869 / 1871 }
Lees Mills (Mason Valley)	48C	4,350	1876
Little Valley	47D	6,417	1876
Little Valley and Mills Station, divide between	47D	6,939	1876
Lodi	48D	5,356	1876
Log Cabin (Carson River)	48C	4,070	1876
Long and Surprise Valleys, divide between	38D	7,170	1877
Lyonsville (Rose Valley)	58D	5,401	1869
McBrides Ranch	57C	5,561	1878
McMahons Ranch	57B	6,552	1876
McLarnahans Bridge	47D	a4,597	1877
McLarnahans Road and road to Brunswick Mill, junction of	47D	6,008	1876
Mackey and Fairs Tailing Dump, on creek above	47D	5,246	1877
Marlettes Ranch	47D	8,074	1876
Mastens Ranch (Central Pacific Railroad)	47D	4,678	1876
Matty Roachs, near Mineral Hill	47D	6,864	1877
Matty Roachs, divide on road north of	47D	6,987	1876
Mexican Mining Claim	47D	6,154	1876
Middle Gate, Lookout Mountains, Captain Simpsons wagon route	48C	a4,703	1876
Mineral Hill Station, Eureka and Palisade Railroad	49	6,508	1871
Monte Christo Mill (Astronomical Monument)	49C	7,596	1869
Moore Campbells Ranch	48D	6,267	1876
Morey Mines, near Shoshone Peak	58	7,384	1871
Mound House Station (Virginia and Truckee Railroad)	47D	5,032	1877
New Yellow Jacket Mine, east shaft	47D	6,050	1877
New York House, near Dayton	47D	a4,810	1877
Occidental Mill	47D	5,480	1876
Old Kentuck Ranch (Sutro Tunnel Road)	47D	5,684	1876
Omega Mill (Washoe District)	47D	5,351	18,6
Ophir Mine	47D	6,130	1877
Overman Mine	47D	5,731	1877

U. S. GEOGRAPHICAL SURVEYS. 161

TABLE III.—CITIES, TOWNS, SETTLEMENTS, ETC.—Continued.

Locality and name.	Atlas sheet.	Altitude in feet above sea.	Expeditionary year.
NEVADA—Continued.			
Owyhee	40C	5,392	1871
Palmyra (abandoned)	47D	6,592	1877
Panacca, near	58D	4,718	1869
Pattersons Ranch	48D	5,213	1876
Peavine Ranch	47D	4,952	{ 1876 / 1877 }
Peko (Astronomical Monument)	40C	5,180	1869
Petersons Ranch	48D	6,137	1876
Peytona Mine	47D	6,639	1876
Pioche (Astronomical Monument)	58D	5,942	1872
Pinto Spring, flat below	38D	5,600	1877
Poeville Mine, near Peavine Peak	47D	6,408	1876
Poormans Mining Claim	47D	6,000	1876
Proctors Ranch (Truckee River)	47D	3,963	1837
Prospect Mine	47D	5,866	1876
Pyramid Lake (Indian Agency)	47D	3,980	1877
Quinn Cañon, near Railroad Valley	58	6,256	1871
Race Course, near Virginia City	47D	6,157	1876
Ragtown (Carson River)	48C	4,002	1876
Ramsell Mill, near Silver City	47D	5,324	1877
Red Jacket Mine, road below	47D	5,190	1877
Reliance Mining Companys Shaft	47D	6,047	1877
Reno (Central Pacific Railroad)	47D	4,484	1876
Ritches Cabin, near Grant Peak	48C	7,474	1876
Rock Island Mine	47D	5,678	1877
Rookers Corral	48D	6,708	1878
Rookers Ranch	48D	7,148	1878
Saint Clair (New River)	48C	a3,989	1876
Saint Thomas	66B	1,600	1869
San Antonio	57	5,280	1871
Sand Spring Station	48C	3,926	1876
Savage Mine	47D	/5,179	1877
Schmidtleins Ranch, mouth of Kingston Cañon	48D	6,220	1876
Sellers Ranch, near Reno	47D	4,439	1877
Sheridan (post-office)	56B	a4,794	1876
Sierra Nevada Mine (new shaft)	47D	/6,031	1877
Sierra Nevada, Mexican and Union Mines (joint shaft)	47D	/6,067	1877
Silver Age Station	48D	6,014	1876
Silver City, church in	47D	5,098	1877
Silver City, old foundry	47D	4,940	1877
Silver Hill Mine	47D	/5,285	1877
Silver Peak Mine	57	4,257	1871
Slaughter House, creek near	47D	5,118	1877
Slaughter House, on road between Virginia City race-course and toll-gate	47D	6,414	1876
Smoke Creek Depot	47B	4,163	1877
Snow Shed, Virginia and Truckee Railroad	47D	5,685	1877
Spanish Springs Ranch	47D	a4,469	1876
Sterling Mill, near Schmidtleins Ranch	48D	6,818	1876
Stillwater, on the Slough	48C	3,954	1876
Stones Cabin	57B	6,390	1871
Stones Ferry (Colorado River)	66	1,108	1875
Stumps Ranch	49	4,749	1871
Sturtevants Ranch (Truckee River)	47D	4,303	1876
Superior Gold and Silver Mine	47D	6,415	1877
Sutro	47D	a4,392	1877

1874 WH——11

BAROMETRIC ALTITUDES.

TABLE III.—CITIES, TOWNS, SETTLEMENTS, ETC.—Continued.

Locality and name.	Atlas sheet.	Altitude in feet above sea.	Expeditionary year.
NEVADA—Continued.			
Sutro Monument, divide between Emma and Rose Peaks	47D	5,837	1876
Sutro Tunnel:			
Mouth of	47D	*4,482	1876
Shaft No. 1	47D	4,998	1876
Shaft No. 2	47D	*5,539	1876
Shaft No. 3	47D	*5,867	1876
Shaft No. 4	47D	*5,998	1876
Swanns Ranch (East Walker River)	57A	5,042	1878
Taylors Ranch	47D	4,720	1878
Tecoma (Central Pacific Railroad)	40D	4,788	1878
Todhunters Ranch (Long Valley)	38D	5,851	1877
Trojan Mine	47D	6,086	1877
Tunnel (Virginia and Truckee Railroad), base of American Flat Peak	47D	5,821	1877
Twelve-Mile House	56B	a4,801	1877
Upper Caledonia Mine	47D	5,987	1877
Underdown Cañon, mouth of Reese River	48D	6,181	1878
Utah Mine	47D	5,996	1876
United States Coast Survey Stake, 82–85	47D	5,858	1876
Vaughans Ranch	48D	5,316	1878
Verdi (Central Pacific Railroad)	47D	4,894	1876
Virginia City:			
Astronomical Monument	47D	6,339	1876
Biddlemans Milk Ranch	47D	5,825	1876
Foot of B street	47D	6,294	1876
165 G street	47D	6,118	1876
Virginia City and Washoe, divide between	47D	7,242	1876
Virginia and Gold Hill Water Flume, near Virginia City	47D	6,559	1877
Vista (Central Pacific Railroad)	47D	4,406	1876
Vivian Mine	47D	5,414	1877
Vulcan Mine, flume near	47D	5,187	1877
Wadsworth (Central Pacific Railroad)	47D	4,095	{ 1876 1877
Walkers Ranch	40	5,146	1869
Walker River Indian Agency	48C	4,120	1876
Wallaces Ranch	48D	5,787	1878
Ward Mine	47D	*6,117	1877
Washington (San Pedro Cañon)	48D	6,992	1876
Washoe (Virginia and Truckee Railroad)	47D	5,021	1876
Washoe Grade, foot of	47D	5,850	1877
Washoe Grade, Station 7	47D	7,202	1877
Weimer Mud Meadows	39C	4,318	1877
Welchs Ranch	48D	5,771	1878
West Belcher Mine	47D	6,098	1877
West Gate, Lookout Mountains, Captain Simpsons wagon route	48C	4,504	1876
West Point	66B	1,755	1869
White Rock	48C	a4,818	1876
Wilcox Ranch	47D	5,396	1876
Wm. Penn Mine	47D	5,235	1877
Winnemucca (Astronomical Monument)	39D	4,355	1877
Winter Ranch (Dry Valley)	47B	5,145	1877
Woods Ranch, Pyramid Lake (Emerson, by King)	47B	3,861	1877
Yellow Jacket Mine	47D	*5,959	1877
Youngs Ranch, Snake Creek	49	5,642	1872

U. S. GEOGRAPHICAL SURVEYS.

TABLE III.—CITIES, TOWNS, SETTLEMENTS, ETC.—Continued.

Locality and name.	Atlas sheet.	Altitude in feet above sea.	Expeditionary year.
NEW MEXICO.			
Abiquiu	69D	5,930	1874
Acoma	77A	*6,700	1873
Acoma, Camp at	77A	6,423	1873
Agua Azul, or Blue Water	77A	6,683	{ 1873 1874
Alameda	77B	4,985	1877
Alamillo (Rio Grande)	77C	4,600	1878
Alamocita (Rio Grande)	84A	4,256	1877
Alamosa (Alamosa Cañon)	84A	a5,177	1878
Albuquerque	77B	4,919	{ 1873 1874 1875 1877 1878
Aleman, or Martins Well, on Jornado del Muerto	84C	4,594	1878
Algodones (Rio Grande)	77B	5,104	{ 1873 1877
Andrews Mine (Rio Galisteo)	77B	5,585	1875
Anton Chico	78A	5,480	1875
Apache Tejo	84C	5,478	1878
Apachita	83B	a7,324	1878
Agua Fria	77B	6,486	1873
Arms Ranch (Canadian River)	70A	5,972	1874
Belen	77D	4,785	{ 1876 1878
Bernal	78A	6,162	1875
Bernal Arroya	78A	6,078	1874
Bernalillo (Rio Grande)	77B	5,083	1875
Blazers Mill (Indian Agency)	84D	6,449	{ 1877 1878
Boundary Monument, Mexico and United States	90B	4,444	1878
Brazos and San Antonio Creeks, divide between	69B	9,887	1874
Brents Ranch	84C	4,118	1878
Burbanks Ranch	70C	6,882	1876
Camerons Corner (Vermejo Creek)	70A	7,133	1876
Camp Stampede (Mimbres River)	84C	6,208	1873
Cañada Ranch (Alamosa Cañon)	84A	5,088	1878
Cañon Blanco, head of	69C	7,116	1875
Cañon Largo, head of	69C	6,513	1874
Cañoncito	77B	7,023	1875
Capitan and East Carrizo Peaks, divide between	84B	6,847	1877
Carrizillo and Niggerhead Springs, flat between	90A	4,198	1878
Casa Colorada	77D	4,679	1877
Casa Salazar	77A	5,668	1875
Cattle Ranch (Rio Grande)	69B	7,387	1878
Chamisal	69D	a7,528	1874
Chavez	77D	4,775	1873
Chili (Rio Chama)	69D	5,648	1874
Chilili	77B	a6,838	1875
Chupadero Ranch	77D	5,825	1877
Cibolletta	77A	6,411	1874
Cieneguilla	77B	6,026	1874
Cieneguilla, near Rio Grande	69D	6,348	1878
Cimarron (Astronomical Monument)	70A	6,384	1874
Clifton (Canadian River)	70A	6,292	1874

*Approximate, on bluff about 300 feet higher than camp.

BAROMETRIC ALTITUDES.

TABLE III.—CITIES, TOWNS, SETTLEMENTS, ETC.—Continued.

Locality and name.	Atlas sheet.	Altitude in feet above sea.	Expeditionary year.
NEW MEXICO—Continued.			
Colorado Plaza (Rio Grande)	84C	4,008	1878
Constancia (Rio Grande)	77D	4,711	1877
Corrales (Rio Grande)	77B	5,091	1873
Coyote (Coyote Creek)	70C	7,055	1874
Crittendens Ranch	84C	5,004	1878
Crow Creek Stage Station	70A	6,454	1874
Cubero	77A	6,122	1873
Cuchilla	69D	a5,680	1874
Cuchillo	77B	5,195	1874
Don Rafael Plaza	77A	6,509	1873
Dowlins Mill (Rindoso Creek)	84B	6,496	{ 1877 1878
El Chorro	77B	6,021	1875
El Rito	69D	6,792	1875
El Rito	77A	5,639	{ 1873 1874
Elizabethtown	70A	8,465	1874
Ellis Ranch (Animas River)	84C	4,692	1878
Embuda (Rio Grande)	69D	5,891	1874
Estancia Ranch and Spring	77D	6,177	1876
Emerys Ranch	70B	6,080	1876
Fests Ferry (Rio Grande)	84A	4,184	1878
Florida Mountains and Tres Hermanas, flat between	90A	4,022	1878
Fort Cummings and Mimbres River, divide between	84C	5,224	1878
Francisco Ranches (Rio Grande de Taos)	69D	6,983	1877
Galisteo	77B	6,117	1875
Gallinas Ranch	77D	6,912	1877
Gavilan Cañon, divide in	84C	a6,581	1878
Georgetown	84C	6,455	1878
Gran Quivira Ruins	77D	6,407	1877
Greens Ranch	78A	6,422	1874
Guadalupita	70C	7,677	1874
Hillsboro	84C	5,224	1878
Hot Springs and Mimbres Settlement, divide	84C	5,274	1878
Indian Ranch	77B	5,290	1878
Isleta, three-fourths of a mile south of	77B	4,798	1875
Jaroso	70C	6,744	1875
Jackson Ranch (Cottonwoods)	90B	3,738	1878
Jemez	77B	5,479	1875
Johnsons Ranch, near	70A	6,215	1874
Kozlowski Ranch	77B	6,905	1875
La Bajada	77B	5,514	{ 1873 1877
La Glorieta	77B	7,424	1874
La Joya (Rio Grande)	69D	5,712	{ 1876 1877 1878
La Junta (Mora River)	70C	6,612	1874
La Tenaja	90A	4,748	1878
Las Coloñas (Vaca Creek)	77B	6,768	1874
Las Cruces	90B	3,808	1878
Las Nutritas (Tierra Amarilla)	69B	7,455	1875
Las Truchas	69D	a7,622	1874
Las Vegas (Astronomical Monument)	78A	6,418	1874
Lincoln	85A	5,679	1877
Lomitas	77D	5,731	1877
Los Alamos (Sapello Creek)	70C	6,789	1876

U. S. GEOGRAPHICAL SURVEYS.

TABLE III.—CITIES, TOWNS, SETTLEMENTS, ETC.—Continued.

Locality and name.	Atlas sheet.	Altitude in feet above sea.	Expeditionary year.
NEW MEXICO—Continued.			
Los Brazos (Tierra Amarilla)	69B	7,324	1874
Los Fuertos de San Augustin	78A	6,002	1875
Los Griegos (Laguna)	78A	6,656	1875
Los Lentes	83B	a6,542	1878
Los Lunas	77D	4,803	{ 1873 / 1876 / 1878
Los Ojos (Tierra Amarilla)	69B	7,273	1874
Los Pinos (Rio Grande)	77B	4,675	1877
Los Quelites	77A	5,134	{ 1873 / 1875
Los Machos (Rio Pecos)	69D	7,290	1874
Los Posos del Pino	77D	6,055	{ 1876 / 1877 / 1878
McCarthys Ranch (San Jose Creek)	77A	6,099	{ 1873 / 1874
McEvers Ranch (Berenda Creek)	84C	5,086	1878
McKnights Ranch (North Star road)	84C	6,237	1878
Magruders Silver Mine	84C	5,864	1878
Masons Ranch	84C	4,771	1878
Mesilla Crossing (Rio Grande)	90B	3,754	1878
Mesteñito	77D	6,268	1876
Mimbres River Ford, near Hot Springs	84C	5,028	1878
Mimbres Settlement	84C	a4,920	1878
Mora	70C	7,043	1874
Myers Ferry (Rio Grande)	69B	7,434	1878
Nacimiento	69C	7,300	1874
Nambe Pueblo	69D	a6,045	1874
Ocate (Ocate Creek)	70C	7,077	1874
Ojo Caliente	69D	6,126	1874
Ojo Caliente	84A	6,081	1878
Palomas (Rio Grande)	84C	4,160	1878
Paraje Ferry (Rio Grande)	84A	4,353	1877
Paraje, on Rio Grande	84A	4,319	1877
Parias Ranch	83B	a6,896	1878
Pattersons Ranch	83B	a6,720	1878
Peña Blanca (Rio Grande)	77B	5,170	1878
Peña Blanca, ford of Rio Grande	77B	5,107	1878
Peralta	77B	4,661	1877
Piedra Pintado Cañon (El Puerto)	78A	a5,477	1875
Picacho de Sabinal	77D	4,721	{ 1876 / 1878
Picuris Pueblo	69D	7,108	1874
Pinos Altos	84C	6,845	1878
Placitas	77B	5,129	1873
Plaza del Alcalde	69D	5,625	{ 1874 / 1876 / 1877 / 1878
Point of Rocks, on Jornado del Muerto	84C	4,268	1878
Pojoaque	69D	a5,750	{ 1876 / 1877
Pojuate	77A	a6,269	1874
Pueblo Colorado	76	6,368	1873

BAROMETRIC ALTITUDES.

TABLE III.—CITIES, TOWNS, SETTLEMENTS, ETC.—Continued.

Locality and name.	Atlas sheet.	Altitude in feet above sea.	Expeditionary year.
NEW MEXICO—Continued.			
Pueblo Pintado	69C	6,506	1875
Puertocito	77B	a6,079	1875
Puertocito, near Fort Stanton	84B	6,428	1877
Punta del Agua	77D	6,599	1877
Ragado	70C	6,532	1874
Ralston	89B	a4,488	1873
Real de Dolores (Old Placer)	77B	6,802	1873
Real de San Francisco (New Gold Placers)	77B	6,659	1875
Rincon, Colorado, mouth of	78A	5,358	1877
Rio Grande Ford, near Fort Craig	84A	4,441	1876
Rio Grande, 14 miles above Fort Craig	84A	4,537	1876
Rito Quemado	76D	a6,827	1878
Rindoso and North Fork Tulerosa Creeks, divide	84B	7,686	1877
San Augustin (Shedds Ranch)	84D	4,378	1878
San Antonio	69D	a5,625	1874
San Cristobal Crossing (Rio Grande)	69B	6,575	{ 1874 / 1878 }
San Cristobal Crossing, Highbank, west of	69B	7,139	{ 1874 / 1878 }
San Felipe Pueblo (Rio Grande)	77B	a5,007	1878
San Felipe de Santiago	70C	5,110	1874
San Fernandez de Taos	69D	6,949	1875
San Francisco, upper plaza	83B	a5,688	1878
San Ignacio	77A	a5,515	1874
San Ildefonso (Rio Grande)	69D	5,458	1874
San Jose	69D	a5,648	1874
San Jose, on Rio Grande	84A	4,313	1877
San Juan	69D	a5,601	1874
San Lorenzo (Oso Creek)	69D	a6,107	1874
San Luis Rey	77B	5,152	1878
San Mateo	77A	7,323	1874
San Pedro, 1 mile below	77B	6,364	1875
San Pedro	84B	4,488	1877
San Simeon, cienega of	89B	a3,855	1873
San Ysidro	77B	5,460	{ 1873 / 1874 }
Sanchez Ranch	77A	7,298	1873
Sandia (Rio Grande)	77B	5,011	1877
Sayres Ranch (Willow Creek), (United States forage station)	70A	6,694	1874
Santa Aña	77B	5,292	{ 1873 / 1874 / 1878 }
Santa Cruz	69D	5,590	1875
Santa Fe	69D	6,965	{ 1874 / 1875 / 1877 }
Santa Rita Copper Mines	84C	6,161	1878
Santa Rita and Upper Mimbres, divide between	84C	6,779	1878
Santa Rosa	78A	a4,766	1875
Santo Domingo (Rio Grande)	77B	5,191	1877
Santo Niño del Rincon	70C	7,418	1874
Shaws Ranch	84A	7,256	1878
Silla	77B	6,677	1873
Silver City	83D	5,771	1878
Slocums Ranch	84C	4,519	1878
Socorro	77C	4,594	{ 1876 / 1877 }

U. S. GEOGRAPHICAL SURVEYS.   167

TABLE III.—CITIES, TOWNS, SETTLEMENTS, ETC.—Continued.

Locality and name.	Atlas sheet.	Altitude in feet above sea.	Expeditionary year.
NEW MEXICO—Continued.			
Socorro Ford	77C	4,534	1877
Stone Ranch (Franklin Ranch) (Canadian River)	70C	5,844	1876
Taos	69D	6,949	{ 1874 / 1877
Taos Pueblos	69D	7,015	1874
Taos, Rancho de (Francisco Ranches)	69D	6,983	1877
Taylor Ranch	78A	5,831	1875
Tesuque	69D	6,668	{ 1874 / 1877
Tesuque Pueblo	69D	a6,245	1874
Tijeras	77B	6,214	1875
Toasketc Indian Camp	68D	6,506	1873
Toussaints Ranch	84B	4,634	1877
Tulerosa (Forage Agency)	84D	4,358	{ 1877 / 1878
Vermejo	70A	6,259	1874
W ite Rock Cañon, head of divide	84A	8,960	1878
W iters Ranch	84B	6,582	1877
Yucca Camp	89	a4,374	1873
Zuñi	76	6,392	{ 1873 / 1874
OREGON.			
Antelope (post-office)	20A	2,844	1878
Barlow Tollgate (Stricklands Ranch)	20A	a2,096	1878
Barnums Ranch	20A	1,795	1878
Big Meadows	29A	4,124	1878
Big Prairie (Salmon River)	20A	3,335	1878
Big Summit Prairie	20D	5,124	1878
Brattons Ranch	29D	4,495	1878
Bridge Creek (post-office)	20D	a1,830	1878
Burnt Ranch (John Day River)	20D	1,561	1878
Buttons Ranch	29A	4,237	1878
Buzzard Cañon	29D	4,762	1878
Carmicals Ranch (Crooked River)	20C	a2,794	1878
Cherry and Muddy Creeks, divide between	20D	2,603	1878
Crater Lake road, summit of	28D	6,412	1878
Cross Hollows (post-office)	20A	3,197	1878
Currant Creek (Stage Station)	20B	2,142	1878
Currys camp on Silver Creek, abandoned	29B	4,273	1878
Dalles City	20A	180	1878
Dalles:			
North Base	20A	188	1878
South Base	20A	215	1878
Deschutes and John Day Rivers, divide on Shears road	20A	3,515	1878
Deschutes River, toll-bridge near Carmicals	20C	2,563	1878
Dillard and Renshaws Ranch	29B	4,657	1878
Drakes Ranch	38B	a4,559	1878
Drew Valley (post-office)	38A	4,953	1877
Dufur post-office (Fifteen-mile Creek)	20A	1,267	1878
Durands Ranch, near Silver Lake	29C	4,312	1878
Eaton Ranch (post-office)	20A	a1,160	1878
Farewell Bend (Deschutes River)	20C	3,621	1878
Five-mile House, near The Dalles	20A	a246	1878
Fitzpatrick Ranch	20A	a2,624	1878
Fosters Ranch, on Summer Lake	29C	4,174	1878

TABLE III.—CITIES, TOWNS, SETTLEMENTS, ETC.—Continued.

Locality and name.	Atlas sheet.	Altitude in feet above sea.	Expeditionary year.
OREGON—Continued.			
Goose Lake Valley	38B	5,128	1878
Grants Landing (Columbia River)	11C	336	1878
Greens Ranch	20C	4,479	1878
Haights Ranch (Cottonwood Cañon)	20A	3,026	1878
Halds Ranch	20D	3,287	1878
Half-way Camp (East Deschutes River)	29A	4,081	1878
Haystack, or Finnegans Ranch	20A	2,144	1878
Hiltons Ranch	20A	3,007	1878
Hood River (post-office)	20A	a388	1878
Hoskins Ranch (Silver Creek)	29B	4,139	1878
Invarieties Ranch, one mile above	20A	2,018	1878
Jones Ranch (Honey Creek)	29D	4,466	1878
Kamas Prairie	20A	3,020	1878
Kamas Prairie (Warner Creek)	38B	5,525	1877
Klamath Indian Agency	29C	a4,156	1878
Lakeview	38B	4,851	{ 1877 1878
Langtons Ranch (Great Oregon Desert)	29A	5,163	1878
Little Meadows (East Deschutes River)	29A	4,258	1878
Little Prairie	29A	4,428	1878
Lone Pine Ranch	20C	a3,064	1878
McNeals Ranch	20D	a4,003	1878
Metoles River, ford of	20C	1,902	1878
Millers Bridge (Deschutes River)	20A	166	1878
Millers Ranch, near Summer Lake	29C	4,420	1878
Moss Ranch	29D	4,828	1878
Mount Hood (post-office), (Columbia River)	11C	260	1878
Oak Grove, one mile above	20A	2,414	1878
Oak Grove Settlement (post-office)	20A	a2,148	1878
Parrish Ranch	20C	3,330	1878
Partons Ranch (Rim Rock Mountains)	29C	4,498	1878
Pauline Valley, ranch in	20D	a3,872	1878
Prineville	20C	2,899	1878
Rim Rock Mountains and Summer Lake, divide between	29C	6,868	1878
Saw Mill (Mill Creek)	20A	3,307	1878
Sherars Bridge (Deschutes River), (post-office)	20A	702	1878
Sherars Mill, Falls on White River	20A	a1,012	1878
Summit Prairie	20A	3,694	1878
Sycan Marsh, south end	29C	4,960	1878
The Dalles (Astronomical Monument)	20A	180	1878
Tygh Valley Settlement	20A	1,089	1878
Upper Cascades Ranch (Columbia River)	20A	127	1878
Wallace Ranch (Deep Creek)	38B	4,487	1878
Warm Spring Indian Agency	20C	1,514	1878
Warner Lake Flat	29D	4,544	1878
Wasco	20A	a1,109	1878
Williamson River Ford, near Klamath	29C	4,387	1878
TEXAS.			
El Paso, or Franklin	90B	3,623	1878
UTAH.			
Alder, or Big Cañon, mouth of	41A	6,441	1877
Alma, near Weber River	41D	4,262	1878
American Fork	50B	4,578	1872

U. S. GEOGRAPHICAL SURVEYS.

TABLE III.—CITIES, TOWNS, SETTLEMENTS, ETC.—Continued.

Locality and name.	Atlas sheet.	Altitude in feet above sea.	Expeditionary year.
UTAH—Continued.			
Bear Valley	66C	7,072	1872
Beaver	59A	6,060	1873
Beaver (Astronomical Monument)	59A	5,916	1872
Birch and Paria Creeks, divide between	59	7,591	1872
Blanchards (Salt Spring)	41B	4,634	1877
Blue Creek Station (Central Pacific Railroad)	41A	l4,379	1877
Bovine (Central Pacific Railroad)	41C	4,363	1878
Brigham City (court-house)	41B	4,476	1877
Cedar City	59C	5,727	1872
Centreville	41D	4,275	1878
Circleville (Sevier River)	59	5,625	1872
Clarkston	41B	a4,853	1877
Clear Creek Stage Station	41A	a5,536	1877
Coles Farm (on Mesa)	41B	4,233	1878
Corinne (Central Pacific Railroad)	41B	l4,233	1873
Corinne (Signal Office)	41B	l4,244	1877
Cove Creek Station (Beaver Range)	59	6,960	1872
Curlew	41A	4,396	1877
Danishtown	41B	a4,408	1877
Deep Creek (Astronomical Monument)	49B	5,237	1872
Deseret City	50C	4,642	1872
Deweyville	41B	4,415	1877
Diamond City	50B	6,369	1872
East Valley (Snowy Range)	50B	7,539	1872
El Vado de los Padres	67	3,194	1872
Ephraim City	50D	5,633	1872
Fairfield (Camp Floyd)	50B	4,866	1872
Fausts Station	50A	5,296	1872
Fillmore	59B	6,026	1872
Fillmore (Astronomical Monument)*	59B	6,120	1872
Fountain Green	50D	5,873	1872
Glenwood, near Richfield	59	5,221	1872
Goshen, northwest of, near Utah Lake	50B	4,482	1872
Goulds Ranch	67	4,052	1872
Gunnison (Astronomical Monument)	50D	5,145	1872
Hackberrys Ranch (Promontory Range)	41D	4,171	1878
Hamptons Bridge	41B	4,371	1877
Hay Spring Ranch	59A	5,092	1872
Heber, near	50B	5,571	1872
Hebron	58	5,475	1872
Hooperville (School-house)	41D	4,239	1878
Hunterville	41D	5,011	1877
Hyde Park	41B	a4,412	1877
Iron City	59	6,099	1872
Joes Valley (east side of), Snowy Range	50D	8,420	1873
Kanab (Astronomical Monument)	67A	4,909	1872
Kanara	59C	5,449	1872
Kamas, near	50B	6,301	1872
Kaysville, Hills Farm, near	41D	4,252	1878
Keiths Ranch	41A	a4,737	1877
Kelton (Central Pacific Railroad)	41A	l4,226	1877
Lakeside (Great Salt Lake)	41D	4,260	1878
Lakeside Station (Central Pacific Railroad)	41A	l4,218	1877
Laketown	41B	5,993	1877
Lehi (Utah Southern Railroad)	50B	4,596	1873
Lewiston	41B	a4,489	1877

*On Chalk Creek, three miles east of Fillmore.

TABLE III.—CITIES, TOWNS, SETTLEMENTS, ETC.—Continued.

Locality and name.	Atlas sheet.	Altitude in feet above sea.	Expeditionary year.
UTAH—Continued.			
Little Cottonwood	50B	4,359	1872
Little Mountain	41D	4,264	1878
Logan	41B	4,533	1877
Lucin (Central Pacific Railroad)	40D	*4,495	1872
Mammoth Mill (Needle Range)	58	6,947	1878
Marshs Ranch (Promontory Range)	41C	4,230	1878
Matlin (Central Pacific Railroad)	41A	*4,599	1877
Meadowville	41B	5,975	1877
Mendon	41B	4,553	1877
Monument (Central Pacific Railroad)	41A	*4,230	1877
Mountain Meadows	59	5,742	1872
Mount Pleasant, near	50D	6,089	1873
Nephi	50D	4,920	1872
North Ogden Cañon, mouth of	41D	4,890	1877
North Ogden (Co-operative store)	41D	4,509	1877
North Willard	41D	4,276	1877
Oak Creek Settlement	50C	5,159	1877
Ogden Observatory (Astronomical Monument)	41D	*4,374	{ 1873 1874 1877
Ogden (Central Pacific Railroad)	41D	*4,300	{ 1873 1877
Ombe (Central Pacific Railroad)	41A	*4,724	1877
Panquitch, near	59	6,273	1872
Paradise	41B	4,863	1877
Paragoonah	59	6,223	1872
Paria	67	4,562	{ 1872 1873
Parowan	59C	5,910	1872
Payson	50B	4,523	1872
Pettingills Ranch (Promontory Range)	41D	4,208	1878
Pilot Springs	41A	4,704	1877
Plain City	41A	4,224	1878
Pleasant Valley post-office	41B	a6,065	1877
Point Lookout	41B	4,565	1877
Pons Ranch	41A	a4,737	1877
Potatoe Valley, head of	59D	8,610	1872
Promontory (Central Pacific Railroad)	41A	*4,908	1877
Provo (Astronomical Monument)	50B	4,567	1873
Rabbit Valley, south end	59	6,849	1873
Richfield, near Sevier River Bridge (Astronomical Monument)	59B	5,283	1872
Richmond	41B	4,636	1877
Ricks Bridge (Logan Creek)	41B	4,452	1877
Rosebiers, on Dove Creek	41A	a4,999	1877
Rozel (Central Pacific Railroad)	41A	4,597	1877
Saint George (Astronomical Monument)	67A	2,611	1871
Salt Lake City (Observatory), (Temple Pier)	41D	*4,330	{ 1873 1877
Salt Lake City (Signal Office)	41D	*4,352	1878
Scipio, near	50D	5,113	1872
Shoonesburg	67A	3,920	1872
Skeens Ranch	41A	4,266	1877
Skumpah	67A	6,000	{ 1872 1873
Smithfield	41B	4,623	1877
Stauffers (North Fork Raft River)	41A	a4,795	1877

TABLE III.—CITIES, TOWNS, SETTLEMENTS, ETC.—Continued.

Locality and name.	Atlas sheet.	Altitude in feet above sea.	Expeditionary year.
UTAH—Continued.			
Strawberry Valley	50B	7,717	1872
Ten-mile Station	41A	5,086	1877
Terrace (Central Pacific Railroad)	41A	4,551	1878
Tibballs Ranch	41A	4,204	1877
Toponce Ranch	41B	4,583	1877
Van Hellers Ranch	41A	a4,807	1877
Washington	67	2,906	1872
Willard City	41D	4,311	1878
Willow Creek (Utah Southern Railroad)	50B	4,409	1872
Winegar Ranch, near mouth Jordan River	41D	4,206	1878
WASHINGTON.			
Walla Walla (Astronomical Monument)	12C	1,034	1878
WYOMING.			
Cheyenne (Astronomical Monument)	44C	l6,041	1872
Green River Station (Union Pacific Railroad, Astronomical Monument)	42B	6,096	1873
Evanston (Union Pacific Railroad, Richard's Astronomical Monument)	42C	l6,757	1877
Laramie (Union Pacific Railroad, Astronomical Monument)	43D	7,123	1872
MEXICO.			
Algodones Station	81D	188	1876
New River Station	81C	80	1876

TABLE IV.—LAKES, SPRINGS, ETC.

Locality and name.	Atlas sheet.	Altitude in feet above sea.	Expeditionary year.
ARIZONA.			
Antelope Spring, near Humphreys Peak	75	8,065	1871
Apache Spring	76	6,125	1873
Blue Spring	76	7,796	1873
Cave Springs	76	6,031	1873
Cottonwood Spring, near White Cliff Creek	75	4,170	1871
Coyote Spring	76D	a6,874	1878
Deer Spring	76	5,982	{ 1873 1874
Desert Tanks (Great Colorado Plateau)	76C	5,192	1873
Diamond Creek, mouth of	67	1,350	1871
Eureka Springs	83	4,239	1873
Green Spring	67	4,931	1873
Limestone Waterpocket	67	5,405	1873
Lockwood Spring, near Bill Williams Mountain (Relief Spring)	75	5,527	1871
Mineral Springs	76	6,670	1873
Mountain Spring	74D	3,596	1875
Navajo Spring	67	4,110	1873
Nelson Tanks	75	6,216	1871
Peach Orchard Spring	68C	6,273	1873
Pine Tanks	83	5,649	1871
Reservoir Lake	83	9,056	1873
Silver Spring	76	6,169	1873
Summit Springs	76	7,867	1873
Sunset Tanks	76	5,797	1871
Tanks, near Fort Apache	83A	5,717	{ 1873 1874
Tin-nah-kah Spring (Colorado Plateau)	66	4,080	1871
Truxton Springs	75	3,886	1871
Tule Spring	76	5,925	1873
Tule Spring, near La Tilla	76D	a5,861	1878
Volunteer Spring, near Humphreys Peak	75	7,106	1871
White-rock Spring	68C	a6,301	1873
Willow Spring	76	7,295	{ 1873 1874
CALIFORNIA.			
Antelope Spring (Amador road)	56B	4,272	1878
Arab Springs (Coso Mountains)	65D	5,697	1871
Ash Springs	65A	1,810	1878
Bah-le-bah Spring	65B	6,284	1875
Bird Spring	73A	3,949	1878
Bennetts Well (Death Valley)	65D	—6	1875
Black Spring, on Big Tree road	56B	6,421	1877
Blue Lake, upper	56B	8,094	1877
Bridal Veil Creek, one-half mile above Yosemite Trail	56D	6,938	1879
Bridal Veil Fall, Merced River, opposite	56D	3,823	1878
Bridal Veil Fall, pool at foot of	56D	4,150	1878
Bridal Veil Fall, top	56D	4,769	1878
Caliente Springs	73A	3,688	1875
Cañon Springs	81A	1,238	{ 1875 1876

U. S. GEOGRAPHICAL SURVEYS. 173

TABLE IV.—LAKES, SPRINGS, ETC.—Continued.

Locality and name.	Atlas sheet.	Altitude in feet above sea.	Expeditionary year.
CALIFORNIA—Continued.			
Carnelian Hot Springs (Lake Tahoe)	47D	6,237	1876
Carson River, east fork, and Silver King Creek, junction of	56B	6,392	1877
Chip Creek head of	47A	5,934	1878
Cinder Cone, lake east of	47A	a6,085	1878
Clear Lake (Warner Range)	38D	5,808	1877
Cold Spring, east of Stonebreakers	56B	5,512	1877
Conness Peak, lake 2 miles northwest of	56D	9,646	1878
Cooks Well	81D	/88	1876
Cow Head Lake	38B	5,329	1878
Cow Spring	65C	3,876	1871
Dahlonega Hot Springs	73A	2,162	1878
Deep Spring	65A	4,957	1871
Desert Spring	73A	1,989	1871
Donner Lake	47D	5,885	1876
Double Springs	56B	5,998	1877
Dry Lake, near Bitter Springs	81A	—28	1875
Eagle Lake	47A	5,114	1877
Eleanor Lake	56D	4,630	1879
Francis Springs	74A	.4,220	1875
Gardners Well	81C	/55	1876
Geyser, near Willow Lake	47A	5,864	1878
Goose Lake	38B	4,697	1877
Granite Springs	73B	4,015	1875
Grant Wells	73B	2,180	1875
Grapevine Spring (Grapevine Mountains)	65B	2,432	1871
Halloran Springs	74A	3,272	1875
Hat and Lost Creeks, junction of	38C	a4,277	1878
Herring Creek and Stanislaus River, junction of	56B	5,421	1878
Highland Lake, north, tributary to Mokelumne River	56B	8,567	1877
Highland Lake, south, tributary to Stanislaus River	56B	8,620	1877
Hines Hot Spring	56B	4,670	1877
Honey Lake	47B	3,949	1876
Horn Spring	38D	5,476	1877
Horse Lake	{ 47B 38D }	5,039	1877
Hot Springs	47A	6,080	1878
Hot Springs, east of Honey Lake	47B	3,959	1877
Hot Spring, north of Honey Lake	47B	3,851	1877
Hot Springs (Lake Tahoe)	47D	6,237	1876
Hot Spring, 3 miles west of Markleeville	56B	6,005	1877
Indian Wells	{ 65C 65D 73A 73B }	2,608	1875
Indian Wells	81C	—20	1876
Keg Spring (Willow Creek)	47B	5,757	1876
Laguna Grande (San Jacinto Valley)	80B	1,292	1876
Lake Annie	38B	5,060	1877
Lake Tahoe	47D	6,202	1876
Lamberts Soda Spring	56D	8,558	1878
Last Chance and Squaw Queen Creeks, junction of	47B	5,268	1876
Last Chance and Thompson Creeks, junction of	47B	5,431	1876
Leek Spring, old emigrant trail to Pleasant Valley	56B	7,242	1877
Little Lake	65C	3,086	1875
Lyell Creek, mouth of	56D	8,575	1878

BAROMETRIC ALTITUDES.

TABLE IV.—LAKES, SPRINGS, ETC.—Continued.

Locality and name.	Atlas sheet.	Altitude in feet above sea.	Expeditionary year.
CALIFORNIA—Continued.			
Mazurka Creek Springs	65A	6,202	1875
Meadow Lake	47D	7,377	1877
Mesquite Spring	73B	2,010	1871
Middle Alkali Lake (Surprise Valley)	38D	4,551	1877
Mirror Lake	56D	a4,025	1878
Mud Spring (Amador road ..)	56B	5,973	1878
Mud Spring, Noble Pass road	47B	a4,671	1877
Nevada Fall, foot of, Yosemite Valley	56D	5,203	1878
Nevada Fall, top of, Yosemite Valley	56D	5,808	1878
Owens Lake	65C	3,567	1871
Packers Lake, near	47C	6,041	1876
Pah-ute Spring	74B	2,849	1871
Peach Spring	47A	5,303	1878
Rattlesnake Lake	47D	6,881	1877
Rose Spring	65C	3,545	1875
Sacketts Wells	81C	210	1876
San Joaquin, north fork, head of	56D	7,184	1878
Saratoga Springs	66C	264	1871
Secret Valley Creek, head of	47B	4,934	1877
Seven Wells	81C	760	1876
Silver Lake (reservoir of El Dorado and Deep Gravel Mining Company)	56B	7,174	1877
Silver Spring, near Lookout Hill	65D	a4,110	1875
Soap Spring	73A	706	1878
Soda Lake, sink of Mohave River	74A	1,128	1875
Soda Springs	47D	5,882	1877
Surveyors Wells	73B	3,567	1875
Tragedy Spring	56B	7,989	1877
Twin Lake, near Tejon Pass	73A	5,106	1878
Vernal Fall, foot of, Yosemite Valley	56D	4,633	1878
Vernal Fall, top of, Yosemite Valley	56D	4,976	1878
Virginia Creek Trail, lake near summit of	56D	10,090	1878
Warm Spring (Sonora road)	56B	7,384	{ 1877 1878
Webber Lake	47D	6,808	{ 1876 1877
Wild Rose Spring	65D	a4,683	1875
Willow Creek, mouth of Petes Valley	47B	4,467	1877
Willow Lake	47A	5,382	1875
Willow Spring, near Ehrenberg	81B	420	{ 1875 1876
Willow Spring, 13½ miles southwest of Mohave Station	73A	2,573	1875
Yosemite Falls, foot of lower	56D	4,018	1878
Yosemite Falls, foot of upper	56D	t4,980	1878
Yosemite Falls, top of upper	56D	t6,482	1878
Yosemite Falls, top of lower	56D	t4,421	1878
COLORADO.			
Beaver Creek, mouth of	61D	8,416	1874
Buffalo Springs (South Park)	61B	a8,952	1876
Chicoso Spring	70A	6,076	1874
Cold Spring, 4½ miles north of Rosita	62C	9,063	1874
Crystal Creek, near head of	61A	9,482	1877
Cuerno Verde Lake	62C	11,365	1874
Granite Falls	61C	a8,960	1875

TABLE IV.—LAKES, SPRINGS, ETC.—Continued.

Locality and name.	Atlas sheet.	Altitude in feet above sea.	Expeditionary year.
COLORADO—Continued.			
Hardscrabble Creek, head of	62C	9,102	1873
Hensen Creek, head of	61C	12,066	1875
Idaho Springs	52D	7,284	1873
Lime Creek, head of	61C	9,581	1875
Mosca Pass, lake in	61D	7,495	1875
Pagosa Hot Springs	69A	7,057	1873 / 1874
San Juan, head of middle fork	61D	10,429	1874
San Luis Lake (largest)	61D	7,477	1874
Tell Lake	61B	9,977	1873
Trout Lake	61C	9,700	1875
Twin Lakes	52D	9,187	1873
Ute Creek, forks of	61C	10,801	1874
Vincennes Creek, head of	61A	10,185	1877
Wagon Creek, mouth of	62C	8,199	1874
Williams Creek, headwaters of	62C	10,528	1876
IDAHO.			
Bear Lake	41B	5,955	1877
Bonneville Bench Mark:			
No. 1, near Barrys Ranch	41A	5,132	1877
No. 2, southeast Barrys Ranch	41A	5,113	1877
No. 3, 1¼ miles south Barrys Ranch	41A	5,061	1877
No. 4, Meander Station 5	41A	4,936	1877
No. 5, Meander Station 8	41A	4,836	1877
Under Topog. IX	41A	5,192	1877
Near Meander Station 3	41A	5,159	1877
R. near Meander Station 10	41A	5,264	1877
Danilsons Springs	32C	4,350	1877
Deep Creek (head spring)	41A	4,761	1877
Fly Spring	32C	5,912	1877
Fountain Spring	32C	5,235	1877
John Days Lake	32D	6,400	1877
Malade Springs	32C	5,150	1877
Marsh Lake (Sams Ranch)	32C	4,323	1877
Mule Spring, head of Gentile Valley	32D	5,245	1877
Palisade Spring	32C	a4,528	1877
Pine Spring	32C	a6,178	1877
Shadow Lake	32C	4,310	1877
Spring, 4 miles from Fort Hall	32D	5,142	1877
Ten-Mile Spring	32D	5,548	1877
Twin Spring	41A	5,207	1877
Warm Spring, near Samaria	41B	4,506	1877
NEVADA.			
Alkali Lake, mouth of High Rock Cañon	38D	4,967	1877
Allens Spring	48C	4,051	1876
Antelope Spring	49C	7,201	1869
Antelope Spring	57B	6,445	1876
Barkley Spring	38D	5,906	1877
Campbells Spring	57B	7,366	1876
Carson Hot Spring (at jail)	47D	4,592	1876
Carson Lake	48C	3,950	1876
Cedar Hill Cañon, spring at head	47D	7,045	1876

TABLE IV.—LAKES, SPRINGS, ETC.—Continued.

Locality and name.	Atlas sheet.	Altitude in feet above sea.	Expeditionary year.
NEVADA—Continued.			
Cold Spring, near Borax Flat	57A	4,200	1876
Cottonwood Spring (Spring Mountain range)	66	3,450	1871
Coyote Spring	58	3,674	1871
Crossman Spring	74A	4,391	1875
Crystal Spring, near Olcott Peak	66	5,782	1871
Dead Mans Spring	47D	4,512	1877
Desert Wells	57	4,696	1871
Disappointment Spring	66	4,835	1871
Fish Lake	57C	4,745	1871
Fish Lake	58A	6,866	1871
Fish Spring (Andersons Ranch)	47B	4,041	1878
Friday Creek, mouth of (Lake Tahoe)	56B	6,202	1876
Genoa Hot Springs	56B	4,802	1877
Hot Spring	48D	4,731	1871
Indian Spring (Monument Canon)	58B	6,114	1869
Marlette Lake	47D	7,750	1876
Mountain Spring	66C	5,501	1872
Mud Spring	66A	4,900	1869
Naquinta Springs (Tim-pah-ute range)	58	6,892	1871
Penoyer Spring	58	6,652	1871
Pinto Spring	38D	5,639	1877
Pyramid Lake (north end)	47B	3,848	1877
Rattlesnake Spring	58B	6,038	1869
Sacramento Spring	49D	6,575	1869
Sheep Head Spring	47B	3,914	1878
Spring Valley Spring, near Eureka	49	7,768	1871
Steamboat Springs	47D	4,595	1876
Sulphur Spring in Sand Spring (Alkali Flat)	48C	3,973	1876
Sutro Spring	47D	5,366	1876
Tib-ba-bah Spring	48C	6,248	1876
Tis-sa-pok Spring	48C	5,832	1876
Todhunters Spring (Long Valley)	38D	5,779	1877
Twin Lakes	47D	7,843	1876
Virgin River, mouth of	66D	1,200	1869
Wah-wah-bah Spring, near Slate Peak	48C	5,188	1876
Wall Spring	38D	3,912	1877
Washoe Lake	47D	5,046	1876
Welchs Spring	57B	5,236	1876
White Bluff Spring (Beaver Mountains)	66	5,020	1871
Winnemucca Lake	47B	3,825	1877
NEW MEXICO.			
Agua Negra and Mora Creeks, junction of	70C	8,194	1874
Aguajes-de-los Guajalotes	78A	6,202	1875
Alamo Cañon (Warm Spring)	84A	6,593	1878
American and Cieneguilla Creeks, junction of	70C	8,183	1874
Annaya Spring	84A	4,717	1877
Antelope Spring	77B	6,291	1875
Bacon Spring	76	7,190	1873
Black Rock Tank	90A	4,180	1878
Boulder Lake	69B	7,204	1874
Buffalo Springs, 2 miles east of	77B	6,346	1875
Cañon Spring	83D	5,498	1873

Table IV.—LAKES, SPRINGS, ETC.—Continued.

Locality and name.	Atlas sheet.	Altitude in feet above sea.	Expeditionary year.
New Mexico—Continued.			
Cañoncito Tanks	77D	5,083	1877
Carrizo Spring:			
Head of Carrizo Creek	84B	8,831	1877
Southwest of San Magdalena	84A	a6,332	1877
Carrizoso Spring (Murphy's Ranch)	84B	5,300	{ 1877 / 1878 }
Carrizillo Spring	90A	4,457	1878
Cattle Spring	90A	4,540	1878
Chupadero Spring	77D	6,241	1877
Cottonwood Spring (Franklin Range)	90B	4,773	1878
Cow Spring (Antelope Plains)	84C	5,001	{ 1873 / 1878 }
Cross Spring	77A	6,265	1874
Culebra Spring	77C	5,707	1876
Datil Spring	77C	7,419	1873
Deer Spring	68D	7,683	1873
Dripping Spring (San Andreas Range)	84B	5,623	1877
Elk Spring (Sacramento Range)	84D	7,414	1878
Empedrados Tanks	78A	6,457	1876
Gallo Spring (Datil Range)	76	a7,925	1873
Gallo Spring	77A	7,943	1875
Gallo Spring	83B	a7,586	1878
Gallinas Water-holes	77D	6,393	1877
Hedionda Lake	69B	7,149	1874
Hedionda Lake, Water-holes (near)	69B	7,181	1874
Hell Cañon, spring in	77B	6,082	1876
Horse Spring	84A	7,045	{ 1873 / 1874 }
Hot Spring, foot of Needle Point (south)	68D	5,594	1874
Hot Spring (Hudsons)	84C	5,008	1878
Hot Spring, 1 mile west of Hudsons	84C	5,065	1878
Indian Cañon Water-holes	77A	a7,847	1874
Indian Spring	77A	9,289	1874
Jakes Spring	84B	a5,217	1877
Jaraloso Spring	84B	4,783	1877
Kettle Spring	90A	4,540	1878
La Lacha Spring	89B	4,756	1878
Laguna	77A	6,266	1874
Laguna Colorada	77B	7,000	1875
Llano Spring	84B	5,348	1877
Leitendorfs Well	89B	a4,601	1873
Los Aguajes (Mesa Jumanes)	77D	6,524	1877
Los Cazos Spring	77B	7,615	1875
Luera Spring	84A	7,585	{ 1873 / 1874 / 1878 }
Malpais Spring	84B	4,106	1877
Mangos Spring	83D	4,799	1873
Mesa Spring, near San Mateo	77A	7,851	1874
Monica Spring	84A	7,602	{ 1873 / 1878 }
Mound Spring	84B	4,336	1877
Mule, or Macho Springs	84C	5,261	{ 1873 / 1878 }
Mule Spring, No. 2	84C	5,652	1878

BAROMETRIC ALTITUDES.

TABLE IV.—LAKES, SPRINGS, ETC.—Continued.

Locality and name.	Atlas sheet.	Altitude in feet above sea.	Expeditionary year.
NEW MEXICO—Continued.			
Niggerhead Spring	90A	4,861	1878
Nutria Spring	76	6,934	{ 1873 1874 1875
Oak Spring	76	7,946	1873
Oak Spring	76D	a7,741	1878
Oak Spring (Encinosa)	76D	7,204	1878
Oak Spring	84B	a7,448	1877
Ojo Amarilla	69C	6,384	1874
Ojo Berenda (Turkey Mountains)	77D	7,494	1877
Ojo Caliente, near Zuñi	76	6,291	1873
Ojo Chameleon	77D	6,401	1878
Ojo de Estancia	77D	6,177	1876
Ojo de Nuestra Señora	69C	6,606	1875
Ojo del Cibolo	77D	5,640	1877
Ojo del Oso	77D	7,786	1876
Ojo de la Casa	77D	6,243	1876
Ojo de la Parida	77D	4,929	1877
Ojo de la Quinca	77C	5,673	1876
Ojo de las Cañas	77D	5,130	1876
Ojo de Los Pinos	69C	7,005	1874
Ojo Milagro	84B	5,172	1877
Ojo Seco	85A	5,258	1877
Oscuro Water-holes	84B	5,561	1877
Pato Pond (Jicarilla Mountains)	84B	a6,279	1877
Pato Spring (Jicarilla Mountains)	84B	a6,290	1877
Pedernal Spring	77B	6,804	1877
Pedernal Water-holes	77B	6,850	1875
Penasco Creek, head of	84D	7,159	1878
Pescado Spring	76	6,546	1873
Pueblo Spring	77C	6,398	{ 1873 1878
Rock Springs	76	6,849	1873
Salt Lake (Alkaline Ponds)	77D	6,047	1876
Salt Lake, near Sweet Water Spring	76	6,344	1873
San Andreas Water-holes, or Dripping Spring	84B	4,960	1877
San Diego Hot Springs	69D	8,320	1874
San Lorenzo Spring	77C	a5,326	1878
San Marco Spring	77B	6,056	1876
San Nicolas Spring	84D	4,218	1878
Sapillo and Manuelit Creeks, junction of	70C	6,876	1874
Silver Springs	84D	7,638	1878
Stinking Springs	76	6,690	1873
Stinking Springs	77B	6,249	1875
Taylor Spring	84B	6,988	1877
Thompsons Spring, 7 miles northwest Oak Spring	76	7,607	1873
Tomasceños Water-holes	77D	5,502	1876
Torreon Spring	84A	5,980	1877
Tres Cerros Springs	84B	6,128	1877
Two Cave Spring	77A	5,902	1874
Valley Spring	77B	6,979	1875
Warm Springs, mouth San Diego Cañon	69D	8,366	1874
Waterpool in Chasco Mountains	68D	6,380	1873
West Gallinas Spring	77D	7,673	1877
White Oak Spring	84B	6,618	1877

U. S. GEOGRAPHICAL SURVEYS. 179

TABLE IV.—LAKES, SPRINGS, ETC.—Continued.

Locality and name.	Atlas sheet.	Altitude in feet above sea.	Expeditionary year.
NEW MEXICO—Continued.			
White Tail Spring	84B	7,517	1877
White Water Spring, near	84D	3,888	1878
Willow Springs	77A	6,677	1874
OREGON.			
Abert Lake (Alkaline)	29D	4,209	1878
Big Spring (Klamath Marsh)	29C	4,552	1878
Corral Springs, on Oregon road	29A	4,569	1878
Corral Spring, camp near source	29A	4,783	1878
Crater Lake, edge of cliff, 900 feet above	28D	7,143	1878
Crescent Lake	{ 28B / 29A }	a4,753	1878
Davis Lake	29A	4,466	1878
Fall Creek Cascade	29A	4,178	1878
Fish Lake	20C	3,155	1878
Four-mile Lake, near Mount Pitt	28D	5,610	1878
Fort Klamath Reservation, spring in	29C	4,597	1878
Goose Lake	38B	4,697	1877
Horsehead Spring	29A	a4,186	1878
Lodge Pole Spring	20C	1,648	1878
Mule Spring	29D	4,738	1878
North Twin Lake	28D	a5,117	1878
Odell Lake	28B	4,873	1878
Pauline Lake	29A	6,336	1878
Summer Lake	29C	4,163	1878
Summit Lake	28B	5,610	1878
Warm Springs (Warm Spring River)	20A	1,529	1878
Warm Spring Indian Agency	20C	1,514	1878
Willow Spring, near Round Butte	29C	a4,696	1878
UTAH.			
Antelope Spring (House Range)	50B	6,701	1872
Antelope Spring (Promontory Range)	41A	4,858	1878
Antelope Spring, upper	50	7,144	1872
Bear Lake	41B	5,955	1877
Berrys Spring	67	2,810	1872
Big Dam Springs	41A	4,317	1877
Blue Spring	41A	4,613	1877
Buckhorn Spring	59C	5,688	1872
Connors Spring	41D	4,251	1878
Desert Spring, near Hebron	58	5,887	1872
Emigrant Springs	41A	5,271	1877
Fish Lake	59	8,763	1872
Fish Springs	50A	4,269	1872
Good Indian Spring	50A	5,771	1872
Great Salt Lake	41A	l4,210	1872
Ha-wah-wah Springs	59	5,551	1872
Hansel Spring (Dilleys Ranch)	41A	5,043	1877
Hay Patch Spring	50A	5,590	1872
Indian Spring (Champlin Mountains)	50A	5,283	1872
Mill Spring (Ha-wah-wah Range)	59	6,504	1872
Pah-ghun Spring	66	2,282	1871
Raft River, head of south fork	41A	6,723	1877
Salt Springs	41A	4,203	1877
San Francisco Springs (Picacho Mountains)	59	6,527	1872

BAROMETRIC ALTITUDES.

TABLE IV.—LAKES, SPRINGS, ETC.—Continued.

Locality and name.	Atlas sheet.	Altitude in feet above sea.	Expeditionary year.
UTAH—Continued.			
Sevier Lake	{ 50 / 59	} 4,600	{ 1872 / 1873
Skumpah Spring, near	67A	5,558	1872
Washie pah-ghun Spring	66D	4,421	1872
Weber River, mouth of	41D	6,202	1877
White River Junction, north and south forks	51	7,088	1873
Willow Springs	50A	4,421	1872
WYOMING.			
Canteen Springs	41B	6,722	1877
MEXICO.			
Cookes Wells	81D	177	1876
Gardners Wells	81C	132	1876
Seven Wells	81D	125	1876

TABLE V.—MOUNTAIN PASSES.

No.	Name of pass.	Range.	State or Territory.	Atlas sheet.	Altitude in feet above sea.	Remarks.
1	Abo	Manzano	New Mexico	77D	6,431	Wagon-road between Punta del Agua and Abo Ruins.
2	Alpine Tunnel	Saguache	Colorado	61B	†11,722	Denver and South Park Railroad.
3	Alturas	Pacific and Great Interior Basin divide.	California	38D	a5,500	Alturas and Susanville road.
4	Antler	Great Interior Basin divide, low and indefinite.	Oregon	38B	4,929	Wagon-road from Drews Valley to Antler post-office.
5	Aragones	Zuni Mountains	New Mexico	77A	8,509	Wagon-road from Fort Wingate to Agua Fria.
6	Argentine	Front	Colorado	52D	13,286	On wagon-road from Georgetown to Montezuma.
7	Arkansas	Park	do	52D	11,445	Denver and Rio Grande Railroad.
8	Beales	Hualapais Mountains	do	74	5,127	Altitude from Kansas Pacific Railroad survey.
9	Bear Creek	San Juan	do	61C	11,606	Trail across divide between Bear and Lime Creeks.
10	Bear Valley	San Bernardino	California	73D	6,850	Summit of wagon-road about three-fourths of a mile north of Bear Valley Mining Camp.
11	Beckworth	Sierra Nevada	do	47D	5,193	Wagon-road from Reno to Beckworths Store.
12	Bidwell	Warner	do	38B	7,204	Ayers wagon-road, between Bidwell and Lakeview.
13	Bird Spring	Sierra Nevada	do	73B	5,417	Old wagon-road from Weldon to Mohave Desert, probably same as Humpahyamup Pass of Williamson; altitude 5,351.
14	Black Pine	Between Black Pine and Deep Creek Mountains.	Idaho	41A	5,537	Wagon-road from Curlew to Sublette Creek.
15	Blackwood	Sierra Nevada	California	47D	7,704	Trail to head of Blackwood Creek.
16	Blue Lake	do	do	56B	*8,960	Northwest of Upper Blue Lake on old wagon-road near Summit City Mining Camp.
17	Breckenridge	Park	Colorado	52D	11,503	On wagon-road from Breckenridge to Fairplay.
18	Buffalo Cañon	Between Granite and Warner.	California	38D	5,391	Reno and Surprise Valley road.
19	Burns, point in	Sunday Cone Ridge	New Mexico	84	†4,689	Atchison, Topeka and Santa Fe Railroad.

*Estimated. †Altitude of Nutt Station on Atchison, Topeka and Santa Fe Railroad.

BAROMETRIC ALTITUDES—TABLE V.

TABLE V.—MOUNTAIN PASSES—Continued.

No.	Name of pass.	Range.	State or Territory.	Atlas sheet.	Altitude in feet above sea.	Remarks.
20	Burton	Sierra Nevada	California	47D	7,164	Millers Ranch, Georgetown, and Lake Tahoe trail. Whitney gives 7,119, and railroad levels 7,373 as altitude for this pass.
21	Cactus	Between Aquarius and Peacock.	Arizona	75	*4,224	Wagon-road between Willow Creek and Tanks.
22	Cahuenga	San Fernando	California	73C	750	On wagon-road from Los Angeles to San Fernando Mission.
23	Cajon, west	San Bernardino	do	73D	4,841	Crossed by trail at head of Cajon Creek.
24	Cajon, middle	do	do	73D	4,676	Summit of old Salt Lake wagon-road; altitude from Williamsons Pacific Railroad report.
25	Cajon, east	do	do	73D	4,196	Summit of present wagon-road from San Bernardino to Panamint.
26	Caliente	Sierra Nevada	do	73A	5,497	Trail from Caliente Springs to Kelso Valley.
27	Campbells	Zuni Mountains	New Mexico	76	7,152	Altitude from Atlantic and Pacific Railroad survey; on Atlantic and Pacific Railroad.
28	Camp Curry	Crest of Great Plain of Central Oregon.	Oregon	29B	a5,513	Prineville and Harney wagon-road.
29	Canada de las Uvas	Tejon Mountains	California	73C	4,206	Wagon-road from Elizabeth Lake to Bakersfield. Williamson gives 4,356 feet.
30	Canada de las Uvas	do	do	73C	3,306	Wagon-road from Elizabeth Lake to Bakersfield.
31	Capitan	Capitan	New Mexico	85A	7,398	Wagon-road from Fort Stanton southward.
32	Carson	Sierra Nevada	California	56B	8,634	Summit of Amador and Nevada wagon-road. Whitney gives 8,759 feet as altitude of this pass.
33	Casitas	Sulphur Mountains	do	73C	1,605	Wagon-road from Caritas to Santa Paula.
34	Cedarville	Warner	do	38B	6,356	Alturas and Cedarville road.
35	Cerro Gordo	Sierra Nevada	do	65B	8,874	Wagon-road from Swansea to Bird Springs.
36	Charity	do	do	56B	8,292	Summit of wagon-road from Charity to Hermit Valley.
37	Chewaucan	Great Interior Basin divide.	Oregon	29C	a5,731	Lakeview and Prineville road.
38	Cinnamon Gulch	San Juan	Colorado	61C	12,659	On wagon-road from Burrows Park to Animas River.

* Level of station on A. and P. R. R.

U. S. GEOGRAPHICAL SURVEYS.   183

TABLE V.—MOUNTAIN PASSES—Continued.

No.	Name of pass.	Range.	State or Territory.	Atlas sheet.	Altitude in feet above sea.	Remarks.
39	Cochetopa	Cochetopa Hills	Colorado	61B	10,032	Summit of wagon-road from Los Pinos Indian agency to Saguache.
40	Comanche Cañon	Manzano	New Mexico	77D	8,284	Trail from Torreon to Ojuelos.
41	Costilla	Costilla	do	70A	10,188	Wagon-road from head of Costilla Creek to Vermejo Creek.
42	Cove Creek	Between Beaver and Pahvant.	Utah	59	6,456	Wagon-road from Cove Creek to Richfield.
43	Crooks	Warner, southward	Oregon	29D	26,864	Trail from Antler post-office (Chandlers) to Camp Warner.
44	Cucharas	Culebra	Colorado	70A	9,994	Wagon-road east of Trinchera Peak, from Spring Valley post-office northward.
45	Currant Creek	Between Park and Front	do	61B	9,654	Branch of Poncho Pass road to South Park.
46	Daggets	Genoa	Nevada	56B	7,297	Also called Kingsbury Grade. Simpson gives 7,180 for summit.
47	Devils Cañon	San Bernardino	California	73D	4,683	Summit of road from San Bernardino.
48	Diamond	Cascade	Oregon	20C	5,624	Eugene City and Fort Klamath, (Oregon Central) road.
49	Donner	Sierra Nevada	California	47D	6,983	Central Pacific Railroad, Summit Station. Whitney gives 7,056, and railroad levels 7,018 feet for summit.
50	Donner	do	do	47D	7,043	Summit of wagon-road from Truckee to Emigrant Gap.
51	Eagle	St. Teresa and Pinaleño	Arizona	83C	4,282	On wagon-road from old Camp Goodwin to Camp Grant.
52	Emigrant	Black Pine and Clear Creek.	Utah and Idaho	41A	6,887	Montana stage route between Raft River and Clear Creek stations.
53	Emigrant	Reese River Mountains	Nevada	48D	6,604	Old overland route.
54	Forty-nine Cañon	Mesa-like ridge east of Simpsons Valley.	California	38B	6,306	Surprise Valley and Summit Lake road.
55	Franktown	Tahoe Mountains, Sierra Nevada.	Nevada	47D	7,960	On trail between Hot Springs (Lake Tahoe) and Franktown.
56	Fredonyer	Sierra Nevada	California	47A	5,670	Cross road between Susanville and Fort Crook and Susanville and Red Bluff road.
57	Freels	Lake Tahoe Group, Sierra Nevada.	do	56B	8,685	Summit of trail from Lake Valley to Hope Valley.

TABLE V.—MOUNTAIN PASSES—Continued.

No.	Name of pass.	Range.	State or Territory.	Atlas sheet.	Altitude in feet above sea.	Remarks.
58	Fremont	Beaver and Parowan	Utah	59	6,883	On wagon-road from Day Valley to Parowan Valley.
59	French	Park	Colorado	52D	12,044	On wagon-road from Michigan Creek to French Creek.
60	Gate	Augusta	Nevada	48C	4,743	Wagon-road between Spring Pass and White Rock.
61	Georgia	Between Park and Front	Colorado	52D	11,778	Wagon-road from Michigan Creek to Swan River.
62	Gold Run	Sierra Nevada	California	47A	6,428	Susanville and Taylorville road.
63	Gosiute	Gosiute	Nevada	49	*6,065	Between Gosiute Monuntains and northern spur of Antelope Mountains.
64	Gray & Torry	Front	Colorado	52D	13,929	Gap between Grays and Torreys Peak.
65	Green Creek	Sierra Nevada	California	56D	10,161	On trail from Bridgeport to Yosemite Valley. Pass is on main divide, small lake in pass.
66	Hamilton	Continental divide between Rio Grande and Animas Rivers.	Colorado	61C	12,413	On wagon-road from Deep Creek to Howardville.
67	Handcart	Hansel Mountains	...do	52D	12,263	Head of Halfmoon Creek.
68	Hansel	Hansel Mountains	Utah	41A	5,138	On wagon-road from Blue Springs to Snowsville.
69	Hardscrabble	Wet Mountains	Colorado	62A	9,159	Wagon-road from the Arkansas to Wet Mountain Valley.
70	Haskells	Sierra Nevada	California	47A	5,315	Wagon-road from Sierra Valley to Quincy.
71	Hastings	Humboldt	Nevada	49	‡6,580	} Old overland stage route between Old Camp Ruby and Jacobs Wells.
72	Hay Cañon	Mesa-like ridge east of Simpsons Valley.	California	38D	16,425 7,170	Trail, Eagleville to Todhunter.
73	Hayden Creek	Sangre de Cristo	Colorado	61B	10,780	Trail at head of Hayden Creek across divide to San Luis Valley.
74	Henness	Sierra Nevada	California	47D	6,958	Henness Pass wagon-road, Whitney gives altitude of 6,994 feet.
75	Holcomb Valley	Cascade	...do	73D	7,131	At Placer Mines, on summit of road west of Bear Valley.
76	Hood	Cascade	Oregon	20A	3,694	At Summit Prairie, on wagon-road between Willamette and Tygh Valleys.
77	Hoosier	Park	Colorado	52D	11,627	On wagon road from Alma to Breckenridge.

*From Union Pacific Railroad levels. †Simpson. ‡Pacific Railroad Report.

U. S. GEOGRAPHICAL SURVEYS.   185

TABLE V.—MOUNTAIN PASSES—Continued.

No.	Name of pass.	Range.	State or Territory.	Atlas sheet.	Altitude in feet above sea.	Remarks.
78	Horse Lake	Divide between Horse Lake and Madeline Plains.	California	38D	5,798	Alturas and Susanville Road.
79	Indian Creek	Veta Mountains	Colorado	62C	9,720	Wagon-road from Veta to Garland.
80	Inscription Rock	Zuni Mountains	New Mexico	77A	8,444	On road to Zuñi.
81	Johnsons	Sierra Nevada	California	56B	7,266	Simpson gives 7,222, Central Pacific Railroad survey 7,373, as altitude for this pass.
82	Johnstone	Onaquin	Utah	50	*6,237	On old overland stage route between Fausts and Davis stations.
83	Kenosha	Front	Colorado	52D	9,981	Denver and South Park Railroad.
84	Lake City	Warner	California	38B	7,034	Surprise Valley and Goose Lake road.
85	Lake Creek	Saguache	Colorado	61B	12,226	Across Continental Divide east of Red Mountain.
86	Lake Tahoe	Sierra Nevada	Nevada	47D	7,186	On wagon-road between Carson and Glenbrook.
87	Langtons	Crest of Great Plain of Central Oregon.	Oregon	29A	a5,225	Northeast of Langtons ranch, on Lakeview and Prineville road.
88	Lassens	Warner	California	38B	6,201	Old Bidwell and Goose Lake road. Altitude above Fort Bidwell from Lydeckers tables.
89	Last Chance	Sierra Nevada	do	47B	6,006	Local road from Last Chance Valley to Long Valley.
90	Longs Cañon	Raton Plateau	New Mexico	70A	8,134	On wagon-road from Trinidad southward via Upper Canadian.
91	Los Valles, Colorados	Continental divide of Zuni Mountains.	do	77A	8,350	On wagon-road from Agua Fria to Wingate.
92	Loveland	Front	Colorado	52D	h11,876	North of Torreys and Grays Peaks.
93	Loyalton	Sierra Nevada	California	47D	7,075	Wagon-road between Loyalton and Reno.
94	Luthers	do	do	56B	a7,681	On stage road from Hope Valley to Lake Valley. Simpson gives 7,505 for altitude of this pass.
95	McFadden	do	do	47B	5,999	Ranch road from Honey Lake Valley to Thompson Creek Basin.

* Whitney.

TABLE V.—MOUNTAIN PASSES—Continued.

No.	Name of pass.	Range.	State or Territory.	Atlas sheet.	Altitude in feet above sea.	Remarks.
96	McLanes	Sierra Nevada	California	56D	10,165	Summit of Great Sierra wagon-road; altitude estimated from Whitney.
97	Madeline	Between Sierra Nevada and Warner.	do	38C	5,736	Lieutenant Beckwiths route (Central Pacific Railroad Report).
98	Madmans	Sierra Blanca	Colorado	62C	9,724	Wagon-road across divide from Middle Creek to Wagon Creek.
99	Magdalena	Magdalena	New Mexico	84C	4,755	On wagon-road from Clifton to San Isadore.
100	Manco Burro	Raton Plateau	do	70A	9,040	On wagon-road from Silver City to Old Fort West on Gila River.
101	Mangos	Diablo	do	83	1,798	
102	Marcellina	West Elk Mountains	Colorado	61A	10,944	On wagon-road from Haverly to head of Oak Creek.
103	Marlette	Sierra Nevada	Nevada	47D	8,265	Summit of wagon-road from Carson to Marlette Lake via Ash Cañon.
104	Marshall	Saguache	Colorado	61B	10,852	From Poncho Creek to Tumichi Valley.
105	Massacre Creek	Divide between Massacre Lakes and High Rock Cañon.	California	38B	6,334	Old Emigrant road.
106	Meadow Lake	Sierra Nevada	do	47B	7,677	Branch road from Hennes Pass road to Meadow Lake Mining District.
107	Mineral	do	Nevada	47D	6,864	McTarnahan road.
108	Mono	do	California	57	*10,765	Summit of Mono trail, head of Bloody Cañon.
109	Mosca	Sierra Blanca	Colorado	62C	9,787	Wagon-road from Poison Creek to San Luis Valley.
110	Mosquito	Park	do	52D	13,308	On wagon-road from Mosquito Creek to Leadville.
111	Moreno	Culebra	New Mexico	70A	9,770	Trail from Elizabethtown northward via head of Comanche and Moreno Creeks.
112	Mountain Spring	Spring Mountain	Nevada	66	5,508	Wagon-road, south end of Spring Mountain Range, between Cottonwood Springs and Stump Springs.
113	Mountain Wells	Pah-ute	do	48C	6,258	On wagon-road from Stillwater to West Gate.
114	Muddy Creek	Wet Mountains	Colorado	62C	8,890	Wagon-road across low divide at southern end of Wet Mountain Valley.

* Whitney.

TABLE V.—MOUNTAIN PASSES—Continued.

No.	Name of pass.	Range.	State or Territory.	Atlas sheet.	Altitude in feet above sea.	Remarks.
115	Nells	Mimbres	New Mexico	84C	7,698	Trail from headwaters of Cuchillo Negro to headwaters of Gila River.
116	New	Desatoya	Nevada	48D	8,370	On wagon-road from Pattersons to Jacobsville.
117	Noble	Sierra Nevada	California	47A	a5,963	Wagon-road from Deer Flat to head of Canoe Creek.
118	North Cañon	West Mountains	Idaho	41B	5,964	Central Pacific Railroad Survey. Wagon-road from Green on Malade Creek, westward.
119	Oak Creek	Tejon Mountains	California	73A	6,904	Trail from Nations, Tejon Creek to Oak Creek.
120	Palmyra	Pine Nut	Nevada	47D	7,226	
121	Pedernal	Pedernal Mountains	New Mexico	77B	7,181	Wagon-road from Anton Chico southward.
122	Pine Nut	Pine Nut	do	47D	7,211	McTarnahan road.
123	Pirches	Mimbres	Colorado	84C	8,264	Trail from Hillsboro to Chicken Creek.
124	Placer	Sangre de Cristo	do	62C	a9,526	From Upper Huerfano to Placer Creek.
125	Poison	Sangre de Cristo	do	62C	8,672	Wagon-road from Gardiners Post-office via Poisoned Cañon to Mosca Pass road.
126	Poison Lake	Sierra Nevada	California	47A	5,409	Honey Lake Valley, Susanville and Fort Crook road.
127	Pole Creek	Continental Divide	Colorado	61C	12,296	Divide between Pole Creek and Maggie Gulch, near head of Rio Grande.
128	Poncho	Saguache	do	61B	8,946	Old Cañon City Toll road.
129	Ponil	Cimarron and Costilla	New Mexico	70A	9,848	On wagon-road from Ponil Park to Elizabethtown.
130	Port Neuf	Port Neuf	Idaho	32D	6,610	Utah Northern Railroad, outlet of ancient Lake Bonneville.
131	Promontory	Promontory	Utah	41A	*4,800	Central Pacific Railroad.
132	Quinn Cañon	Quinn Cañon Range	Nevada	58	6,256	On road from White Pine District to Pahranagat Valley.
133	Ragtown	Kawsoh Mountains	do	48C	4,303	On wagon-road from Ragtown to Wadsworth.
134	Raton	Raton Plateau	New Mexico	70A	b7,861	On stage-road from Trinidad southward.
135	Railroad	Pinaleño	Arizona	83	4,490	Altitude from Texas and Pacific Railroad survey. Wagon-road from San Simeon Plains to Arivapa Valley.
136	Red River	Taos and Cimarron	New Mexico	70A	a9,764	On wagon-road from Elizabethtown westward.

*Approximated.

TABLE V.—MOUNTAIN PASSES—Continued.

No.	Name of pass.	Range.	State or Territory.	Atlas sheet.	Altitude in feet above sea.	Remarks.
137	Red Rock, east	Warner, south end	California	38D	a6,236	Susanville and Surprise Valley road, on divide between Madeline Plains and headwaters south fork of Pitt River.
138	Red Rock, west	do	do	38D	a6,052	Same road as above, on the divide between Red Rock Valley and Tuledad.
139	Red Rock	Port Neuf	Idaho	32D	4,893	Lake Bonneville outlet.
140	Relief (north)	Sierra Nevada	California	56D	9,805	
141	Relief (south)	do	do	56D	9,585	
142	Rock Creek	Coast Range	do	73D	6,703	Trail between Rock Creek and Prairie Fork.
143	San Augustin	Organ and San Andreas	New Mexico	84B	5,654	Wagon-road from Fort Selden to San Augustine.
144	San Andreas	San Andreas	do	84B	5,543	Wagon-road to Annaya Spring, northern end of range, Forts Craig and Stanton road.
145	San Fernando	San Fernando	California	73C	1,951	Head of Brophys Creek, on trail west of railroad tunnel.
146	San Fernando (tunnel)	do	do	73C	1,479	North end of tunnel from railroad levels.
147	San Fernando	do	do	73C	1,871	Wagon-road, summit cut, east of railroad tunnel.
148	San Francisquito	Sierra Nevada	do	73C	3,833	Summit of wagon-road from Newhall to Elizabeth Lake. Williamsons altitude 3,718 feet.
149	San Gorgonio	San Jacinto	do	80B	2,746	Southern Pacific Railroad.
150	San Joaquin	Sierra Nevada	do	57C	12,400	Summit of trail from San Joaquin Basin to Owens River Valley. Altitude from Whitney.
151	Sand Hill	Sangre de Cristo	Colorado	62C	9,772	From Cucharas Creek to San Luis Valley.
152	Sand Spring	Tarogua	Nevada	48C	4,533	On wagon-road from Sand Springs to West Gate.
153	Sangre de Cristo	Veta Mountains	Colorado	62C	9,578	Wagon-road from Badito to Stearnes Ranch.
154	Sardine Valley	Sierra Nevada	California	47B	6,346	Truckee and Loyalton road.
155	Sevier	Cañon	Utah	50	4,767	Sevier Cañon.
156	Sierra Valley	Sierra Nevada	California	47D	6,321	Wagon-road from Truckee to south end of Sierra Valley.
157	Sierraville	do	do	47D	6,893	Wagon-road from Reno to south end Sierra Valley.
158	Silver Mountain or Ebbetts	do	Nevada	56B	7,630	Big Tree wagon-road between Sonora and Silver Mountain.
159	Shoshone Creek	Augusta Mountains	do	48D	5,481	Branch from New Pass road northward.
160	Soda Spring	Sierra Nevada	California	47D	7,906	On trail between Squaw Valley and Soda Springs.

TABLE V.—MOUNTAIN PASSES—Continued.

No.	Name of pass.	Range.	State or Territory.	Atlas sheet.	Altitude in feet above sea.	Remarks.
161	Soledad	Sierra Nevada	California	73C	l3, 210	Southern Pacific Railroad. Williamson gives 3,164 feet. This pass is also called Williamsons "New Pass."
162	Sonora	do	do	56B	9,660	Summit of Sonora and Mono Stage-road.
163	Squaw Valley	do	do	47D	8,630	Trail from Squaw Valley to American Valley runs over this gap.
164	Saint Johns Mine	do	do	65C	5,083	Wagon-road from Weldon to Kelso Valley.
165	Strawberry	San Bernardino	do	73D	5,186	Summit of road from San Bernardino to Little Bear Valley.
166	Sunset Gap	Mogollon Mesa	Arizona	76	5,755	Wagon-road from the Colorado Chiquito to Camp Apache, Ariz.
167	Susanville	Sierra Nevada	California	47A	5,507	On Red Bluff and Susanville road.
168	Swarthouts Cañon	do	do	73D	6,870	Road head of Swarthouts Cañon.
169	Sycan	Winter Ridge	Oregon	29C	6,868	Trail from Summit Lake to Old Eugene road.
170	Taos	Mora and Taos	New Mexico	70C	9,282	On wagon-road from Taos to Elizabethtown.
171	Tehachapai	Tehachapai Mountains	California	73A	l4,025	Southern Pacific Railroad. Williamsons altitude 4,020 feet.
172	Tejon	Tejon Mountains	do	73A	5,485	Summit of trail between Tejon Creek and Dearborns Ranch.
173	Telegraph	Bear River	Idaho	41B	*7,800	On wagon-road from Bloomington to Franklin.
174	Tennessee	Saguache and Park	Colorado	52D	10,702	From head of Arkansas to head of Eagle River.
175	Thompsons	Sierra Nevada	California	47B	6,022	Ranch road from Thompson Creek to Honey Lake Valley.
176	Trout Creek	Park	Colorado	61B	9,613	Wagon-road from South Park to Upper Arkansas Valley.
177	Tuledad	Pacific and International Basin Divide.	California	38D	a6,362	Road from Tuledad to Painters Flat.
178	Tulerosa	Datil	New Mexico	76D	7,452	Wagon-road from Fort Tulerosa to Camp Apache.
179	Twin Creek	Saguache	Colorado	62A	8,568	Trail across divide between South Fork of Twin Creek and Rule Creek.
180	Tygh	Tygh Hills	Oregon	20A	3,119	Summit of wagon-road between Sherars Bridge (Deschutes river) and The Dalles.
181	Uiyabe	Deep Creek Mountains	Nevada	49	6,233	Altitude from Pacific Railroad report.
182	Union	Blue Ridge Mountains	Arizona	74B	3,600	Wagon-road from the Colorado to Sacramento Valley.

* Estimated.

BAROMETRIC ALTITUDES—TABLE V.

Table V.—MOUNTAIN PASSES—Continued.

No.	Name of pass.	Range.	State or Territory.	Atlas sheet.	Altitude in feet above sea.	Remarks.
183	U. S. Mountain No. 1	Mora	Colorado	69D	8,414	Trails from Taos northward.
184	U. S. Mountain No. 2	do	do	69D	9,252	Do.
185	Ute	Front	do	62A	8,551	Wagon-road from Florissant to Colorado Springs.
186	Vermejo or Francisco	Calebra Range	do	70A	9,172	Divide between Vermejo and Purgatoire Rivers.
187	Veta	Veta Mountains	do	62C	b, 392	Denver and Rio Grande Railroad.
188	Visalia	Sierra Nevada	California	65A	10,175	Visalia and Lone Pine Trail; also called "Hockett Trail."
189	Virginia Creek	Sierra Nevada	do	56D	11,046	Summit of Bridgeport and Yosemite Trail, divide of Virginia and Green Creeks
190	Wagon-wheel Gap	Between Lagarita and San Juan.	Colorado	61D	8,459	On wagon-road from head of Rio Grande to Aldens Junction.
191	Walkers	Sierra Nevada	California	73A	5,322	Wagon-road from Weldon to Coyote Holes. Williamson gives 5,302.
192	Warm Springs	Mutton Mountains	Oregon	20A	3,670	Summit of road between Warm Spring Indian Agency and The Dalles.
193	Warner	San Jacinto	California	80B	3,734	Wagon-road between Warners Ranch and Oak Grove.
194	Warner	Warner	Oregon	38D	a5,820	Old Oregon Central Military road. Present road from Lakeview to Warner Lakes.
195	Washington	Chusco Mountains	New Mexico	68I	8,826	Trail at head of Cañon de Chelle.
196	Washington Gulch	Elk Mountains	Colorado	61A	10,132	Wagon-road from Belleview to Gunnison.
197	Watermans	San Bernardino	California	73D	4,721	Summit of trail head of Watermans Cañon.
198	Westons	Park	Colorado	52D	12,109	Wagon-road from South Park to Leadville.
199	White Earth Creek	San Juan	do	61C	11,314	On wagon-road from head of White Earth Creek to Clear Creek and Argenton Falls.
200	{ Wolf Creek, north	} Sierra Nevada	California	56B	{ 8,438	} These gaps are at the head of Wolf Creek and are crossed by trails.
	{ Wolf Creek, south				{ 8,729	
201	Yuba Gap	Sierra Nevada	do	47B	6,700	Wagon-road from Sierra Valley to Sierra City. Whitney gives 6,642.
202	Zani	Zani Mountains, Continental Divide.	New Mexico	77A	a8,459	Wagon-road from Fort Wingate to Agua Fria.

PART IV.

ITINERARIES OF IMPORTANT ROUTES

IN

CALIFORNIA, NEVADA, OREGON, UTAH, ARIZONA, NEW MEXICO, COLORADO, AND WYOMING.

ITINERARIES OF IMPORTANT ROUTES IN CALIFORNIA, OREGON, NEVADA, UTAH, ARIZONA, NEW MEXICO, COLORADO, AND WYOMING.

The following itineraries embrace a small portion only of the results of the odometer measurements made by the various parties of the survey. The original intention was to publish, under this heading, the final results of the odometric and barometric measurements gathered along all the principal wagon-routes surveyed, but at the date of going to press only the tables here given were in a sufficiently complete state for the printer. Most of the material here presented has not before been published, and refers mainly to California and Nevada, while the routes of Arizona, New Mexico, and Colorado, Utah, and Idaho have already been more or less carefully examined and the results published in the annual reports of this office for 1877 to 1879, inclusive.

The distances given are the results of odometric measurements, unless otherwise stated, while the altitudes of all the main points are from cistern-barometer determinations, the minor ones being from aneroid readings, checked by daily comparisons with the cistern barometer, and computed by the method described in the Meteorological Instructions issued by this office.

M. M. M.

ENGINEER OFFICE,
   U. S. GEOGRAPHICAL SURVEYS.

U. S. GEOGRAPHICAL SURVEYS. 193

Route No.	Itineraries.	Distance.	Page.
		Miles.	
1	Reno, Nev., to Fort Bidwell, Cal	190.42	194–5
2	..... do	230.84	196–7
3	Susanville, Cal., to Sheeps Head, Nev	56.05	198
4	Susanville, Cal., to Lake View, Oreg	143.82	199–200
5	Fort Bidwell, Cal., to Forth Klamath, Oreg	140.68	201
6	Fort Klamath, Oreg., to Fort Bidwell, Cal	180.70	202
7	Fort Bidwell, Cal., to The Dalles, Oreg	406.77	203–4
7a	Summit Lake, Oreg., to Beatties Butte, Oreg	257.70	205
7b	Prineville, Oreg., to Fish Lake, Cascade Mountains, Oreg	71.45	206
7c	Oak Grove, Oreg., to Tollgate, Mount Hood, Oreg	45.42	207
7d	Tygh Valley, Oreg., to Tollgate, Mount Hood, Oreg	49.75	208
8	Fort Bidwell, Cal., to The Dalles, Oreg	324.40	209–10
9	..... do	365.42	211–13
10	Cottonwood, Cal., to Susanville, Cal	116.91	214–15
11	Red Bluff, Cal., to Susanville, Cal	101.79	216–17
12	Chico, Cal., to Susanville, Cal	98.13	218–19
13	Chico, Cal., to Reno, Nev	173.44	220–21
14	Oroville, Cal., to Susanville, Cal	118.55	222
15	Truckee, Cal., to Quincy, Cal	74.92	223
16	Reno, Cal., to Milton, Cal	50.08	224
17	Reno, Cal., to Emigrant Gap, Cal	64.31	225
18	Virginia, Nev., to Placerville, Cal	101.12	226
18a	Carson, Nev., to Rowlands, Cal	27.49	227
18b	..... do	27.65	228
19	Carson, Nev., to Volcano, Cal	97.00	229
20	Carson, Nev., to Milton, Cal	140.37	230–1
21	Milton, Cal., to Bodie, Cal	153.88	232
22	..... do	157.74	233–4
23	Calaveras Big Tree Route, Milton, Cal., to Yosemite, Cal	152.45	235–6
24	Big Oak Flat Route, Milton, Cal., to Yosemite, Cal	94.61	237–8
25	Coulterville Route, Merced, Cal., to Yosemite, Cal	99.34	239–40
26	Mariposa Route, Merced, Cal., to Yosemite, Cal	93.95	241–2
27	Madera Route, Madera, Cal., to Yosemite, Cal	96.29	243
28	Caliente, Cal., to Coyote Holes, Cal	70.88	244
29	Bakersfield, Cal., to Forks of Road Station	66.88	245
30	Los Angeles, Cal., to Caliente, Cal	114.61	246
31	Newhall, Cal., to Bakersfield, Cal	119.02	247
32	Newhall, Cal., to San Buena Ventura, Cal	48.00	248
33	Los Angeles, Cal., to San Buena Ventura, Cal	70.85	249
34	Mohave Station, Cal., to Independence, Cal	131.82	250
35	Independence, Cal., to Panamint, Cal	90.56	251–2
36	Los Angeles, Cal., to Panamint, Cal	211.68	253–4
37	Mohave Station, Cal., to Darwin, Cal	100.82	255
38	Los Angeles, Cal., to Fort Yuma, Cal	275.94	256
39	San Bernardino, Cal., to Ehrenberg, Ariz	190.70	257
40	Pueblo, Colo., to Santa Fe, N. Mex	297.90	258–9
41	Carson, Nev., to Austin, Nev	178.19	260

1874 WII——13

194   ITINERARIES OF ROUTES.

ROUTE No. 1.—*Reno, Nev., to Fort Bidwell, Cal.*

[Atlas sheets Nos. 38B and D, 47B and D.]

Stations.	Distance.		Altitude above sea-level.	Remarks.
	Between consecutive points.	From Reno.	From Camp Bidwell.		
	Miles.	*Miles.*	*Miles.*	*Feet.*	
Reno	0.00	0.00	190.42	4,484	Town of about 3,000 inhabitants; station on Central Pacific Railroad, at junction of Virginia and Truckee Railroad.
Forks of road near quartz mill	1.93	1.93	188.49	4,600	North edge of Truckee Meadows.
Deep Wells	10.84	12.77	177.65	4,561	Good water; forage for sale.
Junction House	4.92	17.69	172.73	4,497	Good water; forage for sale. Road to Pyramid (mining camp west of Pyramid Lake) forks to northeast. Upper Pyramid about 10 miles from Junction House.
Warm Spring	6.03	23.72	166.70	4,287	Good water and grass near head of Winnemucca Valley.
Chapmans	8.68	32.40	158.02	4,932	Good water; forage for sale.
Tule Franks	0.70	33.10	157.32	5,141	Do.
Winters Ranch	1.57	34.67	155.75	5,145	Good water and grass.
Giles and Bickfords Ranch	0.80	35.47	154.95	5,394	Good water.
Newcombs Ranch	2.15	37.62	152.80	5,320	Good water; forage for sale.
Fish Spring	9.98	47.60	142.82	4,041	Do.
Sheep Head[1]	27.55	75.15	115.27	3,914	Do.
Buffalo Salt Works (Murphys)[2]	7.56	82.71	107.71	3,845	Very bad water. Deep Hole, by right-hand road, 22.94 miles.
Buffalo Station	14.73	97.44	92.98	4,378	Water and grass.
Spring in Cedar Cañon	13.06	110.50	79.92	4,946	Do.
Clarks Ranch	16.04	126.54	63.88	4,677	Good water and grass.
Forks of road	2.87	129.41	61.01	4,709	Road to Tuledad, Madeline Plains, Cold Springs, and Susanville turns southwest.
Bares Ranch	8.42	137.83	52.59	4,679	South end of Surprise Valley, on Silver Creek.

[1] If the Smoke Creek road be taken at Sheeps Head the distance to forks of road will be as follows: Sheep Head to Smoke Creek Depot, 9.76 miles; Smoke Creek Depot to Painters Flat, 21.75; Painters Flat to Tuledad, 17.15; Tuledad to forks of road, 9.00. Total, Sheep Head to forks of road, 57.66, or 3.4 miles greater than by stage road.
[2] For distances from Susanville to Buffalo Salt Works and Sheep Head see Route No. 3.

ROUTE No. 1.—*Reno, Nev., to Fort Bidwell, Cal.*—Continued.

[Atlas sheets Nos. 38B and D, 47B and D.]

Stations.	Distance.			Altitude above sea-level.	Remarks.
	Between consecutive points.	From Reno.	From Camp Bidwell.		
	Miles.	*Miles.*	*Miles.*	*Feet.*	
Eagleville (post-office)	11.72	149.55	40.87	4,632	On Eagle Creek, west side of Surprise Valley; largest village in the valley.
Cedarville (post-office)	15.90	165.45	24.97	4,674	Village west side Surprise Valley.
Lake City (post-office)	8.65	174.10	16.32	4,624	Do.
Fort Bidwell	16.32	190.42	0.00	4,647	Military post and settlement.

NOTE.—The distance from Deep Wells here given is by the new road. By the road generally traveled the distance is 2.63 miles greater. The above roads were surveyed in 1877 and 1878 and from the present mail route (1883) and the most direct one from Reno to Bidwell.

ITINERARIES OF ROUTES.

ROUTE No. 2.—*Reno, Nev., to Fort Bidwell, Cal., via Susanville, Cal.*

[Atlas sheets Nos. 38B and 38D, 47B and 47D.]

Stations.	Distance.			Altitude above sea-level.	Remarks.
	Between consecutive points.	From Reno.	From Fort Bidwell.		
	Miles.	*Miles.*	*Miles.*	*Feet.*	
Reno, Nev	0.00	0.00	230.84	4,484	Large town on Central Pacific Railroad; seat of Washoe county.
Old Stage Station	8.43	8.43	222.41	5,133	Well-water; no wood nor grass; Poeville mines 3.26 miles to southwest, on slope of Peavine Mountain.
Peavine Ranch	2.31	10.74	220.10	4,952	Forage for sale.
Pine Stage Station, near California and Nevada State line.[1]	5.78	16.52	214.32	5,133	Water; altitude taken at State line monument, 0.33 mile southeast of Pine Station.
Junction House[2]	8.48	25.00	205.84	4,639	Forage for sale.
Dunnings Ranch	7.43	32.43	198.41	4,571	Do.
Willow Ranch	14.24	46.67	184.17	4,275	Forage for sale; road westward to Last Chance Valley.
McFaddens Ranch	16.51	63.18	167.66	4,420	Forage for sale; west shore Honey Lake.
Milford	1.51	64.69	166.15	4,204	Do.
Clarks Ranch	6.42	71.11	159.73	4,028	Do.
Buntingville (store)	4.03	75.14	155.70	4,278	Do.
Janesville (post-office)	2.23	77.37	153.47	4,386	Settlement; forage for sale.
Susanville	13.56	90.93	139.91	4,195	Town of about 600 inhabitants; land office and seat of Lassen county.
Willow Creek Crossing	*14.00	104.93	125.91		Forks of road—left-hand road to Eagle Lake.
Shumways Ranch	*13.00	117.93	112.91	5,067	North of Horse Lake; forage for sale.
Forks of road to Alturas[3]	*10.50	128.43	102.41	5,257	Alturas road turns north across Madeline Plains.
Cold Spring	*17.65	146.08	84.76		Water, wood, and grass.

* Distance from plot.
[1] The State line monument (longitude 120° west of Greenwich) is 0.31 mile southeast of Pine Station, Cal.; 0.33 mile to the northwest and 0.74 mile to the southeast of Pine Station are roads turning westward via Loyalton Pass to points in Sierra Valley.
[2] At junction a road forks westward via Beckworth Pass for Summit and Beckworth post-office, Sierra Valley (see Route 3). From Junction to Susanville there are numerous settlements where forage can be had.
[3] This is the most direct road from Susanville to Alturas (see Route No. 4).

ROUTE No. 2.—*Reno, Nev., to Fort Bidwell, Cal., via Susanville, Cal.*—Continued.

[Atlas sheets Nos. 38B and D, 47B and D.]

Stations.	Distance.			Altitude above sea-level.	Remarks.
	Between consecutive points.	From Reno.	From Fort Bidwell.		
	Miles.	*Miles.*	*Miles.*	*Feet.*	
Tuledad Ranch	14.75	160.83	70.01	5,046	Cattle ranch; California and Nevada State line; old road comes in from south from Sheep Head via Smoke Creek Depot.
Junction with Bidwell road	9.00	169.83	61.01	4,709	Reno and Bidwell stage and mail road. See Route No. 1.
Bares Ranch, south end Surprise Valley	8.42	178.25	52.59	4,679	Forage for sale.
Eagleville (post-office)	11.72	189.97	40.87	4,632	Principal village of Surprise Valley.
Cedarville (post-office)	15.90	205.87	24.97	4,674	Settlement in Surprise Valley.
Lake City (post-office)	8.65	214.52	16.32	4,624	Do.
Fort Bidwell	16.32	230.84	0.00	4,647	North end of Surprise Valley; military post and settlement.

NOTE.—From Reno to Susanville the road is the mail and stage road; general direction, northwest. From Susanville to junction with Reno and Bidwell road is a good stage-road; general direction, northeast. Thence to Bidwell is over the Reno road (Route 1) surveyed in 1877.

ROUTE No. 3.—*Susanville, Cal., to Sheep Head and Buffalo Salt Works, Reno and Bidwell road.*

[Atlas sheet No. 47B.]

Stations.	Distance.			Altitude above sea-level.	Remarks.
	Between consecutive points.	From Susanville.	From Sheep Head.		
	Miles.	*Miles.*	*Miles.*	*Feet.*	
Susanville	0.00	0.00	56.05	4,195	Seat of Lassen County.
Willow Creek Crossing	12.20	12.20	43.85	4,150	North of Honey Lake.
Shaffers Ranch	6.35	18.55	37.50	4,026	Old emigrant camping place; wood, water, and grass; north of Honey Lake, south of Shaffers Peak.
Forks of road[1]	8.00	26.55	29.50	4,411	Road north to Secret Valley, Painters Flat, and Tuledad.
Mud Spring	8.66	35.21	20.84	4,671	No grass; water scanty.
Camp on Rush Creek	6.14	41.35	14.70	4,437	Water.
Smoke Creek Depot[2]	4.94	46.29	9.76	4,163	Old military depot, water and feed.
Sheep Head Springs (post-office), via east branch of road	9.76	56.05	0.00	3,914	Station on Reno and Bidwell mail road.

[1] Forks to south end Secret Valley, 8.50; Secret Valley to Shams Ranch, 12.00; Shams Ranch to Painters Flat (Cattle Ranch, California and Nevada State line), 12.00; Painters Flat to Tuledad Valley (California and Nevada State line), 16.00. Total: Susanville to Tuledad Valley, 75.05 miles.
[2] By the west branch of road (about .75 mile below depot) Buffalo Salt Works (Murphys) is reached in 12.57 miles. Total: Susanville to Buffalo Salt Works (Reno and Bidwell road), 58.45 miles.

U. S. GEOGRAPHICAL SURVEYS. 199

ROUTE No. 4.—*Susanville, Cal., to Lake View, Oreg.*

[Atlas sheets Nos. 47A and B, 38A and B.]

Stations.	Distance.			Altitude above sea-level.	Remarks.
	Between consecutive points.	From Susanville.	From Lake View.		
	Miles.	*Miles.*	*Miles.*	*Feet.*	
Susanville	0.00	0.00	143.82	4,195	Lassen County seat.
Shumways Ranch	27.00	27.00	116.82	5,067	North of Horse Lake.
Forks of road	10.50	37.50	106.32	5,257	Madeline Plains; road turns northeast to Cold Spring, 17.65 miles.
McDonalds Ranch	12.00	49.50	94.32	5,297	Northern arm of Madeline Plains.
Low Pass	7.40	56.90	86.92	5,466	Pacific and Great Interior Basin divide.
Dry Creek	5.40	62.30	81.52	5,087	Camping place; wood, water, and grass.
Forks of road, valley of South Fork Pit River.	5.77	68.07	75.75	4,462	Road eastward to Jeso Valley.
Fitzhugh Creek	9.00	77.07	66.75	4,431	Ranch in valley of South Fork Pit River.
Alturas (formerly Dorris Bridge)	9.50	86.57	57.25	4,365	Village of about 300 inhabitants; seat of Modoc County.
Pit River Slough	5.00	91.57	52.25	4,407	North Fork Pit River.
Cedarville road[1]	1.38	92.95	50.87	4,443	Mail route to Cedarville, via Cedarville Pass (Warner Mountains).
Martins Ranch	5.50	98.45	45.37	4,662	Joseph Creek.
Lindale (post-office), Swearingen Creek[2]	3.58	102.03	41.79	4,666	Road to Lake City turns northeast up creek, via Lake City Pass.
Lake City road	2.00	104.03	39.79		Road to Lake City turns southeast; Lake City 10.5 miles distant.
Davis Creek (post-office)	4.19	108.22	35.60	4,855	On Davis Creek; wood, water, and grass.
Fort Bidwell road	10.33	118.55	25.27	5,221	Fort Bidwell, via Lassens Pass, 14.3 miles.
Willow Ranch (post-office)	2.58	121.13	22.69	4,925	Fandango Creek.

[1] This is the best road from Alturas to Bidwell. The distances are: Alturas to forks of road, 6.38 miles; forks to summit (6,356 feet), 11.57 miles; summit to Cedarville, 5.29 miles; Cedarville to Fort Bidwell, 24.97. Total, Alturas to Bidwell, 48.21 miles.
[2] This road affords a shorter route from Alturas to Bidwell, but the pass is higher. The distances are: Alturas to Lindale, 15.76 miles; Lindale to summit (7,034 feet), 5.35 miles; summit to Lake City, 5.23 miles; Lake City to Bidwell, 16.32 miles. Total distance to Bidwell, 42.66 miles.

ROUTE No. 4.—*Susanville, Cal., to Lake View, Oreg.*—Continued.

[Atlas sheets Nos. 47A and B, 38A and B.]

Stations.	Distance.			Altitude above sea-level.	Remarks.
	Between consecutive points.	From Susanville.	From Lake View.		
	Miles.	*Miles.*	*Miles.*	*Feet.*	
Ayres grade to Fort Bidwell	4.20	125.33	18.49	4,844	Road runs southeast up Cottonwood Creek. Fort Bidwell, 12.49 miles.
California and Oregon State line	3.58	128.91	14.91		State line monument, No. 12, on 42d parallel.
New Pine Creek (post-office)	1.61	130.52	13.30	4,940	Kelly Creek, Oregon.
Cogswell Creek	4.11	134.63	9.19	4,891	Wood, water, and grass; camping place half-mile up creek.
Crane Creek	3.87	138.50	5.32	4,907	Wood, water, and grass.
Hot Springs	3.25	141.75	2.07	4,760	Ranch.
Lake View, Oreg[1]	2.07	143.82	0.00	4,851	Land-office and seat of Lake County.

[1] For continuation of this route northward to The Dalles, see Route No. 7.

NOTE.—This route was surveyed in 1871, and is the most direct route from Susanville to Alturas and Lake View. Road generally good. From Davis to Crane Creek the road runs just east of Goose Lake, 30 miles long by 5 to 10 wide; water unfit for drinking; superficial area about 198 square miles; altitude, 4,697 feet above sea.

ROUTE No. 5.—*Fort Bidwell, Cal., to Fort Klamath, Oreg., via Ayres Grade (surveyed in 1876).*

[Atlas sheets Nos. 38 and 29.]

Stations.	Distance.			Altitude above sea-level.	Remarks.
	Between consecutive points.	From Fort Bidwell.	From Fort Klamath.		
	Miles.	*Miles.*	*Miles.*	*Feet.*	
Fort Bidwell	0.00	0.00	140.68	4,647	Settlement and military post.
Summit (Bidwell pass, Ayres grade)	8.19	8.19	132.49	7,204	Warner Mountains, divide between Goose Lake (Pit River or Sacramento Basin) and Surprise Valley (Great Interior Basin).
Alturas and Lakeview road	4.30	12.49	128.19	4,844	Eastern shore of Goose Lake.
California and Oregon line	3.58	16.07	124.61	4,940	State line monument No. 12 on 42d parallel.
Kelly Creek, Oreg	1.61	17.68	123.00	4,891	New Pine Creek post-office.
Cogswell Creek	4.11	21.79	118.89	4,907	Good camping place up creek one-half mile.
Crane Creek	3.87	25.66	115.02		
Hot Springs	3.25	28.91	111.77	4,760	Sulphur Springs.
Lakeview, Oreg	2.07	30.98	109.70	4,851	Land office and seat of Lake County.
Warner road	11.84	42.82	97.86	4,920	Road to Warner turns north; part of old Oregon and California military road.
Phelps Ranch	8.50	51.32	89.36	4,953	Wood, water, and grass.
Drews Valley (post-office)					
Prines Ranch	28.39	79.71	60.97		Wood, water, and grass; forage for sale.
Sprague River Valley	16.34	96.05	44.63	4,250	Sub-agency for Klamath Indians; forage for sale.
Vainax	13.73	109.78	30.90	4,143	Eugene road turns north toward Klamath marsh.
Eugene City road[1]	20.00	129.78	10.90		Good water, wood, and grass.
Williamsons River Bridge	4.80	134.58	6.10	4,156	Wood, water, and grass; road to north for The Dalles
Klamath Indian Agency	6.10	140.68	0.00	4,108	Military post; water, wood, and grazing.
Fort Klamath					

[1] For distances northward to The Dalles, see Routes Nos. 7, 8, and 9.

NOTE.—Ayres road, completed in 1878, affords the most direct route from Fort Bidwell to Fort Klamath. The distance via the older Lassens Pass road is 8.59 miles greater, as shown below, viz: Fort Bidwell southward to forks of road, 4.12 miles; forks of road westward to summit Warner Range (6,201 feet), 2.33 miles; summit to junction with Alturas and Lakeview road, 7.85 miles; junction to Willow Ranch post-office, 2.38 miles; Willow Ranch to Lakeview, 32.69 miles. Total, Bidwell to Lakeview, 39.57 miles.

ITINERARIES OF ROUTES.

ROUTE No. 6.—*Fort Klamath, Oreg., to Fort Bidwell, Cal., via Old Camp Warner, Oregon.*

[Atlas sheets Nos. 29 and 38.]

Stations.	Distance.			Altitude above sea-level.	Remarks.
	Between consecutive points.	From Klamath.	From Bidwell.		
	Miles.	*Miles.*	*Miles.*	*Feet.*	
Fort Klamath	0.00	0.00	180.70	4,108	Military post.
Yainax	44.63	44.63	136.07		Sub-agency for Klamath Indians.
Drews Valley	44.73	89.36	91.34	4,953	Phelps ranch; wood, water, and grass.
Forks of road	8.50	97.86	82.84	4,920	To Lakeview eastward 11.84 miles.
Cross-road	14.45	112.31	68.39	4,856	Main road from Lakeview northward. (See Route No. 8).
Summit	1.70	114.01	66.69	4,930	Divide between Goose Lake (Sacramento Basin) and Crooked Creek (Great Interior Basin).
Antler	1.06	115.07	65.63	4,719	Post-office in 1877, now discontinued.
Crooked Creek	1.95	117.02	63.68	4,818	Camping place.
Summit	3.89	120.91	59.79	6,864	Crest of Warner Mountains; divide between Crooked and Honey Creeks, and Great Interior Basin.
Camp Warner	6.81	127.72	52.98	5,760	Abandoned post; wood, water, and grass.
Forks of road	7.18	134.90	45.80	5,374	Eastward to Jones Ranch, 9.4 miles. (See Route No. 9.) Road to Bidwell turns south.
Do	1.80	136.70	44.00	5,335	Northeastward to Jones Ranch, 9.57 miles. These forks come together 6.57 miles west of Jones Ranch.
Forks of road, east of Sugar Loaf Peak[1]	5.35	142.05	38.65	5,662	To Lakeview, via Kamas Prairie and Warner Cañon, 25.49 miles. Bidwell road keeps south.
Warner Creek	7.70	149.75	30.95		Joins Deep Creek about 1½ miles to southward.
Deep Creek	5.00	154.75	25.95		Northeast corner Long Valley.
Forks of road near State line	12.40	167.15	13.55	5,443	Winter road from Bidwell. (See Route No. 9.)
Lake Annie	8.88	176.03	4.67	5,060	Pond east of road.
Fort Bidwell	4.67	180.70	0.00	4,647	Settlement and military post.

[1] If the wagon-road, via Lakeview, Warner Cañon, and Kamas Prairie, be taken, the distance would be: Fort Klamath to Lakeview, 109.70 miles; Lakeview to ranch at mouth of Warner Cañon (5,060 feet), 15.65 miles; ranch to summit of Warner Mountains (5,820 feet), 4 miles; summit to junction with Bidwell road (5,662 feet), 15.84 miles; junction of roads to Camp Warner, 5, 14.33 miles. Total, 154.52 miles. Camp Warner (*via* Lakeview), 149.52 miles. Road open during summer and fall; camping facilities good.

NOTE.—These routes were surveyed in 1877 and 1878. They are the most direct from Fort Klamath to Old Camp Warner, and from Old Camp Warner to Fort Bidwell. The latter is called the summer road, and averages 1,000 feet higher than the route to Bidwell, via Warner Lake Valley, and is about 12 miles shorter. (See Route No. 9.) From Crooked Creek to Old Camp Warner (10.7 miles) is by trail.

ROUTE No. 7.—*Fort Bidwell, Cal., to The Dalles, Oreg., via Klamath Indian Agency.*

[Atlas sheets Nos. 38, 29, and 20.]

Stations.	Distance. Between consecutive points.	Distance. From Bidwell.	Distance. From The Dalles.	Altitude above sealevel.	Remarks.
	Miles.	*Miles.*	*Miles.*	*Feet.*	
Fort Bidwell	0.00	0.00	406.77	4,647	Settlement and military post.
Klamath Indian Agency	134.58	134.58	272.19	4,156	To Fort Klamath, 6.1 miles. (See Route No. 5 for details).
Williamson River (west bank)	11.70	146.28	260.49	4,387	West bank of river; wood, water, and grass.
Big Spring	22.85	169.13	237.64	4,552	Wood, water, and grass.
Corral Spring[1]	21.64	190.77	216.00	4,783	Wood, water, and grass; on Eugene road. (See Route No. 7a.)
Little Meadows, east fork Deschutes River	17.10	207.87	198.90	4,258	Wood, water, and grass; to Summit Lake, westward, 26 miles.
Deschutes River (east bank)	21.74	229.61	177.16	4,081	Wood, water, and grass.
Big Meadows	13.90	243.51	163.26	4,124	Do.
Farewell Bend[2]	15.80	259.31	147.46	3,621	Ranch east bank Deschutes River; forage for sale.
Prineville road	10.80	270.11	136.66	3,311	To Prineville, 22 miles northeast.
Carnicals Ranch, Crooked River	15.04	285.15	121.62	2,794	Forage for sale; to Prineville, eastward, 13.3 miles.
Lucra Ranch	15.10	300.25	106.52	2,443	Forage for sale.
Sheep Ranch	10.83	311.08	95.69		Do.
Lodge Pole Creek	13.73	324.81	81.96	1,648	Water and grass; wood scarce.
Deschutes Ferry	3.61	328.42	78.35	1,358	Great Cañon of Deschutes River (here about 1,000 feet deep).
Warm Spring Agency	2.31	330.73	76.04	1,514	Wood scarce; grass on neighboring hills.
Warm Springs	*10.00	340.73	66.04	1,529	Warm Springs River.
Road to Sinamese marsh	*4.75	345.48	61.29	3,670	Sinamese Indian settlement, 7.5 miles.
Neene Spring	*7.50	352.98	53.79	2,914	Water, wood, and grass.

* Distances from plot.

[1] To Summit Lake (5,420 feet) 29.1 miles northwest; southward to Willow Spring on Eugene road, 15 miles; Willow Spring to Silver Lake post-office, 36 miles. (See Route 7a.)
[2] Old Emigrant Ford (river about 400 feet wide and 2 feet deep; rocky bottom). For side roads to Oak Grove and Tygh Valley, see 7c and 7c.

ROUTE No. 7.—*Fort Bidwell, Cal., to The Dalles, Oreg., via Klamath Indian Agency*—Continued.

[Atlas sheets Nos. 38, 39, and 20.]

Stations.	Distance.			Altitude above sea-level.	Remarks.
	Between consecutive points.	From Bidwell.	From The Dalles.		
	Miles.	*Miles.*	*Miles.*	*Feet.*	
Oak Grove (store)	*7.40	360.38	46.39	2,148	Stage station in valley of Wapenitia Creek; wood, water and grass.
Wapenitia (post-office)	*2.00	362.38	44.39		Agricultural settlement.
Tygh Valley	*13.50	375.88	30.89	1,089	Agricultural settlement; forage for sale.
Kingsley (post-office)	*5.60	381.48	25.29		Settlement on Fifteen Mile Creek.
Dufur (post-office)	*10.50	391.98	14.79	1,267	
The Dalles	14.79	406.77	0.00	180	Large town on south bank of Columbia River; seat of Wasco County; station on Northern Pacific Railroad.

* Distances from plot.

NOTE.—This road was surveyed in 1878. It follows the eastern base of the Cascade Range, keeping between those mountains and the western rim of the Great Interior Basin. For side routes from Prineville, Oak Grove, and Tygh Valley, see Routes 7 *b, c,* and 7.

ROUTE No. 7a.—*Summit Lake, Cascade Mountains, to Beatties Butte, Oreg., via old Oregon and California military road.*

[Atlas sheets Nos. 29 and 30.]

Stations.	Distance.			Altitude above sea-level.	Remarks.
	Between consecutive points.	From Summit Lake.	From Beatties Butte.		
	Miles.	*Miles.*	*Miles.*	*Feet.*	
Summit Lake	0.0	0.0	257.7	5,610	Pass south of Diamond Peak, Cascade Range.
Corral Spring	29.1	29.1	228.6	4,783	Road south to Klamath and north to Prineville.
Willow Spring	15.0	44.1	213.6	4,682	West of Round Butte. Road runs south parallel to Klamath road.
Old Bridge	*20.0	64.1	193.6	4,350	South of Klamath marsh.
Junction with Klamath and Bidwell road	17.6	81.7	176.0	4,250	Sprague River Valley.
Yainax	13.7	95.4	162.3		Sprague River Valley. (See Routes Nos. 5 and 6.)
Forks of road east of Lakeview	67.0	162.4	95.3	4,920	To Lakeview, 11.8 miles. (See Routes Nos. 5 and 6.)
Ranch at mouth of Warner Cañon	*12.0	174.4	83.3	5,060	See Route No. 6.
Jones Ranch	34.8	209.2	48.5	4,466	See Route No. 9.
Crooks Bridge	*8.5	217.7	40.0		Old stone bridge, Warner Lakes.
Old Camp Warner	*18.0	235.7	22.0		Abandoned post.
Beatties Butte	*22.0	257.7	0.0	5,730	Due north of Beatties Butte.

* Distances from plot.

NOTE.—This table shows the portion examined by this survey of the old military land-grant road, extending from Oregon City and Eugene in the Willamette Valley over the Cascade Range across Southern Oregon to the Idaho line west of Silver City, via Sprague River Valley, Warner Lake Valley, Old Camp Warner, and Old Camp C. F. Smith. Portions of this old road are still in use, as shown in Routes Nos. 5 and 6; it is generally referred to as the "Eugene Road." Route No. 7b shows part of another old land-grant road extending across Central Oregon, known as the Willamette Valley and Cascade military road. Route No. 9 shows part of a third land-grant road running from The Dalles via Cañon City to the Oregon and Idaho line at Old Fort Boise on the Snake River. It is known as The Dalles military road.

ROUTE No. 7 b.—*Prineville, Oreg., to Fish Lake, Cascade Mountains, Oregon.*

[Atlas sheet No. 20C.]

Stations.	Distance.			Altitude above sea-level.	Remarks.
	Between consecutive points.	From Prineville.	From Fish Lake.		
	Miles.	*Miles.*	*Miles.*	*Feet.*	
Prineville	0.00	0.00	71.45	2,899	Thriving village, seat of Crook County.
Carmicals Ranch	13.20	13.20	58.25	2,794	Water and wood; forage can be bought.
Deschutes Bridge	13.10	26.30	45.15	2,563	Water and wood; forage can be bought; toll-bridge.
Old Camp Polk (post-office)[1]	14.45	40.75	30.70	3,079	Water and wood; grass scarce.
Parrish Ranch[2]	5.30	46.05	25.40	3,330	Water and wood; forage can be bought.
Cash Creek	9.40	55.45	16.00	3,963	Water, wood, and grass.
Summit Cascade Mountains	4.00	59.45	12.00	4,843	Locally "summit of first range."
Fish Lake	12.00	71.45	0.00	3,155	Water, wood, and grass; store.

[1] From here the McKenzie road turns southwestward, crossing the Cascade range south of the Three Sisters and passing down the McKenzie River to Springfield, in the Willamette Valley. From Springfield to McKenzie's Bridge is a mail route (once a week).
[2] From here an Indian trail leads to Warm Spring Agency, which is seldom traveled on account of the dangerous fording of Matoles River. The distances are: To Matoles River ford, 20.1 miles; ford to Warm Spring Agency, 22.9 miles. Total, 43 miles.

NOTE.—This table shows part of the old land grant road known as the Willamette Valley and Cascade military road. A portion of the same road is shown on Route No. 9, from Beaver Creek to Old Camp Curry. The road extends from Albany, in the Willamette Valley, over the Cascade range, through Central Oregon to Old Fort Boise, on the Snake River, via Prineville, Ochoco, and Fort Harney. The greater portion is still in use for local travel and mails.

ROUTE No. 7 c.—*Oak Grove Settlement, Oreg., to toll-gate west of Mount Hood on Barlow road.*

[Atlas sheet No. 20A.]

Stations.	Distance.			Altitude above sea-level.	Remarks.
	Between consecutive points.	From Oak Grove.	From toll-gate.		
	Miles.	*Miles.*	*Miles.*	*Feet.*	
Oak Grove	0.00	0.00	45.42	2,414	Large settlement, store, and post-office; water, wood, and grass.
Kamas Prairie	17.50	17.50	27.92	3,020	Water, wood, and grass.
Big Prairie	12.71	30.21	15.21	3,335	Water, wood, and grass; swampy.
Summit Prairie[1]	4.50	34.71	10.71	3,694	Water and wood; grass scarce; store; forage can be obtained.
Cascade Range	2.27	36.98	8.44	3,748	Water, wood, and grass; swampy.
Government Prairie	8.44	45.42	0.00	1,675	Water and wood; forage can be bought.

[1] Best point from which to make the ascent of Mount Hood. The Barlow road from Tygh Valley comes in here. At 1.2 miles west of Summit Prairie is the highest point of the road, 3,918 feet above sea. The road continues westward to the Willamette Valley.

ROUTE No. 7 d.—*Tygh Valley, Oregon, to toll-gate west of Mount Hood, via Barlow toll-gate.*

[Atlas sheet No. 20A.]

Stations.	Distance.			Altitude above sea-level.	Remarks.
	Between consecutive points.	From Tygh Valley.	From toll-gate.		
	Miles.	*Miles.*	*Miles.*	*Feet.*	
Tygh Valley	0.00	0.00	49.75	1,089	Large settlement; forage can be bought.
Barlows Toll-gate, or Stricklands Ranch	12.88	12.88	36.87	2,096	Water, wood, and grass.
White River Crossing	14.52	27.40	22.35	2,939	Water and wood; grass scarce.
Summit Prairie[1]	11.64	39.04	10.71	3,694	Water and wood; grass scarce; store; forage can be bought.
Government Prairie	2.27	41.31	8.44	3,748	Water, wood, and grass.
Toll-gate foot of grade	8.44	49.75	0.00	1,674	

[1] Best point from which to make the ascent of Mount Hood. Road from Oak Grove joins Barlow road here.

ROUTE No. 8.—*Fort Bidwell, Cal., to The Dalles, Oreg. (desert route).*

[Atlas sheets Nos. 38, 29, and 20.]

Stations.	Distance.			Altitude above sea-level.	Remarks.
	Between consecutive points.	From Fort Bidwell.	From The Dalles.		
	Miles.	*Miles.*	*Miles.*	*Feet.*	
Fort Bidwell	0.00	0.00	324.40	4,647	Military post and settlement.
California and Oregon line	16.07	16.07	308.33	4,940	State line monument No. 12, on 42d parallel.
Lakeview	14.91	30.98	293.42	4,851	Seat of Lake County, Oreg.; land office.
Ranch at mouth of Warner Cañon	5.65	36.63	287.77	5,060	Old Oregon and California military (or Eugene) road turns up cañon eastward to Old Camp Warner, 34-17 miles; to Jones Ranch (Route No. 9), 34.76 miles.
Cross-roads	3.60	40.23	284.17	4,850	Drews Valley and Antler road; to Drews Valley, southwest, 22.95 miles; to Antler, northeast, 2.76 miles.
Summit	6.27	46.50	277.90	5,280	Great Interior Basin divide; heavy timber.
Sawmill	2.35	48.85	275.55	5,262	Wood, water, and grass.
Moss Ranch	9.52	58.37	266.03	4,828	No wood; water and grass.
Chewaucan (post-office)	8.63	67.00	257.40	4,495	Wood, water, and grass.
Paisley (post-office)	3.96	70.96	253.44	4,456	Do.
Millers Ranch	9.13	80.09	244.31	4,420	Wood, water, and grass; south shore Summer Lake.
Summer Lake (post-office)	17.30	97.39	227.01	4,163	Wood, water, and grass; Partons Ranch.
Forks of road[1]	12.30	109.69	214.71		Road turns westward to Silver Lake post-office.
Durands Ranch	3.58	113.27	211.13	4,312	East shore Silver Lake (fresh water); forage and fuel for sale.
Road to Buttons Ranch[2]	16.94	130.21	194.19		East to Buttons Ranch (Christmas Lake), 3 miles; forage and fuel for sale.
Road to Buttons	1.70	131.91	192.49	4,235	East to Buttons Ranch, 2.6 miles.
Langtons Ranch	20.28	152.19	172.21	5,163	Wood and grass; small water-hole; water scant and poor.
Summit (Langtons Pass)	1.00	153.19	171.21	5,225	Great Interior Basin divide.
Water-hole	19.24	172.43	151.97	4,480	No wood; grass scarce; water not permanent.
Greens Ranch	10.34	182.77	141.63	4,479	Wood, water, and grass plenty.

[1] Westward to Silver Lake post-office (mail once a week), 15.7 miles. [2] In the sandy desert, about 11 miles east of Buttons Ranch, petrified animal remains are to be found.

210   ITINERARIES OF ROUTES.

ROUTE No. 8.—*Fort Bidwell, Cal., to The Dalles, Oreg. (desert route)*—Continued.

[Atlas sheets Nos. 18, 19, and 20.]

Stations.	Distance.			Altitude above sea-level.	Remarks.
	Between consecutive points.	From Fort Bidwell.	From The Dalles.		
	Miles.	*Miles.*	*Miles.*	*Feet.*	
Prineville (post-office)	25.93	208.70	115.70	2,899	Thriving village at junction of Ochoco and Crooked Rivers; seat of Crook County.
Willow Creek	18.10	226.80	97.60		Wood, water, and grass.
Hay Creek (post-office)	*9.00	235.80	88.60		Settlement.
Cross Keys	*8.00	243.80	80.60		Do.
Forks of road	*21.25	265.05	59.35	3,252	To Cross Hollow, by eastern fork, 8¼ miles.
Bake Oven (post-office)	*10.00	275.05	49.35	2,672	On Dalles military road.
Sherars Bridge (Deschutes River)	*19.25	294.30	30.10	702	Lower end of Tygh Valley; forage for sale.
The Dalles	*30.10	324.40	0.00	180	Rapidly growing town; seat of Wasco County; on Columbia River; head of navigation of portion of river between the Cascades and Narrows east of town; principal supply depot for Central Oregon.

* Distance from plot.

NOTE.—The above route, surveyed in 1876, crosses Central Oregon in a general north and south direction, and is the most direct road from Bidwell and Lakeview to The Dalles. Good camping facilities and numerous settlements are to be found from Bidwell to Durands Ranch, on Silver Lake; hence to Prineville, the road is over the desert country of Central Oregon. It is a desolate region; in some places rocky, in others with a scant growth of sage-brush, and some juniper on the hills. This desert country, especially the hilly parts about Bear Creek and Bear Creek Butte (near Greens), is a winter range for the deer of the Cascade Range. From Prineville north the route is through a well settled region. From The Dalles to Prineville there is a mail thrice, and from Lakeview to Summer Lake twice a week.

ROUTE No. 9.—*Fort Bidwell, Cal., to The Dalles, Oreg., via Old Camp Curry.*

[Atlas sheets Nos. 38, 29, and 20.]

Stations.	Distance.			Altitude above sea-level.	Remarks.
	Between consecutive points.	From Fort Bidwell.	From The Dalles.		
	Miles.	*Miles.*	*Miles.*	*Feet.*	
Fort Bidwell	0.00	0.00	365.42	4,647	Settlement and military post.
Lake Annie	4.67	4.67	360.75	5,060	Pond east of road.
Forks of road [1]	8.88	13.55	351.87	5,443	On north bank of Twelve-mile Creek, near California and Oregon State line.
Wallace Ranch (Deep Creek)	15.85	29.40	336.02	4,487	Warner Lake Valley; water and grass.
Drakes Ranch	11.00	40.40	325.02	4,559	Warner Lake Valley; road forks eastward to Old Camp Warner.
Jones Ranch [2]	8.00	48.40	317.02	4,466	On Honey Creek; good water and grass.
Forks of road north of Warner Lakes	33.00	81.40	284.02	4,738	Road southward to Old Camp Warner.
Mule Spring	11.70	93.10	272.32	4,738	Good water and grass.
Buzzard Cañon	25.00	118.10	247.32	4,762	Water and grass.

[1] Summer road from Fort Bidwell to Old Camp Warner turns north. (See Route No. 6.)
[2] Here the Old Camp Warner road turns westward, forming with the above the winter road from Bidwell, viz:

Stations.	Distance.			Altitude above sea-level.	Remarks.
		From Fort Bidwell.	From The Dalles.		
		Miles.	*Miles.*	*Feet.*	
Fort Bidwell		0.00	0.00	4,647	
Jones Ranch		48.40	48.40	4,467	
Forks of road		6.57	54.97	5,335	To Bidwell, 44 miles; to Lakeview (via Warner Cañon), 33.84 miles.
Summer road from Bidwell		2.90	57.87	5,374	
Old Camp Warner		7.18	65.05	5,730	Abandoned as military post.

ROUTE No. 9.—*Fort Bidwell, Cal., to The Dalles, Oreg., via Old Camp Curry*—Continued.

[Atlas sheets Nos. 38, 39, and 20.]

Stations.	Distance.			Altitude above sea-level.	Remarks.
	Between consecutive points.	From Fort Bidwell.	From The Dalles.		
	Miles.	*Miles.*	*Miles.*	*Feet.*	
Warm Spring	14.00	132.10	233.32	4,071	Good water and grass; Harney road turns eastward.
Hoskins Ranch	9.70	141.80	223.62	4,139	On Silver Creek; good water and grass.
Willamette Valley and Cascade military road.	13.30	155.10	210.32		Old military road from Albany, Willamette Valley, to Old Fort Boise, Snake River, via Camp Polk, Prineville (Ochoco), Old Camp Curry, and Old Fort Harney.
Old Camp Curry	11.00	166.10	199.32	4,273	Evergreen post-office, on Silver Creek; good water and grass.
Buck Creek	15.50	181.60	183.82	5,297	Headwaters of creek; good grass.
Hardin (post-office), on Twelve-mile Creek	13.00	194.60	170.82	4,657	Good water and grass.
Prineville road	6.50	201.10	164.32		Road to Prineville forks northwest.
Cross-roads	2.80	203.90	161.52	4,137	West to Prineville: east down Grindstone Creek to settlement near junction of Wolf and Beaver Creeks.
Paulina (post-office)	5.20	209.10	156.32		Settlement on Willamette Valley and Cascade military road; 0.5 mile above mouth of Paulina Creek and 1.6 mile below Wolf Creek.
Beaver Creek Crossing	3.00	212.10	153.32		
Forks of road	2.00	214.10	151.32	3,840	South end of Paulina Valley; Willamette Valley and Cascade military road turns westward to upper Ochoco and Prineville.
Big Summit Prairie	16.75	230.85	134.57		Good water and grass.
Forks of road	11.00	241.85	123.57	5,124	Left road and traveled by trail to McNeals Ranch, on Dalles military road.
McNeals Ranch[1]	5.00	246.85	118.57	4,003	Military road from Dalles to Boise, via Camp Watson and Cañon City.
Mountain House	1.75	248.60	116.82	4,038	On Mountain Creek; good water and grass.
Mitchell (post-office)[2]	8.75	257.35	108.07	2,737	Settlement at forks of Bridge Creek; forage for sale.
Bridge Creek Station	11.02	268.37	97.05	1,830	Good water; forage for sale.

[1] Eastward to Old Camp Watson (Edgars), 4 miles.   [2] A road turns up south fork Bridge Creek and strikes fork of Mountain (Badger) Creek in 5.25 miles.

ROUTE No. 9.—*Fort Bidwell, Cal., to The Dalles, Oreg., via Old Camp Curry*—Continued.

[Atlas sheets Nos. 38, 29, and 20.]

Stations.	Distance.			Altitude above sea-level.	Remarks.
	Between consecutive points.	From Fort Bidwell.	From The Dalles.		
	Miles.	*Miles.*	*Miles.*	*Feet.*	
Burnt Ranch (post-office)	6.25	274.62	90.80	1,561	On John Day River, 1¼ miles below mouth of Bridge Creek.
Cherry Creek	5.80	280.42	85.00	1,612	Good water and grass.
Ranch at mouth of Muddy Creek	7.50	287.92	77.50	1,596	Do.
Currant Creek Station	3.70	291.62	73.80	2,142	Do.
Antelope (post-office)	10.45	302.07	63.35	2,844	Good water; forage for sale.
Cross Hollows (post-office)	6.00	308.07	57.35	3,197	Do.
Bake Oven (post-office)	8.00	316.07	49.35	2,672	Do.
Salt Spring	10.25	326.32	39.10		Good water; forage for sale.
Sherars Bridge (post-office)	9.00	335.32	30.10	702	
Nansene (post-office)	13.00	348.32	17.10	2,750	
The Dalles	17.10	365.42	0.00	180	Important town on south bank of Columbia River, on Northern Pacific Railroad; seat of Wasco County; about 1,500 inhabitants in 1878; now doubles that number.

NOTE.—This table is compiled from surveys of 1878. Between Jones Ranch and The Dalles the distances were estimated and afterwards checked in plotting. The southern half of the route lies in the Great Interior Basin, the northern in the Columbia Basin, the divide being crossed about three miles south of camp on Buck Creek. Altitude of divide, 5,513 feet above sea. From Fort Bidwell to Warm Springs the route is over the Bidwell and Harney road. Twenty-three miles northwestwardly from Warm Springs the Old Willamette Valley and Cascade military road is struck and followed to south end of Paulina Valley. From here the route is north until The Dalles military road is intersected at McNeals and followed to The Dalles. There is a mail three times a week to Cañon City over this part of the route, and a weekly mail from Priceville to Old Camp Harney, via Paulina and Old Camp Curry (Evergreen).

ROUTE No. 10.—*Cottonwood, Tehama County, California, to Susanville, Cal.*

[Atlas sheets Nos. 46B and 47A.]

Stations.	Distance.			Altitude above sea-level.	Remarks.
	Between consecutive points.	From Cottonwood.	From Susanville.		
	Miles.	*Miles.*	*Miles.*	*Feet.*	
Cottonwood	0.00	0.00	116.91		Station on Oregon Division Central Pacific Railroad.
Balls Ferry	*6.00	6.00	100.91		Sacramento River, about midway between Bear and Battle Creeks.
Forks of road[1]				445	North of Balls Ferry. Road turns eastward; river road keeps northwestward toward Old Fort Reading.
Bear Creek crossing	3.70	9.70	107.21		
Schulers Ranch	2.48	12.18	104.73	430	Near Dirschs Ranch.
Forks of road	4.97	17.15	99.76	1,075	
Ogburns Ranch	2.89	20.04	96.87	1,557	Road to Bear Creek Falls and Danahs saw-mill.
Shingletown (post-office)	3.97	24.01	92.90	2,270	Wood, water, and pasturage.
Eureka mill	4.51	28.52	88.39	3,510	Small settlement.
Loomis Ranch	8.62	37.14	79.77	3,988	Saw-mill.
	3.93	41.07	75.84	4,356	Wood and water; pasturage at Smiths Ranch, 0.6 mile westward.
Noble Pass, divide between Canoe and Battle Creeks.	7.79	48.86	68.05	5,963	Northwest from Lassens Butte.
Canoe Creek	11.46	60.32	56.59	5,359	Third or northern crossing. Camping place 2 miles below.
Forks of road	7.18	67.50	49.41	4,991	Road forks northward to Old Fort Crook and Yreka, via Lockharts Ferry.
Poison Lake Pass, Sierra Nevada divide	11.00	78.50	38.41	5,409	Western rim of Great Interior Basin.
Forks of road	2.21	80.71	36.20	5,365	Road to Surprise Valley forks northwestward.
Pine Creek	7.01	87.72	29.19	5,409	Wood, water, and grass; road forks northward to Surprise Valley.
Forks of road[2]	3.76	91.48	25.43	5,365	Cross road southward to Red Bluff and Susanville road.

*Distance from post-office. †Distance from plot.

[1] To Jelleys Ferry (southward), 13.20 miles; Jelleys to Red Bluff, 12 miles. Total, Forks to Red Bluff, 25.20 miles.
[2] Half a mile eastward a road forks northward to Surprise Valley. The distances on the cross-road southward are: Forks of road to Sierra Nevada divide (5,570 feet), 8.02 miles; divide to Red Bluff and Susanville road, 10.41 miles.

U. S. GEOGRAPHICAL SURVEYS. 215

ROUTE No. 10.—*Cottonwood, Tehama County, California, to Susanville, Cal.*—Continued.

[Atlas sheets Nos. 46B and 47A.]

Stations.	Distance.			Altitude above sea-level.	Remarks.
	Between consecutive points.	From Cottonwood.	From Susanville.		
	Miles.	*Miles.*	*Miles.*	*Feet.*	
Bridge Creek	6.24	97.72	19.19	5,509	Wood, water, and grazing. About 1 mile east of Bridge Creek a wagon trail forks eastward to Eagle Lake.
Forks of road [1]	12.00	109.72	7.19	5,036	Wood and water; pasturage at Stocktons Mill.
Forks of road	1.77	111.49	5.42	4,765	Junction with Red Bluff and Susanville road (see Route No. 10).
Susanville	5.42	116.91	0.00	4,195	Seat of Lassen County.

[1] To Stocktons mill, 0.72 mile; Stocktons to Red Bluff and Susanville road, 2 miles.

NOTE.—Route surveyed in 1878. Up to the junction with the Vreka, Old Fort Crook and Susanville road, this is part of the Sacramento and Surprise Valley road. From this to the fork at Poison Lake the roads are one; here the Surprise Valley road turns northeastward, and the Vreka and Old Fort Crook road keeps southeast toward Susanville.

ROUTE No. 11.—*Red Bluff, Cal., to Susanville, Cal., via Tehama County wagon-road.*

[Atlas sheets Nos. 46B, 47A, and 47B.]

Stations.	Distance.			Altitude above sea-level.	Remarks.
	Between consecutive points.	From Red Bluff.	From Susanville.		
	Miles.	*Miles.*	*Miles.*	*Feet.*	
Red Bluff	0.00	0.00	101.79	308	Large town, on west bank of Sacramento River; station of Oregon Division Central Pacific Railroad; seat of Tehama County.
Birds Ranch	*11.60	11.60	90.19		On Paines Creek.
Forks of road[1]	*2.40	14.00	87.79	598	Gates Ranch, one-third mile distant across Paines Creek.
Wilsons Ranch	5.77	19.77	82.02	1,114	Wood, water, and pasturage.
Andersons Ranch	3.50	23.27	78.52	1,837	Road to north for Battle Creek.
Forks of road at Hickmans Ranch	1.19	24.46	77.33	1,925	Wood, water, and pasturage; to Belle Mill by southeast fork, 9.46 miles.
Forks of road	11.77	36.23	65.56	4,353	To Belle Mill via southern fork, 4.78 miles.
Battle Creek Meadows	4.92	41.15	60.64	4,700	Toll-gate; wood, water, and pasturage.
Tylers Ranch	8.45	49.60	52.19	4,802	Wood, water, and pasturage.
Willow Creek[2]	10.25	59.85	41.94	5,038	Wood and water; no pasturage.
Warner Creek Bridge[3]	1.48	61.33	40.46	4,826	Do.
Forks of road near Martins Ranch	5.50	66.83	34.96	4,464	To Prattville via west side Big Meadows, 9.02 miles.
Johnsons Ranch	1.75	68.58	33.21	4,379	To Prattville south 8 miles.
Forks of road east of Johnsons[4]	7.92	71.50	30.29	4,713	To Prattville via east side Big Meadows, also Greenville and Taylorville.
Cross-road	5.58	77.08	24.71	4,968	North to Pine Creek, Yreka road, 18.43 miles.
Prattville road	5.02	82.10	19.69	4,927	Prattville, 15.27 miles southwest (Route 12).

* Distances from plot.
[1] To Jellerys Ferry, 9.41 miles.
[2] Road up Creek to Willow Lake, 6.15 miles; trail thence to Geyser (head of Willow Creek) and to Hot Lake, Hot Springs, and Soda Lake, south of Lassens Butte.
[3] About one-half mile west of bridge road turns up creek to Hot Lake, distant 10½ miles.
[4] To Prattville, 8.72 miles; to Greenville, 19.93 miles.

ROUTE No. 11.—*Red Bluff, Cal., to Susanville, Cal., via Tehama County wagon-road*—Continued.

[Atlas sheets Nos. 46B, 47A, and 47B.]

Stations.	Distance.			Altitude above sea-level.	Remarks.
	Between consecutive points.	From Red Bluff.	From Susanville.		
	Miles.	*Miles.*	*Miles.*	*Feet.*	
Goodrichs	1.77	83.87	17.92	4,883	Wood, water, and pasturage.
Susanville Pass	4.56	88.43	13.36	5,507	Sierra Nevada divide.
Forks of road	4.34	92.77	9.02	4,562	Stocktons Mill, 2 miles northward; Yreka road, 2.72 miles. (See Route 9.)
Do	3.60	96.37	5.42	4,765	Junction with Yreka and Old Fort Crook road.
Susanville (post-office)	5.42	101.79	0.00	4,195	Seat of Lassen County, on Susan Creek.

NOTE.—This road was surveyed in 1878. It is the most direct route (excepting the Belle Mill road) from Red Bluff to Susanville. If the river be crossed directly at Red Bluff the distances via Belle Mill are as follows: Red Bluff to Antelope Creek 5.50 miles; Antelope Creek to Sheep Ranch, 6.37 miles; Sheep Ranch to Williams Ranch, 7.00 miles; Williams Ranch to Belle Mill, 10.62 miles; Belle Mill to junction with Tehama County road, 4.78 miles. Total, Red Bluff to forks of road, 34.29 miles, or 1.94 miles shorter than above.

ROUTE No. 12.—*Chico, Cal., to Susanville, Cal., via Chico Creek toll-road.*

[Atlas sheets Nos. 47C and 47A.]

Stations.	Distance.			Altitude above sea-level.	Remarks.
	Between consecutive points.	From Chico.	From Susanville.		
	Miles.	*Miles.*	*Miles.*	*Feet.*	
Chico (post-office)	0.00	0.00	98.13	177	Large town, seat of Butte County, station on Oregon Division Central Pacific Railroad.
Ten Mile House	10.24	10.24	87.89	1,498	
Toll Gate (Cement Spring)	3.57	13.81	84.32	2,001	
Forest Ranch	2.17	15.98	82.15	2,217	Welds Station; wood and water; no pasturage.
Lomo	13.57	29.55	68.58	3,848	Wood, water, and pasturage.
Bridge over Butte Creek and forks of road.	6.18	35.73	62.40	4,398	Wood and water; to Chaparral House, 4.53 miles southward.
Colbys Ranch	3.71	39.44	58.69	4,990	Wood, water, and pasturage.
Summit	5.25	44.69	53.44	6,619	Divide between Butte Creek and Butt Creek.
Toll House	3.13	47.82	50.31	5,427	Summit Ranch (formerly Dyes); wood, water, and pasturage.
Bridge and forks of road[1]	8.11	55.93	42.20	4,519	Road north to Soldiers Meadow and Deer Creek Meadow.
Forks of road	6.12	62.05	36.08	4,424	Northward to Red Bluff road (near Marlins), 7.90 miles.
Prattville (post-office)	1.12	63.17	34.96	4,394	Village, hotel, pasturage.
Forks of road, 0.13 mile west of Mitchells.	5.80	68.97	29.16	4,285	Altitude of Mitchells Ranch.
Forks of road, 0.12 mile east of Mitchells.	0.25	69.22	28.91		Wood, water, and pasturage at Mitchells.
Landts	4.32	73.54	24.59	4,737	Clear Creek.
Junction of Red Bluff Road, near Coppervale post-office.	4.90	78.44	19.69	4,927	Red Bluff, 82.1 miles westward. (See Route 10.)

[1] This route is part of the old Lassen emigrant route to the Sacramento Valley. After leaving Deer Creek Meadows it follows the ridge between Mill and Deer Creeks to Sesma, Sacramento Valley, and is now impassable for wagons. The distances are: Forks road to foot Deer Creek Meadows, 10.18 miles; Deer Creek Meadows to Sesma, 44.00 miles.

ROUTE No. 12.—*Chico, Cal., to Susanville, Cal., via Chico, Creek Toll-road*—Continued.

[Atlas sheets Nos. 47C and 47A.]

Stations.	Distance.			Altitude above sea-level.	Remarks.
	Between consecutive points.	From Chico.	From Susanville.		
	Miles.	*Miles.*	*Miles.*	*Feet.*	
Goodrichs	1.77	80.21	17.92	4,883	Mountain Meadows.
Susanville Pass	4.56	84.77	13.36	5,507	Sierra Nevada divide.
Susanville (post-office)	13.36	98.13	0.00	4,195	Seat of Lassen County on Susan Creek.

NOTE.—This route was surveyed in 1876. It is a mail route throughout; Chico is the nearest railroad point in the Sacramento Valley by wagon-road to Susanville, Red Bluff being next (Route 11). Reno, Nevada, on the Central Pacific Railroad (Route 2), is nearer than either and is the main mail station for Susanville

ROUTE No. 13.—*Chico, Cal., to Reno, Nev.*

[Atlas sheets Nos. 47A, 47B, 47C, and 47D.]

Stations.	Distance.		Altitude above sea-level.	Remarks.
	Between consecutive points.	From Chico.	From Reno.	
	Miles.	*Miles.*	*Miles.*	*Feet.*	
Chico	0.00	0.00	173.44	177	Seat of Butte County. Station on Oregon Division, Central Pacific Railroad.
Butte Creek	1.97	1.97	171.47	146	Oroville road turns southeast.
Centerville[1]	10.98	12.95	160.49	502	Small settlement.
Toll-gate	1.96	14.91	158.53	1,067	Chico Creek toll-road. Wood, water, and pasturage.
Nimshew (post-office)	4.89	19.80	153.64	2,451	Small settlement. Inn.
Hupps Mill[2]	2.70	22.50	150.94	2,667	Road to Dogtown turns off 0.68 mile south.
Powelton (post-office), junction of Oroville road.	4.52	27.02	146.42	3,631	At Inn. To Lovelocks, on Oroville road, 4½ miles southward.
Inskip (post-office)	6.19	33.21	140.23	4,808	Toll-gate. Wood and water; no pasturage.
Chaparral House[3]	3.90	37.11	136.33	5,076	Wood and water; no pasturage.
Butte Creek House	7.67	44.78	128.66	5,758	Wood, water, and pasturage.
Summit	2.69	47.47	125.97	6,638	Divide between Butte Creek and Yellow Creek.
Longville (post-office). (Toll-gate)	8.94	56.41	117.03	4,309	Humbug Valley. Wood, water, and pasturage.
Forks of road	1.46	57.87	115.57	4,611	To Keddieville Store (near Millers, south end Butte Valley), 6.42 miles.
Forks of road	5.80	63.67	109.77	4,695	To Keddieville Store (south), 7.25 miles; Store to Dutch Hill mining camp, 3.2 miles.
Prattville (post-office)	1.63	65.30	108.14	4,394	Inn. Summer resort, Big Meadows, Cal.

[1] At 0.42 mile north across Butte Creek bridge a road turns up creek to Helltown, 2.5 miles from Centerville.
[2] At Hupps a road turns eastward to Lovelocks (post-office) on Oroville road, distant 2.07 miles. From Lovelocks a road continues eastward 5.81 miles to Dooos saw-mill. From Doons a trail runs eastward 9.25 miles to Old Nimshew, deserted mining camp.
[3] At 0.38 mile southwest a road forks north to Chico road at Butte Creek bridge, distance from Chaparral House 4.53 miles. At 0.43 mile northeast a road turns east to Scotts Diggings, distant 12.33 miles from Chaparral House.
[4] At .75 mile east of Prattville a road turns southward to Dutch Hill Mining Camp, 11.61 miles from Prattville.

ROUTE No. 13.—*Chico, Cal., to Reno, Nev.*—Continued.

[Atlas sheets Nos. 47C, 47A, 47B, and 47D.]

Stations.	Distance.			Altitude above sea-level.	Remarks.
	Between consecutive points.	From Chico.	From Reno.		
	Miles.	*Miles.*	*Miles.*	*Feet.*	
Forks of road 0.47 miles northeast of bridge over north fork of Feather River.	4.49	69.79	103.65	4,479	North to Chico and Susanville road, near Mitchells, 6.36 miles.
Greenville (post-office)	10.42	80.21	93.23	3,544	Village. Forage for sale.
Crescent Mills	4.98	85.19	88.25		Post-office.
Arlington Bridge	1.33	86.52	86.92	3,376	North Fork Feather River.
Taylorville (post-office)	4.85	91.37	82.07	3,479	Inn. Forage for sale.
Genesee Valley	6.87	98.24	75.20	3,635	Hasselkus ranch.
Homnoys Ranch	3.97	102.21	71.23		Pasturage and forage.
Bayleys Ranch	11.50	113.71	59.73	5,387	Pasturage and forage. Red Clover Valley.
Crows Ranch	7.50	121.21	52.23	5,464	Do.
Beckworth (post-office)	9.40	130.61	42.83	4,887	Forage for sale. To Loyalton, 13.69 miles southeast.
Summit (post-office)	14.26	144.87	28.57	4,875	Sierra Valley. To Loyalton, 11.40 miles southwest.
Beckworth Pass	.83	145.70	27.74	5,193	Sierra Nevada Summit.
Junction House	2.74	148.44	25.00	4,639	Reno and Susanville road. (See Route No. 2.)
Reno	25.00	173.44	0.00	4,484	Seat of Washoe County, Nevada, on Central Pacific Railroad.

NOTE.—This table (from surveys of 1877 and 1878) shows mail routes from Chico and Reno to Greenville, Cal.

ROUTE No. 14.—*Oroville, Cal., to Susanville, Cal.*

[Atlas sheets Nos. 47A and 47C.]

Stations.	Distance.			Altitude above sea-level.	Remarks.
	Between consecutive points.	From Oroville.	From Susanville.		
	Miles.	*Miles.*	*Miles.*	*Feet.*	
Oroville	0.00	0.00	118.55	183	At toll bridge over Feather River.
Bidwells Bar	9.50	9.50	109.05	342	Old placer mines; formerly seat of Butte County; good water; forage for sale.
Berry Creek	9.10	18.60	99.95	1,887	Good water; forage for sale.
Junction House	10.51	29.11	89.44	3,562	Good water; forage for sale; limit of snow.
Buckeye	5.33	34.44	84.11	4,938	Stage station.
Bucks Ranch	13.37	47.81	70.74	5,112	Unfit for camping.
Toll gate	5.60	53.41	65.14	5,427	Pasturage.
Meadow Valley	2.38	55.79	62.76	3,757	Wood and water; forage for sale.
Spanish Ranch	1.93	57.72	60.83	3,636	Wood and water; pasturage.
Quincy	6.67	64.39	54.16	3,381	County seat of Plumas; forage and pasturage.
Shoo-fly Toll Bridge	12.90	77.29	41.26	3,071	Feather River (north fork).
Arlington Bridge	3.42	80.71	37.84	3,376	Feather River.
Taylorville	4.85	85.56	32.99	3,479	Village; forage and pasturage.
Forks of road	1.14	86.70	31.85		To Fords via east side of valley, 6.19 miles.
Deadfall Bridge	0.71	87.41	31.14	3,426	To Greenville, 9.73 miles; Greenville to Taylorville via Deadfall Bridge, 11.58 miles.
Fords Greenville road	5.25	92.66	25.89	3,518	Head of northeast arm Indian Valley.
Gold Run Pass	15.68	108.34	10.21	6,428	Main divide (Sierra Nevada).
Johnsons	4.28	112.62	5.93	4,379	Wood, water, and pasturage.
Forks of road	2.46	115.08	3.47	4,113	To Lassens Grove, 2.25 miles.
Susanville (post-office)	3.47	118.55	0.00	4,195	

NOTE.—This route was surveyed in 1878; from Oroville to Quincy there is a mail thrice a week. Distances via the old road from Quincy to Taylorville are, Quincy to Summit, Houghs Ridge, 10.02; Summit (5,959 feet) to Taylorville, 5.28 miles. Total, Quincy to Taylorville, 15.3 miles. This old road, although shorter by 5.85 miles, has been disused for a number of years on account of steep grades.

U. S. GEOGRAPHICAL SURVEYS.

ROUTE No. 15.—*Truckee, Cal., to Quincy, Cal.*

[Atlas sheets Nos. 47A, 47C, and 47D.]

Stations.	Distance.			Altitude above sea-level.	Remarks.
	Between consecutive points.	From Truckee.	From Quincy.		
	Miles.	*Miles.*	*Miles.*	*Feet.*	
Truckee	0.00	0.00	74.92	5,795	Town of about 1,500 inhabitants, Central Pacific Railroad.
Johnsons	4.05	4.05	60.42	5,643	Prosser Creek; wood and water; forage for sale.
Crossing of Henness Pass road [1]	12.45	16.50	58.42	6,228	South Truckee River.
Sierra Valley Pass	0.35	16.85	58.07	6,321	Main Divide, Sierra Nevada.
Randolph	8.36	25.21	49.71	4,991	Village south end Sierra Valley.
Sierraville	1.00	26.21	48.71	4,880	Sierra Valley post-office, village Sierra Valley.
Forks of road near Turners [2]	4.05	30.26	44.66	4,887	Sierra City road turns westwardly.
Sulphur Springs Hotel	12.00	42.76	32.66	4,466	Wash post-office. (See post route map.)
Forks of road [3]	6.00	48.26	26.66	4,325	Junction of Reno and Quincy road.
Jamison road [3]	1.83	50.09	24.83		To Jamison, southwesterly, 2 miles.
Parkers Ranch	8.26	58.35	16.57	4,136	Middle fork Feather River.
Quincy	16.57	74.92	0.00	3,381	Village of about 500 inhabitants in American Valley, seat of Plumas County.

[1] To Crystal Peak, eastward, 17.26 miles; to Webber Lake Hotel, westward, 8.3 miles. (See Route No. 16.)
[2] To Sierra City (4,205 feet) via Yuba Gap (6,700 feet), 18.71 miles. Total Truckee to Sierra City by mail and stage road, 48.97 miles.
    The mail and stage road from Quincy to Heckworth post-office and Reno turns east here. The distances are: Quincy to Forks of road, 26.66 miles; Forks to Delaneys (Crombey post-office), 5.16 miles; Delaneys to Beckworth post-office, 9.40 miles; Beckworth to Reno (see Route 13), 42.83 miles. Total Quincy to Reno by direct mail and stage road, 83.05 miles.
[3] This road was surveyed in 1877 and 1878, and is a mail and stage route.

ROUTE No. 16.—*Reno, Nev., to Milton, Cal., via Henness Pass road.*

[Atlas sheet No. 47D.]

Stations.	Distance.		Altitude above sea-level.	Remarks.
	Between consecutive points.	From Reno.	From Milton.	
	Miles.	*Miles.*	*Miles.*	*Feet.*	
Reno	0.00	0.00	50.08	4,484	Seat of Washoe County, Nevada, at junction of Virginia and Truckee Railroad with Central Pacific Railroad.
Crystal Peak	12.70	12.70	37.38	4,918	Village of Washoe County, Nevada, at California and Nevada State line.
Summit	5.25	17.95	32.13	6,487	Crystal Peak ridge, divide between Dog and Sardine Valleys.
Truckee road[1]	2.50	20.45	29.63	6,049	Junction of Reno and Truckee with Henness Pass road; wood, water, and grass.
Loyalton road[2]	2.51	22.96	27.12	6,051	Sardine Valley.
Sierraville road[3]	1.50	24.46	25.62	6,303	Do.
Truckee and Quincy road	5.50	29.96	20.12	6,228	See Route No. 15 for details.
Webber Lake House	8.30	38.26	11.82	6,808	Inn; lake also called Truckee Lake.
Henness Pass	1.72	39.98	10.10	6,958	Main divide, Sierra Nevada.
Forks of road at Jacksons[4]	6.71	46.69	3.39	5,980	Deserted stage station; wood, water, and grass.
Milton	3.39	50.08	0.00	5,845	Small settlement; grass, wood, and water in vicinity.

[1] For details from Reno to Truckee, see Route No. 17.
[2] To Loyalton, Sierra Valley, via Sardine Valley Pass (6,346 feet), 14.75 miles; Loyalton to Beckwith post-office, 13.69 miles northwest; Loyalton to Summit, 11.40 miles northeast. (See Route No. 18.)
[3] To Sierraville, via Sierraville Pass (6,893 feet), 12.5 miles.
[4] About 2.5 miles southwest Jacksons a road turns eastward, via the English reservoir, to Meadow Lake. Summit City (7,377 feet), mining district, 9.6 miles from Jacksons. A road also turns south to the same point from Webber Lake; distance, 9.5 miles.

NOTE.—This road was surveyed in 1877. It is used principally for local travel, and is known as the Henness Pass road. The southern fork at Jacksons keeps on to Eureka, Nevada City, and Dutch Flat.

U. S. GEOGRAPHICAL SURVEYS.   225

ROUTE No. 17.—*Reno, Nev., to Emigrant Gap, California.*

[Atlas sheet Nos. 46C and 47D.]

Stations.	Distance.			Altitude above sea-level.	Remarks.
	Between consecutive points.	From Reno.	From Emigrant Gap.		
	Miles.	*Miles.*	*Miles.*	*Feet.*	
Reno	0.00	0.00	64.31	4,484	Seat of Washoe County, at junction of Virginia and Truckee Railroad with Central Pacific Railroad.
Crystal Peak	12.70	12.70	51.61	4,918	Village, Washoe County, Nevada, at the State line.
Fork of road	7.75	20.45	43.86	6,049	North Fork to Hennes Pass.
Virginia House	4.58	25.03	39.28	5,689	Stage station; forage for sale.
Johnsons	4.47	29.50	34.81	5,643	On Prosser Creek; forage for sale.
Truckee	4.05	33.55	30.76	5,795	Town of about 1,500 inhabitants, on Central Pacific Railroad.
Donner Lake	3.20	36.75	27.56	5,885	Old inn east end of lake.
Donner Pass	6.58	43.33	20.98	7,043	Wagon-road summit.
Summit Station	0.47	43.80	20.51	6,983	Summit Central Pacific Railroad.
Soda Springs Station	2.19	45.99	18.32	5,882	To Soda Springs south by stage-road, 10 miles.
Cisco[1]	10.32	56.31	8.00	5,654	Site of old village on South Fork Yuba River, opposite mouth of Rattlesnake Creek.
Emigrant Gap	8.00	64.31	0.00		Station, Central Pacific Railroad.

[1] The site of the old town is about one-fourth of a mile north of the present railroad station. From Cisco there is a wagon-road very much out of repair beyond Osseville, and passable only for pack animals to Meadow Lake (Summit City) mining district. The distances are: Cisco to Osseville (deserted mining camp), North Fork of South Fork of Yuba River, 7.9 miles; Osseville to Summit, 3.1 miles. Meadow Lake is in the center of a system of storage reservoirs for mining purposes.

NOTE.—This road was surveyed in 1876-'77. It continues westward from Emigrant Gap into the foot-hills. The approaches to the pass on the east are difficult, and the grade steep and hard to keep in repair. The road is now used for local travel only, although before the completion of the railroad it was a much-used route across the Sierras.

1874 WH——15

ITINERARIES OF ROUTES.

ROUTE No. 18.—*Virginia, Nev., to Placerville, Cal.*
[Atlas sheets Nos. 47D, 56B, and 56A.]

Stations.	Distance.			Altitude above sea-level.	Remarks.
	Between consecutive points.	From Virginia.	From Placerville.		
	Miles.	*Miles.*	*Miles.*	*Feet.*	
Virginia (Consolidated Virginia Mine)	0.00	0.00	101.12	6,155	Mining city of 10,817 inhabitants (1880) on Comstock Lode, eastern slope of Mount Davidson, Washoe Mountains, terminus of Virginia and Truckee Railroad.
American Flat Toll-house	3.75	3.75	97.37	5,349	Mining camp.
Mound House	4.30	8.05	93.07	5,032	Station on Virginia and Truckee Railroad and initial point of Carson and Colorado Railroad.
Empire (hotel at bend of Carson River)	3.45	11.50	89.62	4,593	Mining town.
Carson (at Capitol)	3.68	15.18	85.94	4,634	Capital of Nevada; population 4,229 (1880); station on Virginia and Truckee Railroad.
State Line House	24.90	40.08	61.04		Inn; California and Nevada line; southeast shore Lake Tahoe.
Woodburns	4.89	44.97	56.15		Lake Valley post-office.
Osgoods Toll-house	4.35	49.32	51.80	6,298	Foot of grade near junction of Echo Creek with Upper Truckee.
Johnsons Pass	2.05	51.37	49.75	7,266	Main crest of Sierra Nevada (locally Western Summit).
Phillips	2.81	54.18	46.94	6,871	Inn; wood and water plenty; forage for sale.
Strawberry Toll-house	4.87	59.05	42.07	5,695	Do.
Georgetown Junction	4.28	63.33	37.79	5,440	Road to Georgetown and Surveyors Ranch.
Dicks Ranch (Yarnells Toll-house)	6.28	69.61	31.51	4,113	Slippery Ford post-office.
Perrins Ranch	1.88	71.49	29.63	3,828	Forage for sale.
Moores Station	7.83	79.32	21.80	3,207	Toll-house and bridge over south fork American River.
Pacific House (post-office)	4.28	83.60	17.52	3,451	Inn; forage for sale.
Sportsmans Hall (Fyffe post-office)	6.30	89.90	11.22		Do.
Smith Flat Toll-house	8.00	97.90	3.22		Road south to Newtown and Pleasant Valley.
Placerville (post-office)	3.22	101.12	0.00	1,893	Old mining town; seat of Eldorado County Railroad; station at Shingle Springs, about 10½ miles southwest.

NOTE.—This route was surveyed in 1876–'77. It is the most direct and best from the western foot-hills of the Sierra to the Comstock Mines, and before the completion of the Central Pacific Railroad was an important stage and freighting road. The local travel over it is still considerable, and the road is kept in good repair. The route from Carson across the Tahoe Mountains (eastern summit) may be either via Glenbrook or Genoa and Daggetts Pass, the distance being about the same (for details see Routes 18A and 18B).

ROUTE NO. 18a.—*Carson, Nev., to Rowland's, Cal.,* via Clear Creek road.*

[Atlas sheets Nos. 47D and 56B.]

Stations.	Distance.			Altitude above sea-level.	Remarks.
	Between consecutive points.	From Carson.	From Rowland's.		
	Miles.	*Miles.*	*Miles.*	*Feet.*	
Carson (at Capitol)	0.00	0.00	27.49	4,634	Town of 4,429 inhabitants; capital of Nevada.
Summit of Tahoe Mountains¹	10.96	10.96	16.53	7,186	Locally called "Eastern Summit."
Glenbrook, Camp at	3.24	14.20	13.29	6,282	Village of about 400 inhabitants on east shore of Lake Tahoe.
Cave Rock	3.32	17.52	9.97		Road on trestle around base of bold cliff rising about 200 feet above lake.
Zephyr Cove	2.33	19.85	7.64		Abandoned stage station.
Smalls	4.15	24.00	3.49		Foot of Kingsbury grade.
State Line House	.90	24.90	2.59		California and Nevada State line.
Rowlands²	2.59	27.49	0.00	6,222	Settlement on southern shore of Lake Tahoe; inn; forage or pasturage may be had.

* Surveyed in September 1876; road usually traveled by Carson and Tahoe stages.
¹ From Carson to Summit via Kings Cañon road, 11.96 miles; grades more uniform on this road.
² From Rowlands south to junction with Virginia and Placerville road, 4.25 miles.

ROUTE No. 18b.—*Carson, Nev., to Rowlands, Cal., via Genoa, Nev., and the Kingsbury grade.*

[Atlas sheets Nos. 47D and 56B.]

Stations.	Distance.			Altitude above sea-level.	Remarks.
	Between consecutive points.	From Carson.	From Rowlands.		
	Miles.	*Miles.*	*Miles.*	*Feet.*	
Carson (at Capitol)	0.00	0.00	27.65	4,634	Capital of Nevada.
Genoa	12.96	12.96	14.69	4,802	Village of about 300 inhabitants; seat of Douglas County.
Hot Springs	1.80	14.76	12.89	4,802	Hotel and bath house.
Haines	1.14	15.90	11.75	4,733	Foot of Kingsbury grade.
Daggetts Pass	5.04	20.94	6.71	7,297	Summit of Tahoe Mountains (locally, Eastern Summit).
Smalls	3.22	24.16	3.49		Foot of Kingsbury grade; east shore Lake Tahoe.
State Line House	.90	25.06	2.59		California and Nevada State line.
Rowlands	2.59	27.65	0.00	6,222	Southern shore of Lake Tahoe.

ROUTE No. 19.—*Carson, Nev., to Volcano, Cal.,* * *via Amador and Nevada wagon-road.*

[Atlas sheets Nos. 47D, 56A and B.]

Stations.	Distance.			Altitude above sea-level.	Remarks.
	Between consecutive points.	From Carson.	From Volcano.		
	Miles.	*Miles.*	*Miles.*	*Feet.*	
Carson	0.00	0.00	97.00	4,634	Town of 4,229 inhabitants; capital of Nevada.
Woodfords	30.87	30.87	66.13	5,676	Inn at mouth of cañon of west fork Carson River.
Williams Ranch[1]	13.11	43.98	53.02	7,757	Wood, water, and grass.
Carson Pass (Sierra Nevada)	1.81	45.79	51.21	8,634	Divide between American River (Pacific slope) and Carson River (Great Interior Basin).
Caples Ranch, (Clear Lake)	3.68	49.47	47.53	7,780	Wood, water, and grass.
Silver Lake Hotel	7.37	56.84	40.16	7,174	Inn and toll-house; forage for sale.
Tragedy Spring	3.00	59.84	37.16	7,989	Wood, water, and grass.
Forks of road[2]	4.48	64.32	32.68	7,290	Old emigrant road to right.
Corral Flat	0.78	65.10	31.90		Wood, water, and grass scant.
Peddlers Hill	5.66	70.76	26.24	6,831	Wood; small spring, failing early; no grass.
Cold Spring	4.39	75.15	21.85		Small spring.
Mud Spring	0.39	75.54	21.46	5,973	Small spring and corral.
Hams Station	2.08	77.62	19.38	5,439	Inn; forage for sale.
Wileys Station	3.77	81.39	15.61	5,027	Inn and post-office; forage for sale.
Antelope Spring	3.20	84.59	12.41	4,272	Inn; forage for sale.
Antelope and Pine Grove turnpike	0.32	84.91	12.09		Runs to Jackson, county seat of Amador.
Horsleys Station	1.34	86.25	10.75	3,860	Inn; forage for sale; formerly French camp.
Myers Station	2.23	88.48	8.52	3,759	Inn; forage for sale; formerly Thorps.
Fosters Station[3]	2.17	90.65	6.35	3,265	Inn; forage for sale.
Densers Station[4]	3.07	93.72	3.28	2,922	Do.
Volcano	3.28	97.00	0.00	2,075	Mining town of about 1,000 inhabitants.

* Surveyed in 1877 and 1878. Road generally passable from middle of June to end of October.
[1] From here a road leads to Hermit Valley on the Big Tree road, distance 16.71 miles. From this branch road, at 1 mile from Williams, a road forks to the right and runs to Summit City (abandoned) and Blue Lakes. [2] A side road to the right runs to Leek Spring, Pleasant Valley, and Newton, used principally by cattle and sheep owners. At Leek Spring there is a trail (old emigrant route) to Grizzly Flat. [3] Right-hand road to Fiddletown. [4] Main road keeps to right for Sutter.

ITINERARIES OF ROUTES.

ROUTE No. 20.—*Carson, Nev., to Milton Cal., via Big Tree road and Ebbetts or Silver Mountain Pass.*

[Atlas sheets Nos. 47D, 56B, 56C, and 56D.]

Stations.	Distance.			Altitude above sea-level.	Remarks.
	Between consecutive points.	From Carson.	From Milton.		
	Miles.	*Miles.*	*Miles.*	*Feet.*	
Carson (at Capitol)	0.00	0.00	140.37	4,634	Capital of Nevada, station Virginia and Truckee Railroad.
Genoa	12.96	12.96	127.41	4,802	Seat of Douglas County, Nevada.
Sheridan (post-office)	7.74	20.70	119.67	4,794	Small settlement.
California and Nevada State line	3.50	24.20	116.17	5,001	West side Carson Valley, east of Jobs Peak.
Fredericksburg	1.57	25.77	114.60	5,067	Stage station; forage for sale.
Woodfords (post-office)	5.10	30.87	109.50	5,676	Stage station, mouth Carson Cañon; forage for sale.
Markleeville (post-office)	6.63	37.50	102.87	5,525	Village; seat of Alpine County, California.
Mount Bullion	5.35	42.85	97.52	5,714	Toll-gate; eastward to Union hotel, Monitor, 1.75 miles.
Silver Mountain	5.81	48.66	91.71	6,446	Old mining camp on west bank of Silver Creek.
Silver Mt. or Ebbetts Pass	6.23	54.89	85.48	7,630	Main divide, Sierra Nevada.
Hermit Valley	5.47	60.36	80.01	7,039	Wood and water plenty; forage and pasturage.
Summit	2.71	63.07	77.30	8,157	West of Pacific Valley; divide between Mokelumne and Stanislaus Rivers.
Silver Valley	5.74	68.81	71.56	6,979	Wood, water, and pasturage.
Bloods Toll-house (Bear Valley)	3.74	72.55	67.82	6,464	Wood and water plenty; forage and pasturage.
Big Meadow Creek[1]	5.34	77.89	62.48	6,421	Wood and water plenty; grass scant.
Black Springs	5.70	83.59	56.78	4,756	Wood plenty; water and grass scant.
Gardiners	8.54	92.13	48.24	4,730	Wood and water; forage or pasturage.
Hotel (Calaveras Big Tree Grove)	2.82	94.95	45.42		Summer resort; forage or pasturage.
Fourteen-mile House	1.21	96.16	44.21		Public house.
Forks of road[2]	0.89	97.05	43.32		Roads join again at Halfway House. Distance, via Western Fork, 0.29 mile greater than eastern (given in table).

[1] West of this creek a road used by dairymen and sheep ranchers turns off to West Point. Distances are, Big Meadow Creek to Big Meadow Dairy Ranch, 1.39 miles; Big Meadow Ranch to Folsom & Halls (Hunters Flat), 16.17 miles; Hunters Flat to West Point, 10.05 miles. Total, forks of road to West Point, 21.61 miles.
[2] At about one-half mile southwest of this point, on the western fork, a road turns across San Antonio Creek, to Sheep Ranch (mining camp), 11 miles; to Railroad Flat, 14.63 miles; to West Point, via Railroad Flat, 20.96 miles.

ROUTE No. 20.—*Carson, Nev., to Milton, Cal., via Big Tree road and Ebbetts or Silver Mountain Pass*—Continued.

[Atlas sheets Nos. 47D, 56B, 56C, and 56D.]

Stations.	Distance.			Altitude above sea-level.	Remarks.
	Between consecutive points.	From Carson.	From Milton.		
	Miles.	*Miles.*	*Miles.*	*Feet.*	
Halfway House¹	5.21	102.26	38.11	3,358	Inn; wood and water plenty; forage for sale.
Murphys	8.11	110.37	30.00	2,195	Mining village.
Altaville	*7.50	117.87	22.50	1,560	Do.
Gibsons Station	*5.50	123.37	17.00	*1,570	Inn and stage station; forage for sale.
Reservoir House	*10.87	134.24	6.13	1,013	Inn; forage for sale.
Milton, terminus Stockton and Copperopolis Railroad.	6.13	140.37	0.00	376	Village on east side of Sacramento Valley; distance, 30 miles by rail from Stockton.

* Distances and altitudes marked thus (*) from information furnished by Mr. J. M. Hutchings, guardian Yosemite Valley.
¹ From Halfway House there is a road to San Andreas, via Sheep Ranch and El Dorado. The distances are: Halfway House to Sheep Ranch (2,466 feet), 7.39 miles; Sheep Ranch to El Dorado (2,080 feet), 6.55 miles; El Dorado to San Andreas (1,033 feet), 9.53 miles. Total, Halfway House to San Andreas, 23.47 miles. Total, San Andreas to Big Tree Grove, 30.28 miles.

NOTE.—The above table is from surveys of 1877–'78. It gives what is called the "Big Tree Road" across the Sierra Nevada throughout its entire length. This is a good mountain road, though, like other roads through passes of this altitude in the Sierras, it is blocked by snow from December to June. For details of route from Murphys to Sonora and Yosemite, see Route No. 23.

ROUTE No. 21.—*Milton, Cal., to Bodie, Cal., via Sonora and Mono road.*

[Atlas sheets Nos. 56B, 56C, 56D, and 57A.]

Stations.	Distance.		Altitude above sea-level.	Remarks.
	Between consecutive points.	From Milton.	From Bodie.	
	Miles.	*Miles.*	*Miles.*	*Feet.*	
Milton, terminus Stockton and Copperopolis Railroad.	0.00	0.00	153.88	376	Village east side Sacramento Valley, 30 miles by rail from Stockton.
Copperopolis (post-office)	14.83	14.83	139.05	1,015	Old mining village.
Reynolds Ferry	7.72	22.55	131.33	543	Stanislaus River.
Tuttletown	5.62	28.17	125.71	1,321	Mining village.
Sonora (post-office)	6.48	34.65	119.23	1,816	Old mining town, seat of Tuolumne County.
Baxters Station	13.24	47.89	105.99	4,114	Near Confidence mine (gold quartz).
Northrups (Excelsior Hotel)	1.25	49.14	104.74	4,519	Sugar Pine post-office; forage for sale.
Bradfords saw-mill	4.91	54.05	99.83		Trail turns off.
Strawberry[1]	11.02	65.07	88.81	5,238	Stage station, south fork Stanislaus River.
Summit	2.27	67.34	86.54	6,352	Divide between south and middle forks of Stanislaus River.
Eureka Valley	22.45	89.79	64.09	5,958	Stage station on middle fork of Stanislaus River.
Summit of Sonora Pass	11.20	100.99	52.89	9,660	Crest of Sierra Nevada.
Leavitts	7.59	108.58	45.30		In valley of West Walker.
West Walker River	5.31	113.89	39.99	6,676	Bridge; wood and water plenty; some grazing.
East Branch of West Walker River	2.40	116.29	37.59	6,957	Wood scant; grazing fair.
Hot Springs	3.29	119.58	34.30	7,388	Stage station; wood, water, and grazing in vicinity.
Richeys	7.32	126.90	26.98		Cattle ranch.
Bridgeport	6.98	133.88	20.00		Seat of Mono County.
Bodie	20.00	153.88	0.00	6,424	Large mining town, 40 miles southwest of Hawthorne, Nevada, Carson and Colorado Railroad.

[1] From Strawberry it is possible to reach Leavitts, via what is known as the "Relief Trail," in 42.711 miles.

NOTE.—This road was surveyed in 1877 and 1878. It is a good mountain road, but is closed by snow about half the year.

ROUTE No. 22.—*Milton, Cal., to Bodie, Cal., via Big Oak Flat road and Great Sierra wagon-road.*

[Atlas sheets Nos. 56B, 56C, 56D, and 57A.]

Stations.	Distance.		Altitude above sea-level.	Remarks.
	Between consecutive points.	From Milton.	From Bodie.	
	Miles.	*Miles.*	*Miles.*	*Feet.*	
Milton, terminus Stockton and Copperopolis Railroad.	0.00	0.00	157.74	376	Village on east side of Sacramento Valley, 30 miles by rail from Stockton.
Copperopolis (post-office)	14.83	14.83	142.91	1,015	Old mining village.
Chinese Camp (post-office)	17.16	31.99	125.75	1,299	Do.
Big Oak Flat (post-office)	13.18	45.17	112.57	2,833	Mining village.
Crockers Ranch	25.92	71.09	86.65	4,497	Inn; forage for sale.
South fork Tuolumne	2.20	73.29	84.45		
Aspen Valley	8.36	81.65	76.09		
Middle fork Tuolumne (lower crossing)	4.30	85.95	71.79		Divide between Tuolumne and Merced Basins, on boundary between Tuolumne and Mariposa Counties.
Middle fork Tuolumne (upper crossing)	5.62	91.57	66.17		Westward of the Mount Hoffman group of peaks.
Summit	2.56	94.13	63.61		Southwestern slope of Hoffman group.
Yosemite Creek Crossing	3.85	97.98	59.76		On branch of Glacier Brook, due south of Mount Hoffman.
Porcupine Creek	3.84	101.82	55.92		Divide between Glacier Brook and Lake Tenaiza.
Snow Creek	3.48	105.30	52.44		Murphys cabin, west shore of lake.
Snow Creek Summit	1.71	107.01	50.73		Divide between basins of Tuolumne and Merced Rivers, and point of boundary between counties of same name.
Lake Tenaiza	2.81	109.82	47.92		
Summit	2.95	112.77	44.97	7,971	
Tuolumne River Crossing	5.38	118.15	39.59		In Tuolumne Meadows, about ½ mile west of Lamberts Soda Springs.
McLanes Pass	7.03	125.18	32.56	10,165	Summit of Sierra Nevada; altitude approximate from Whitneys Guide.
Bennettville	2.06	127.24	30.50		Mining camp, terminus Great Sierra wagon-road.

ROUTE No. 22.—*Milton, Cal., to Bodie, Cal., via Big Oak Flat road and Great Sierra wagon-road*—Continued.

[Atlas sheets Nos. 56B, 56C, 56D, and 57A.]

Stations.	Distance.		Altitude above sea-level.	Remarks.
	Between consecutive points.	From Milton.	From Bodie.	
	Miles.	*Miles.*	*Miles.*	*Feet.*	
Lundy	8.50	135.74	22.00		Mining camp in Sierra foot-hills, west of Mono Lake.
Bodie	22.00	157.74	0.00		Mining town in mountains north of Mono Lake, 40 miles southwest of Hawthorne, seat of Esmeralda County, Nevada. Hawthorne is a station on the Carson and Colorado Railroad.

NOTE.—From Milton to Crockers Ranch the route is the same as in Table No. 24, which see; from Crockers to Bennettville it is over the Great Sierra wagon-road, which was to have been completed by the fall of 1883. The distances over this new road are from notes of Mr. H. B. Carpenter, late in charge of surveys for Great Sierra Consolidated Silver Company, furnished through Mr. J. M. Hutchings, of Yosemite. Distances from Bennettville to Bodie from post-route map.

ROUTE No. 23.—(The Calaveras Big Tree route.)—*Milton, Cal., to Yosemite, Cal., via Murphys, Calaveras Big Tree Grove, Sonora, Chinese Camp, and Big Oak Flat.*

[Atlas sheets Nos. 56B and 56D.]

Stations.	Distance.			Altitude above sea-level.	Remarks.
	Between consecutive points.	From Milton.	From Yosemite.		
	Miles.	*Miles.*	*Miles.*	*Feet.*	
Milton (terminus Stockton and Copperopolis Railroad).	0.00	0.00	152.45	376	Village of about 170 inhabitants.
Reservoir House	6.13	6.13	146.32	1,013	Inn; forage for sale.
Gibsons Station	*10.87	17.00	135.45	*1,570	Inn and stage station; forage for sale.
Altaville	*5.50	22.50	129.95	1,560	Mining village of about 150 inhabitants.
Murphys Flat	*7.50	30.00	122.45	2,195	Mining village of about 300 inhabitants; stage station.
Halfway House	8.11	38.11	114.34	3,358	Inn; forage for sale.
Calaveras Big Tree Grove Hotel	7.31	45.42	107.03	4,730	Inn and stage station; forage for sale.
Halfway House (returning)	7.31	52.73	99.72	3,358	Inn; forage for sale.
Murphys Flat	8.11	60.84	91.61	2,195	Mining village.
Vallecito (post-office)	4.16	65.00	87.45	1,748	Mining village; forage for sale.
Trail to Natural Bridges	3.32	68.32	84.13		Natural Bridges on Coyote Creek, distant one-third mile.
Parrotts Ferry	2.27	70.59	81.86	834	Stanislaus River.
Gold Springs	3.17	73.76	78.69	2,014	Old mining village; forage for sale.
Columbia (post-office)	1.15	74.91	77.54	2,157	Mining town of about 1,250 inhabitants.
Sonora (post-office)	4.17	79.08	73.37	1,816	Columbia, via Shaws Flat, 5.75 miles. Town of 1,500 inhabitants; seat of Tuolumne County.
Jamestown	3.20	82.28	70.17	1,473	Manufacturing village of about 150 inhabitants.
Montezuma	1.00	83.28	69.17		Mining settlement.
Chinese camp (‡)	3.80	87.08	65.37	1,294	Mining and agricultural village; about 440 inhabitants.
Gold Spring Cottage	2.75	89.83	62.62	1,299	
Priests Hotel‡	12.11	101.94	50.51	2,558	Stage station and inn; forage for sale.

*The distances and altitudes marked are from information furnished by Mr. J. M. Hutchins, guardian Yosemite Valley. The remaining altitudes and distances are from surveys of this office in 1877 and 1879.
‡For details see Big Oak Flat route.

ROUTE No. 23.—(The Calaveras Big Tree route.)—*Milton, Cal., to Yosemite, Cal., via Murphy's, Calaveras Big Tree Grove, Sonora, Chinese Camp, and Big Oak Flat*—Continued.

[Atlas sheets Nos. 56B and 56D.]

Stations.	Distance.			Altitude above sea-level.	Remarks.
	Between consecutive points.	From Milton.	From Yosemite.		
	Miles.	*Miles.*	*Miles.*	*Feet.*	
Tuolumne Big Tree Grove	33.43	135.37	17.08	5,854	Altitude at base of Tunnel Tree.
Leidigs (via south bank Merced)	16.01	151.38	1.07		Inn of Yosemite Valley.
Cooks	0.30	151.68	0.77		Do.
Barnards	0.77	152.45	0.00	3,934	Do.

ROUTE No. 24.—(The Big Oak Flat route.)—*Milton, Cal., to Yosemite, Cal.*

[Atlas sheets Nos. 56C and 56D.]

Stations.	Distance.			Altitude above sea-level.	Remarks.
	Between consecutive points.	From Milton.	From Yosemite.		
	Miles.	*Miles.*	*Miles.*	*Feet.*	
Milton (terminus of Stockton and Copperopolis Railroad).	0.00	0.00	94.61	376	Village of about 170 inhabitants.
Reservoir House	6.13	6.13	88.48	1,013	Inn; forage for sale.
Copperopolis (post-office)	8.70	14.83	79.78	1,007	Old mining village; about 300 inhabitants.
Byrnes Ferry Bridge	7.60	22.43	72.18	380	Stanislaus River.
Cross-roads (Table Mountain Pass)	4.86	27.29	67.32	1,143	Northern road to Rawhide Camp and Sonora; southern road to Knights Ferry, Stanislaus River.
Chinese Camp	4.70	31.99	62.62	1,299	Village of about 440 inhabitants.
Jacksonville (Tuolumne River)	4.18	36.17	58.47	602	Mining village.
Keiths orchard and vineyard	1.03	37.20	57.41		
Stevens Bar Ferry	1.24	38.44	56.17	614	Tuolumne River.
Culbertsons vineyard	3.45	41.89	52.54	980	Moccasin Creek; forage for sale.
Priests Hotel	2.21	44.10	50.51	2,558	Stage station and inn; forage for sale.
Big Oak Flat (post-office)	1.07	45.17	49.44	2,823	Mining village of about 80 inhabitants.
Groveland	2.24	47.41	47.20	2,828	Mining village; formerly First Garrote.
Second Garrote	2.15	49.56	45.05	2,857	Mining village.
Spragues Ranch	4.97	54.53	40.08	2,950	Inn; forage for sale.
Hamiltons Ranch	3.84	58.37	36.24	2,920	Inn; forage for sale; stage station.
Colfax Spring (Elwells)[1]	2.69	61.06	33.55	3,022	Inn; forage for sale.
South Fork Tuolumne	0.93	61.99	32.62	2,653	Lower bridge.
Hardins Ranch	4.39	66.38	28.23	3,396	Forage for sale.
South Fork Tuolumne	1.37	67.75	26.86		Upper bridge.
Crockers Ranch	3.34	71.09	23.52	4,497	Inn; forage for sale.
Hodgdons Ranch[2]	2.00	73.09	21.22	4,506	Do.

[1] To Hetch Hetchy Valley by road (and trail) turning off east of Lower Tuolumne bridge, 21 miles.
[2] To Hetch Hetchy Valley (cabin at west end of valley), 16.3 miles by trail.

ROUTE No. 24.—(The Big Oak Flat route.)—*Milton, Cal., to Yosemite, Cal.*—Continued.

[Atlas sheets Nos. 56C and 56D.]

Stations.	Distance.			Altitude above sea-level.	Remarks.
	Between consecutive points.	From Milton.	From Yosemite.		
	Miles.	*Miles.*	*Miles.*	*Feet.*	
Tuolumne Big Tree Grove	4.44	77.53	17.08	5,854	Altitude of "Dead Giant" or Tunnel Tree.
Crane Flat	1.00	78.53	16.08	6,054	Inn; forage for sale.
Tamarack Flat	5.07	83.60	11.01	6,234	Meadow; wood, water, and grass.
Gentrys (deserted)	2.81	86.41	8.20	5,694	Old Inn.
Junction Big Oak Flat and Coulterville roads.	4.37	90.78	3.83	3,949	
Leidigs (via south bank of Merced River)	2.76	93.54	1.07		Inn; Yosemite Valley.
Cooks	0.30	93.84	0.77		Do.
Barnards	0.77	94.61	0.00	3,934	Do.

NOTE.—This route was surveyed in 1878-'79. At Crockers Ranch the great Sierra wagon-road turns off. (See Route No. 23.)

ROUTE No. 25.—(The Coulterville route.)—*Merced, Cal., to Yosemite Valley, Cal.**

[Atlas sheet Nos. 56C and 56D.]

Stations.	Distance.			Altitude above sea-level.	Remarks.
	Between consecutive points.	From Merced.	From Yosemite.		
	Miles.	*Miles.*	*Miles.*	*Feet.*	
Merced	0.00	0.00	99.34	171	Town of 1,500 inhabitants on Southern Pacific Railroad; seat of Merced County.
Half-way House	6.35	6.35	92.99	215	Waterloo Inn; forage for sale.
Snelling (post-office, on Merced River)[1]	12.60	18.95	80.39	252	Village of 330 inhabitants; formerly seat of Merced County.
Merced Falls (on Merced River)	6.25	25.20	74.14	360	Manufacturing village of 120 inhabitants.
Cross-roads	8.39	33.59	65.75		To Snelling by southern road, 9.13 miles.
Junction Station	1.26	34.85	64.49	578	Inn; forage for sale.
Lebrights Ranch	5.53	40.38	58.96		Stage station and inn; forage for sale.
Herbecks Ranch	5.74	46.12	53.22	1,621	Inn and blacksmith shop; forage for sale.
Peñon Blanco Ranch	2.93	49.05	50.29	1,807	Inn; forage for sale.
Coulterville	2.64	51.69	47.65	1,665	Village of about 300 inhabitants.
Dudleys Hotel and Ranch	7.58	59.27	40.07	2,959	Stage station and inn; forage for sale.
Bower Cave	4.69	63.96	35.38	2,360	Inn; forage for sale.
Wengers Ranch	3.23	67.19	32.15	3,218	Do.
Watering Trough	4.00	71.19	28.15		On southern slope of Pilot Peak.
Hazel Green[2]	5.51	76.70	22.64	5,550	Stage station and inn; forage for sale.
Merced Grove Big Trees	3.16	79.86	19.48	5,327	Near head of Moss Creek.
Big Meadows (toll-gate)	8.45	88.31	11.03	4,234	Stage station and inn; forage for sale.
Merced River Trail	4.59	92.90	6.44	3,371	Trail down Merced River to Hennessys; Ferguson Mine and Hites Cove Mine.
Forks of road	2.61	95.51	3.73	3,944	Junction of Coulterville and Big Oak Flat roads, north of El Capitan bridge.

* Surveyed in June, 1879.
[1] Distance measured via upper ford; via the lower ford the distance is about 1.25 mile less.
[2] Crane Flat, on Big Oak Flat road, 4.76 miles to east by side road.

ROUTE NO. 25.—(The Coulterville route.)—*Merced, Cal., to Yosemite Valley, Cal.*—Continued.

[Atlas sheet Nos. 96C and 96D.]

Stations.	Distance.			Altitude above sea-level.	Remarks.
	Between consecutive points.	From Merced.	From Yosemite.		
	Miles.	*Miles.*	*Miles.*	*Feet.*	
Leidigs Hotel	2.76	98.27	1.07		
Cooks Hotel	0.30	98.57	0.77		To Leidigs via El Capitan bridge. Inn; Yosemite Valley.
Barnards Hotel	0.77	99.34	0.00	3,934	Do.

ROUTE No. 26.—(The Mariposa route.)—*Merced, Cal., to Yosemite Valley, Cal.**

[Atlas sheets Nos. 56C and 56D.]

Stations.	Distance.			Altitude above sea-level.	Remarks.
	Between consecutive points.	From Merced.	From Yosemite.		
	Miles.	*Miles.*	*Miles.*	*Feet.*	
Merced	0.00	0.00	93.95	171	Town of about 1,500 inhabitants; seat of Merced County.
Half-way House	6.35	6.35	87.60	215	Watering station; forage for sale.
Forks of road to Snelling	0.87	7.22	86.73	219	Snelling to northward.
Lava Bed Station	7.26	14.48	79.47	446	Stage station; forage for sale.
Griffiths Ranch	3.63	18.11	75.84	473	Crossing of old Stockton and Millerton road.
Hornitos	4.35	22.46	71.49	847	Mining village of about 600 inhabitants.
Indian Gulch road	1.52	23.98	69.97	898	Indian gulch, 4.18 miles to southward.
Smiths Ranch	2.44	26.42	57.53	1,047	Side road north to Hunters Valley.
Corbetts Ranch	1.91	28.33	65.62	1,075	Forage for sale.
Toll-house	1.81	30.14	63.81	1,598	
Toll house	2.83	32.97	60.98	1,780	
Summit	1.92	34.89	59.06	2,169	Divide between basins of Bear and Mariposa Creeks.
Princeton	0.73	35.62	58.33	2,104	Old mining village.
Summit	2.35	37.97	55.98	2,417	Divide between Agua Fria and Mariposa Creeks.
Lewis Ranch	1.19	39.16	54.79	2,112	Forage for sale.
Mariposa (post-office)	1.70	40.86	53.09	1,962	Mining village of about 450 inhabitants.
Mormon Bar	1.89	42.75	51.20	1,630	Inn; forage for sale.
Sebastopol Flat	2.76	45.51	48.44	2,210	Do.
Thompsons Ranch	3.51	49.02	44.93	2,114	Do.
Turners Ranch	3.93	52.95	41.00	2,741	
Cold Springs	4.36	57.31	36.64	3,126	Inn; forage for sale; stage station.
Chowchilla Summit	5.24	62.55	31.40	5,605	Divide between Chowchilla and Merced Rivers.
Big Tree Station (Clarks)[1]	4.50	67.05	26.95	3,925	Inn and stage station; forage for sale.

*Surveyed in 1878.
[1] Stopping-place for visitors to Mariposa Big Tree Grove.

ROUTE No. 26.—(The Mariposa route.)—*Merced, Cal., to Yosemite Valley, Cal.*—Continued.

[Atlas sheets Nos. 56C and 56D.]

Stations.	Distance.			Altitude above sea-level.	Remarks.
	Between consecutive points.	From Merced.	From Yosemite.		
	Miles.	*Miles.*	*Miles.*	*Feet.*	
El Capitan Bridge (Yosemite Valley)	23.27	90.32	3.63	3,925	Lower iron bridge over Merced River.
Leidigs Hotel	2.56	92.88	1.07		Inn, Yosemite Valley.
Cooks Hotel	0.30	93.18	0.77		Do.
"Barnards"	0.77	93.95	0.00	3,934	Do.

ROUTE No. 27.—(The Madera route.)—*Madera, Cal., to Yosemite Valley, California.*

[Atlas sheets Nos. 56D and 64B.]

Stations.	Distance.			Altitude above sea-level.	Remarks.
	Between consecutive points.	From Madera.	From Yosemite.		
	Miles.	*Miles.*	*Miles.*	*Feet.*	
Madera	0.00	0.00	96.29	280	Village of about 200 inhabitants, on Southern Pacific Railroad.
Adobe Station (Stitts Ranch)	10.00	10.00	86.29	325	Inn; forage for sale.
Mudgetts Ranch	7.25	17.25	79.04	597	Do.
Greens Ranch	7.25	24.50	71.79	1,100	Inn; forage for sale; stage station.
Doolitiles (Coarse Gold Gulch)	14.00	38.50	57.79	2,085	Do.
Fresno Flats	7.50	46.00	50.29	2,192	Inn; forage for sale.
Buffords	5.00	51.00	45.29	2,094	Do.
Board Ranch	7.99	58.99	37.30	4,645	Inn; forage for sale; stage station.
Chowchilla Summit	3.60	62.59	33.70	5,107	Divide between Big Creek and headwaters of Fresno River.
Forks of road	3.33	65.92	30.37	5,064	To Mariposa Big Tree Grove.
Big Tree Station (Clarks)	3.47	69.39	26.90	3,925	Inn and stage station; forage for sale.
Eleven-Mile Station	10.76	80.15	16.14	5,567	Do.
Chinquapin Flat	2.20	82.35	13.94	5,908	Glacier Point Hotel, by new road, 14 miles.
Opposite El Capitan bridge	10.31	92.66	3.63	3,925	Lower iron bridge, over Merced River, Yosemite Valley.
Leidigs Hotel	2.56	95.22	1.07		Inn; Yosemite Valley.
Cooks Hotel	0.30	95.52	0.77		Do.
Barnards Hotel	0.77	96.29	0.99	3,934	Do.

NOTE.—From Madera to Fresno Flats the distances and altitudes are from information received from J. M. Hutchings, guardian, Yosemite Valley. From Fresno Flats to Yosemite they are from surveys of this office in June, 1879.

ROUTE No. 28.—*Caliente, Cal., to Coyote Holes, Cal.,* * *via Kernville road and Walkers Pass.*

[Atlas sheet No. 73A.]

Stations.	Distance.			Altitude above sea-level.	Remarks.
	Between consecutive points.	From Caliente.	From Coyote Holes.		
	Miles.	*Miles.*	*Miles.*	*Feet.*	
Caliente	0.00	0.00	70.88	1,314	Station on Southern Pacific Railroad, about 160 inhabitants.
Mossmans Ranch	12.66	12.66	58.22	3,157	Walkers Basin; wood, water, and grass.
Havilah	10.09	22.75	48.13	3,150	Mining camp of about 260 inhabitants.
Hot Springs[1]	8.08	30.83	40.05	2,398	Hotel and bath-house.
Kernville road[2]	2.00	32.83	38.05		To Kernville, 5.2 miles.
Weldon (post-office)[3]	10.16	42.99	27.89	2,668	Farming village.
Roberts Ranch	8.75	51.74	19.14	2,775	South Fork Kern River.
The Canebrake	5.63	57.37	13.51	3,904	Ranch; good camping place.
Walkers Pass	6.23	63.60	7.28	5,322	Divide between Kern River Basin and Mohave Desert.
Coyote Holes	7.28	70.88	0.00	3,368	Stage station on Los Angeles and Independence road, west edge of Mohave Desert; water; no wood or grass.

* Surveyed in 1875 and 1878.
[1] From Hot Springs to Pah-ute mine, southeast by trail up Erskine Creek, 13.8 miles.
[2] Kernville, 5.2 miles north by left-hand road. Total distance, Caliente to Kernville, 43.25 miles, via good stage-road.
[3] From Weldon to Coyote Holes, via Bird Spring, 34 miles (road turns south from Weldon up Kelso Creek). Distances are: Weldon to forks of road to St. Johns mine (4,052 feet), 15 miles; forks eastward to pass (5,417 feet), 3.38 miles; pass to Bird Spring (3,950 feet), 3.34 miles; Bird Spring to Coyote Holes, 12.28 miles. From Bird Spring nearly due east to Dixie Stage Station, 5.48 miles. Total, Weldon to Dixie Stage Station (see Route No. 37), 27.20 miles. From Weldon there is a road to St. Johns and Pah-ute mines, viz: Weldon to forks of road on Kelso Creek, 15 miles; forks southward to St. Johns mine (5,085 feet above sea on divide), 5 miles; St. Johns mine to Pah-ute mine, 1 mile north of summit of Pah-ute Peak, 11.61 miles. Total, Weldon to Pah-ute mine, by road, 31.61 miles.

U. S. GEOGRAPHICAL SURVEYS. 245

ROUTE No. 29.*—*Bakersfield, Cal., to Fork of Road Station, Los Angeles and Independence road, via the Tehachapai Pass.*

[Atlas sheet No. 73.]

Stations.	Distance.			Altitude above sea-level.	Remarks.
	Between consecutive points.	From Bakersfield.	From Fork of Road.		
	Miles.	*Miles.*	*Miles.*	*Feet.*	
Bakersfield (Southern Pacific Railroad)	0.00	0.00	66.88	432	Town of 800 inhabitants; seat of Kern County.
Pampa	16.48	16.48	50.40	871	Station on Southern Pacific Railroad.
Caliente (via Kernville road)[1]	12.37	28.85	38.03	1,314	Do.
Coombs Station	10.63	39.48	27.40	2,885	Do.
New Tehachapai	7.35	46.83	20.05	3,926	Tehachapai Pass, west of summit.
Salt Lake	6.50	53.33	13.55	3,832	Ranches; to Oak Creek Stage Station, 5 miles south.
Camerons (Southern Pacific Railroad)	3.30	56.63	10.25	†3,786	Old stage station; water, wood, and grass scarce; to Oak Creek Stage Station, 4.5 miles southwest.
Fork of Road station	10.25	66.88	0.00	2,752	Old Freight Station, Los Angeles and Independence road; west edge of Mohave Desert.

*Surveyed in 1875.   †Railroad.

[1] In 1875 this station was the terminus of the railroad and the main shipping point to the mining country to the north. (See route "Mohave Station to Darwin, Cal.")

ROUTE No. 30.—*Los Angeles, Cal., to Caliente, Cal., via old Los Angeles and Caliente stage road (Tehachapai Pass).*

[Atlas sheets Nos. 73A and 73C.]

Stations.	Distance.			Altitude above sea-level.	Remarks.
	Between consecutive points.	From Los Angeles.	From Caliente.		
	Miles.	*Miles.*	*Miles.*	*Feet.*	
Los Angeles (at Court-house)	0.00	0.00	114.61	290	Large town; county seat of Los Angeles County; population 11,311; altitude at new depot, from railroad levels.
Cross-roads, Los Angeles, River	11.25	11.25	103.36	586	Water plenty; wood scarce; grazing poor, except in rainy season.
San Fernando Mission	11.20	22.45	92.16	1,013	Cultivated country; feed for sale.
Summit (deep cut)	6.30	28.75	85.86	1,871	San Fernando Range; divide between Santa Clara and Los Angeles Creeks.
Lyons Station	1.33	30.08	84.53	1,507	Stage station; good water; wood scarce; feed for sale.
Cross-roads at mouth of San Francisquito Creek.[1]	7.11	37.19	77.42		Newhalls Ranch 3 miles westward; Newhall Railroad Station 1½ miles southeast.
Cañon Station	6.07	43.26	71.35		San Francisquito cañon; water poor; wood and grass scarce.
Stage Station	9.31	52.57	62.04		Do.
Elizabeth Lake (post-office[2])	6.06	58.63	55.98	3,317	Small settlement; to Gormans, 33.4 miles. Total, Los Angeles to Gormans, 89.38 miles.
Willow Springs[3]	16.90	75.53	39.08	2,573	Water good; wood scarce; grazing in rainy season.
Oak Creek Stage Station	12.60	88.13	26.48	3,944	To Salt Lake Ranches north 5 miles; to Cameron Station north 4.5 miles.
New Tehachapai	8.50	96.63	17.98	3,926	In Tehachapai pass west of summit; summit of pass by railroad levels 4,025 feet above sea.
Coombs Station	7.35	103.98	10.63	2,885	Southern Pacific Railroad.
Caliente	10.63	114.61	0.00	1,314	Southern Pacific Railroad; no wood or grass.

This route was surveyed in 1875. It was then the stage route between Los Angeles and Caliente, at that time the terminus of the Southern Pacific Railroad. Before the building of the stage road the route to Willow Springs turned eastward up Soledad Cañon. The distances are, forks to Rileys store (1,477 feet), 6.50 miles; Rileys to Soledad City (or Ravenna Railroad Station, 2,357 feet), 14.20 miles; Soledad to summit of Soledad Pass (3,210 feet), 9.10 miles; summit to Willow Springs, 30.6 miles. Total, 6.4 miles.
[1] The summit of San Francisquito Pass is about 400 feet above Elizabeth Lake post-office and about 2 miles south.
[2] From Willow Springs to Mohave Station, 13.55 miles. Total, Los Angeles to Mohave Station by wagon-road, 89.98 miles. See Route No. 37 for roads north from Mohave Station.

ROUTE No. 31.—*Newhall, Cal., to Bakersfield, Cal.*

[Atlas sheet Nos. 73A and 73C.]

Stations.	Distance.			Altitude above sea-level.	Remarks.
	Between consecutive points.	From Newhall.	From Bakersfield.		
	Miles.	*Miles.*	*Miles.*	*Feet.*	
Newhall	0.00	0.00	119.02	1,151	Station on Southern Pacific Railroad.
Elizabeth Lake (post-office)	23.44	23.44	95.58	3,317	Small settlement.
Gormans[1]	33.40	56.84	62.18	3,838	Forage for sale; water plenty; wood scarce.
Forks of road[2]	2.60	59.44	59.58	4,099	North to Fort Tejon, 5.60 miles.
Forks of road	6.93	66.37	52.65	5,133	To Cuddys Ranch, about 1 mile southwest.
San Emigdio Summit	5.00	71.37	47.65	6,246	Spur of McGills Peak (Mount Pinos); head of San Emigdio Creek.
San Emigdio Ranch	13.00	84.37	34.65	1,855	Near mouth of cañon.
San Emigdio Store[3]	4.40	88.77	30.25	788	Feed for sale; water and wood.
Adobe Station	18.03	106.80	12.22	284	Do.
Bakersfield	12.22	119.02	0.00	432	Seat of Kern County, 1.6 miles west of Sumner Station, Southern Pacific Railroad.

NOTE.—This route was surveyed in 1875. It shows the wagon route via San Emigdio Cañon. The shorter route via Old Fort Tejon and Cañada de los Uvas is given below What is known as Tejon Pass is south of Tehachapai Peak, at the head of Tejon Creek. This was an old emigrant route, and there is still a trail over this pass (altitude 5,485 feet).
[1] About 1½ miles west of Gormans the main divide or southern rim of the Sacramento basin is crossed. It is, by aneroid, about 450 feet above Gormans.
[2] Here the road to Bakersfield via Old Fort Tejon (Cañada de las Uvas) turns north. Distances are: Forks to Fort Tejon (3,246 feet), 5.64 miles; Fort Tejon to Roses Store (1,334 feet), 7.24 miles; Roses to Adobe Station, 17.20; Adobe Station to Bakersfield, 12.22 miles. Total: Gormans to Bakersfield, 45. From Los Angeles to Gormans (via Elizabeth Lake, Route No. 30), 89.38 miles. Total: Los Angeles to Bakersfield, by most direct wagon route, 134.38 miles.
[3] To Roses Store, eastward, 17.40 miles.

ROUTE No. 32.—*Newhall, Cal., to San Buena Ventura, Cal.*
[Atlas sheet No. 73C.]

Stations.	Distance.			Altitude above sea-level.	Remarks.
	Between consecutive points.	From Newhall.	From San Buena Ventura.		
	Miles.	*Miles.*	*Miles.*	*Feet.*	
Newhall	0.00	0.00	48.00	1,151	Station on Southern Pacific Railroad.
Cross-roads near Newhalls Ranch	4.50	4.50	43.50		Santa Clara River.
Camulos Ranch	9.80	14.30	33.70		Do.
Warrens	3.90	18.20	29.80	799	Santa Clara River; Buckhorn Ranch.
Santa Paula	14.50	32.70	15.30	693	Village of about 500 inhabitants; Santa Clara Valley.
Saticoy	7.60	40.30	7.70	384	Small village.
San Buena Ventura	7.70	48.00	0.00		Seat of Ventura County, on sea-coast; population about 2,000.

Mail weekly over this route.

ROUTE No. 33.—*Los Angeles, Cal., to San Buena Ventura, Cal.*

[Atlas sheet Nos. 72 and 73C.]

Stations.	Distance.			Altitude above sea-level.	Remarks.
	Between consecutive points.	From Los Angeles.	From San Buena Ventura.		
	Miles.	*Miles.*	*Miles.*	*Feet.*	
Los Angeles	0.00	0.00	70.85	290	Large town on Southern Pacific Railroad; seat of Los Angeles County.
Cahuenga Pass	9.75	9.75	61.10	750	To Sepulveda, 5.2 miles eastward.
Los Angeles Creek	1.50	11.25	59.60	536	To Sepulveda, 5¼ miles eastward; water plenty; wood scarce; grazing in rainy season.
Encino Ranch	8.11	19.36	51.49	772	Water plenty; wood scarce; grazing.
The Well	12.90	32.26	38.59	729	Road and trail south to Malaga Ranch on sea-coast; south about 11 miles.
Vejais Ranch	3.30	35.56	35.29	847	Cultivated country.
Mills Ranch	4.75	40.31	30.54	820	Do.
Newbury Park	1.97	42.28	28.57	830	Do.
Conejo Hotel	4.39	46.67	24.18	579	Do.
Springville	12.00	58.67	12.18	48	Do.
New Jerusalem	4.10	62.77	8.08	28	
San Buena Ventura	8.08	70.85	0.00		Seat of Ventura County; on sea-coast.

Mail three times a week by this road.

250 ITINERARIES OF ROUTES.

ROUTE No. 34.—(Part of the old Los Angeles and Independence road.)—*Mohave Station, Cal., to Independence, Cal.*

[Atlas sheets Nos. 65 and 73.]

Stations.	Distance.			Altitude above sea-level.	Remarks.
	Between consecutive points.	From Mohave Station.	From Independence.		
	Miles.	*Miles.*	*Miles.*	*Feet.*	
Mohave Station	0.00	0.00	131.82	*2,750	Southern Pacific Railroad.
Indian Wells[1]	48.57	48.57	83.25	2,608	Stage station. Good water; no wood; no grass.
Little Lake Station	18.83	67.40	64.42	3,086	No wood; grass, hay, and water. About ½ mile south of Little Owens Lake.
Rose Spring	12.12	79.52	52.30	3,545	Old house.
Hawai Meadows	4.62	84.14	47.68	3,782	Grass, hay, and water; no wood.
Olancha (post-office)[2]	8.81	92.95	38.87	3,708	Pasmores. Well-water; no wood; forage for sale; some grazing.
Carthage[3]	2.16	95.11	36.71	3,589	Spring-water; forage for sale.
Cottonwood Creek	6.84	101.95	29.87	3,560	Running stream; some grazing; cottonwood timber.
Lone Pine Landing[4]	8.43	110.38	21.44	3,591	No wood; no grass; well.
Johnsons	3.81	114.19	17.63	3,700	Junction of Cerro Gordo road. Well-water, and some grazing and timber.
Lone Pine	2.00	116.19	15.63	3,810	Mining town of about 250 inhabitants. Good running water; some grazing and timber; forage for sale.
Halfway House	7.57	123.76	8.06	3,837	Water and some grazing and timber.
Independence (Court-house)	8.06	131.82	0.00	3,957	Town of about 250 inhabitants. Seat of Inyo County. Forage for sale; some grazing and timber; good running water.

NOTE.—This route was surveyed in 1875. The distance by wagon-road from Los Angeles to Mohave Station (Route No. 30) is 89.08 miles, making a total distance from Los Angeles to Independence of 220.9 miles.

[1] Railroad level.
[2] For intermediate stations see route Mohave Station to Darwin, Cal.
[3] To Cerro Gordo (mining camp) 25.75 miles northeast. To Lone Pine, via east shore Owens Lake, 26.51 miles.
[4] Old steamer landing northwest end of Owens Lake.

Southwest end Owens Lake. Owens Lake is without outlet and is about 15 miles long by 9 wide, with a surface area of about 108 square miles. It is strongly saline, the principal salts being carbonate of soda and common salt. Altitude 3,567 feet above sea.

U S. GEOGRAPHICAL SURVEYS. 251

ROUTE No. 35.—*Independence, Cal., to Panamint, Cal.*
[Atlas sheets Nos. 65A and 65C.]

Stations.	Distance.			Altitude above sea-level.	Remarks.
	Between consecutive points.	From Independence.	From Panamint.		
	Miles.	*Miles.*	*Miles.*	*Feet.*	
Independence (Court-house)	0.00	0.00	98.56	3,957	Mining village of about 250 inhabitants; seat of Inyo County; forage for sale; good running water, some grazing, and a little timber.
Halfway House	8.06	8.06	90.50	3,837	Forage for sale; running water; grazing; scattering timber.
Lone Pine	7.57	15.63	82.93	3,810	Village of about 250 inhabitants; forage for sale; running water; grazing; scattering timber.
Owens River (bridge)	4.55	20.18	78.38	3,618	Forage for sale; running water; grazing; scattering timber.
Duckweilers	7.25	27.43	71.13	3,830	Forage for sale; station on east shore Owens Lake.
Swansea Mills, east shore Owens Lake[1]	0.50	27.93	70.63	3,832	No wood; springs; some grazing near lake.
Cerro Gordo Landing, east shore Owens Lake.[2]	4.91	32.84	65.72	3,656	Freight station; forage for sale; springs; some grazing; no timber.
Tule Station[3]	2.30	35.14	63.42		No wood; forage for sale; water hauled.
Toll house	4.80	39.94	58.62		Do.
Ornes[4]	4.00	43.94	54.62		Do.
Darwin[5]	11.00	54.94	43.62	4,840	Mining town of about 200 inhabitants; established in 1875; water in pipes; forage for sale; no wood.
Tennessee Station	11.00	65.94	32.62		Water from spring.
Junction Station[6]	5.25	71.19	27.37	5,755	No wood; well water; forage for sale.
Toll-gate	5.72	76.91	21.65	4,790	Spring water; no grazing or wood.
Twenty-mile Station	1.44	78.35	20.21	3,886	Spring water; no wood or grass.

*Surveyed in 1875.
[1] Cerro Gordo, mining village of about 250 inhabitants, 8.70 miles to eastward, making a total of 36.63 miles from Independence.
[2] Cerro Gordo, 8.70 miles to northeast by road.
[3] To Olancha, 14.75 miles by road leading southwest, or a total of 49.87 miles from Independence, via east shore Owens Lake.
[4] Olancha, 16.31 miles to southwest, or 27.31 miles from Darwin.
[5] Coso (abandoned mining town), 7.72 miles to southwest, a total of 62.64 miles from Independence.
[6] Coso, 7.61 miles to northwest, or 34.98 miles from Panamint; Indian Wells 36 miles to southeast, or 63.37 miles from Panamint. (See route Mohave Station to Panamint for details.)

ROUTE No. 35.—*Independence, Cal., to Panamint, Cal.*—Continued.

[Atlas sheet Nos. 65A and 65C.]

Stations.	Distance.			Altitude above sea-level.	Remarks.
	Between consecutive points.	From Independence.	From Panamint.		
	Miles.	*Miles.*	*Miles.*	*Feet.*	
Tates Station	12.91	91.26	7.30	1,572	Water formerly brought in pipes from cañon; no wood or grass.
Cañon Station	2.14	93.40	5.16	2,650	Running water; no grazing or wood.
Toll-gate	2.15	95.55	3.01	4,320	Do.
Panamint	3.01	98.56	0.00	6,605	Grazing; timber and water scarce; mining camp; declining in 1875, now practically abandoned.

ROUTE No. 36.—*Los Angeles, Cal., to Panamint, Cal., via Cajon Pass.*

[Atlas sheets Nos. 65 and 73.]

Stations.	Distance.			Altitude above sea-level.	Remarks.
	Between consecutive points.	From Los Angeles.	From Panamint.		
	Miles.	*Miles.*	*Miles.*	*Feet.*	
Los Angeles (Southern Pacific Railroad)	0.00	0.00	211.68	290	Large town (11,183 inhabitants); county seat of Los Angeles County.
Five-mile House	5.25	5.25	206.43	429	Good water; no wood nor grazing.
El Monte (direct road)	6.07	11.32	200.36	329	Water and wood; forage for sale.
Lexington	1.06	12.38	199.30	366	Do.
San Gabriel River	2.86	15.24	196.44	395	Stream dry in early summer; no wood, and little grazing.
San Jose	9.34	24.58	187.10	656	Water in acequia; no wood, little grazing.
Spadra	4.12	28.70	182.98	802	Water, wood, and forage for sale.
Cucamonga[1]	12.23	40.93	170.75	1,248	Good water, little wood; forage for sale. Large vineyards here.
Lytle Creek	11.35	52.28	159.40	2,133	Water; wood scarce; forage for sale.
Martins Station[2]	2.61	54.89	156.79	2,048	Water and wood; forage for sale. Junction with main road north from San Bernardino via Cajon Pass.
Toll-gate	5.28	60.17	151.51	2,666	Good water; wood scarce; forage for sale.
Fears Station	5.40	65.57	146.11	3,278	Do.
Cajon Summit[3]	2.22	67.79	143.89	4,196	The true Cajon Pass is to the westward about 5 miles, and is practicable for a railroad.
Huntingtons, Mohave River	15.09	82.88	128.80	2,899	Water and wells; poor grazing; forage for sale.
Cottonwood	19.47	102.35	109.33	2,488	Water in wells; little wood and grazing.
Blacks Ranch	16.42	118.77	92.91	2,140	Water; some wood; poor grazing.
Grants Wells	2.55	121.32	90.36	2,180	Water in wells; no wood nor grass.
Granite Wells[4]	24.21	145.53	66.15	4,015	Water in wells and spring.

[1] San Bernardino due east across the plains 18.22 miles by road. Total distance Los Angeles to San Bernardino by road, 59.15 miles.
[2] San Bernardino, county town of about 1,800 inhabitants, 12 miles to southeast and 3.2 miles north of Colton on the Southern Pacific Railroad. The route from this point north to Panamint would be as follows: Colton to San Bernardino Court House, 3.24 miles; San Bernardino Court House to Martins, 12 miles; Martins to Panamint (see above), 156.79 miles. Total, Colton on Southern Pacific Railroad to Panamint via Cajon Pass, 172.03 miles.
[3] [4] To avoid the grade from north of Fears the Old Salt Lake road made a detour to the west, coming into this road about 2 miles south of Fears. The Los Angeles and Independence Railroad was projected and partly graded this way.

ROUTE No. 36.—*Los Angeles, Cal., to Panamint, Cal., via Cajon Pass*—Continued.

[Atlas sheets Nos. 65 and 73.]

Stations.	Distance.			Altitude above sea-level.	Remarks.
	Between consecutive points.	From Los Angeles.	From Panamint.		
	Miles.	*Miles.*	*Miles.*	*Feet.*	
Willow Spring	26.00	171.53	40.15	2,573	Water hauled about one mile; no wood or grazing.
Post-office Spring	29.25	200.78	10.90	1,294	Water alkaline; little grazing.
Tates	3.60	204.38	7.30	1,572	Water in pipes.
Cañon Station	2.14	206.52	5.16	2,656	Running water.
Panamint	5.16	211.68	0.00	6,605	Old mining camp.

ROUTE No. 37.—*Mohave Station, Cal., to Darwin Cal.,* and Panamint, Cal.

[Atlas sheets Nos. 65 and 73.]

Stations.	Distance.		Altitude above sea-level.	Remarks.
	Between consecutive points.	From Mohave Station.	From Darwin.		
	Miles.	*Miles.*	*Miles.*	*Feet.*	
Mohave Station	0.00	0.00	100.82	†2,750	Southern Pacific Railroad.
Forks of Road Station	5.80	5.80	95.02	2,752	Old Nadeau Freight Station.
Stage Station[1]	3.62	9.42	91.40	2,570	Old Stage Station.
Forks of road	3.50	12.92	87.90		To Desert Spring, 9.4 miles; to Granite Wells, 55.4.
Red Rock Stage Station	11.41	24.33	76.49	2,211	Water; no wood nor grass.
Red Rock Freight Station	1.23	25.56	75.26	2,394	Water in wells; no wood nor grass.
Red Rock Summit	4.65	30.21	70.61	3,485	Divide between Salt Wells Valley and Kane Spring Flat.
Dixie Stage Station	4.36	34.57	66.25	3,248	Road turns west to Weldon (via Bird Spring), 27.2 miles (see Route No. 28.)
Coyote Holes (stage station)	8.14	42.71	58.11	3,368	Water in well; no wood nor grass.
Panamint Freight Station[2]	0.85	43.56	57.26	3,548	Water in pipes (1875); no wood nor grass.
Indian Wells	5.01	48.57	52.25	2,608	Water; no wood nor grass; southeast across desert to El Paso mines, 1,575 miles.
Desert Wells	12.00	60.57	40.25		Old Stage Station.
Kelleys	12.00	72.57	28.25		Do.
Junction Station[3]	12.00	84.57	16.25	5,755	Well water; no wood nor grass.
Darwin	16.25	100.82	0.00	4,840	Mining town of about 200 inhabitants, established 1875.

*This route was surveyed in 1875, and is the present mail-route to Darwin.
†Railroad.

[1] At about 3¼ miles beyond (northeast) this point a road forks to Desert Spring, lying opposite mouth of Red Rock Cañon, about ¾ miles southeast of Red Rock Stage Station, and continues eastward to Granite Wells, south of Pilot Knob (see Route No. 36). Distances from Los Angeles to Granite Wells by this road would be: Los Angeles to Mohave Railroad Station, 89.08 miles; Mohave to Desert Spring, 22.32 miles; Desert Spring to Kane Spring, 3.30 miles; Kane Spring to Mesquite Spring, 7.30 miles; Mesquite Spring to El Paso Mines road, 10.70 miles; El Paso road to Granite Wells, 25.70 miles. Total, Los Angeles to Granite Wells, 158.40 miles.

[2] From Panamint Freight Station southeast to El Paso mines, 15.11 miles; mines to road from Desert Spring, 5.62 miles; Desert Spring road to Surveyors Hole, 18.40 miles; Surveyors Hole to Granite Wells, near Pilot Knob, 6.90 miles. Total, Freight Station to Granite Well, 46.03 miles. At Panamint Freight Station the Cerro Gordo Freighting Companys road turns eastward to Panamint. The distances are: Freight Station to Salt Wels, 18 miles; Eagle Point (on Borax Lake), 14 miles; borax works, 5 miles; water station, 7.5 miles; Taxes, 18.3 miles; Panamlot, 7.3 miles. Total, Panamint freight station to Panamint, 70.1 miles, or from Mohave Railroad station to Panamint, 113.66 miles.

[3] From Junction Station to Panamint, 27.37 miles (see Route No. 35). Total, Mohave Railroad Station to Panamint, by stage-road, 111.94 miles.

ROUTE No. 38.—*Los Angeles Cal., to Fort Yuma, Cal.*

[Atlas sheets Nos. 81, 80, and 73.]

Stations.	Distance.			Altitude above sea-level.	Remarks.
	Between consecutive points.	From Los Angeles.	From Fort Yuma.		
	Miles.	*Miles.*	*Miles.*	*Feet.*	
Los Angeles	0.00	0.00	275.94	290	Large town, seat of Los Angeles County.
Anaheim	25.25	25.25	250.69	125	German settlement.
Temescal	30.80	56.05	219.89		Wood, water, and grass.
Lagunas Grande	11.19	67.24	208.70	1,292	Do.
Temecula	21.22	88.46	187.48	1,088	Wood scarce; water and grass plenty.
Bergmans	14.95	103.41	172.53	1,807	Wood, water, and grass.
Oak Grove	7.29	110.70	165.24	2,702	Ranch; wood, water, and grass.
La Puerta de la Cruz	10.63	121.33	154.61	2,784	Settlement in Warner Valley.
San Felipe Valley	17.85	139.18	136.76	2,538	Wood, water, and grass; trail saves about 4½ miles to Vallecito.
Vallecito Station	19.79	158.97	116.97	1,574	Water and grass; wood scarce.
Carrijo Creek	17.28	176.25	99.69	466	Deserted house; water and grass; wood scarce.
Old Sacketts Wells	13.87	190.12	85.82	132	Wells filled up by sand in 1876.
Indian Wells	15.87	205.99	69.95	—20	Corral; water scarce.
New River	13.42	219.41	56.53	11	Well (water brackish); wood and forage.
Alamo	12.55	231.96	43.98	54	Wood and water; no grass.
Gardners Well	7.45	239.41	36.53	55	Alkaline water; wood scarce.
Seven Wells	7.74	247.15	28.79	60	Wood and water plenty; grass scarce.
Cooks Wells	6.89	254.04	21.90	88	Good water; wood scarce; no grass.
Algodon Station	11.71	265.75	10.19	114	House and corral; wood and water; no grass.
Fort Yuma	10.19	275.94	0.00	*205	On Colorado River.

* The altitude of bench-mark near Fort Yuma flagstaff, from Southern Pacific Railroad levels, is 204.56 feet. From Yuma to Sacketts Wells the altitudes are from levels depending on 0.s bench. At Los Angeles the altitude at the new depot (Southern Pacific Railroad levels) is given.

NOTE.—This route was surveyed in the spring of 1876. Good camping facilities were found between Los Angeles and San Felipe. From San Felipe to the desert fair camps were found. From Sacketts Wells to the Colorado near Yuma the country is a desert. The road is difficult in several places. Between Anaheim and Temescal the Santa Aña River was crossed seven times, the current being rapid and the bottom with quicksands in places. In very rainy seasons the river is impassable. The road was tolerably good but steep at Vallecito Cañon and Hill. From Vallecito to Indian Wells the road was sandy and very heavy in places, and a severe sand storm was encountered at the latter place. The road is also sandy between Alamo and Yuma.

ROUTE No. 39.—*San Bernardino, Cal., to Ehrenberg, Ariz.*

[Atlas sheets Nos. 73D, 80B, 81A, and 81B.]

Stations.	Distance.			Altitude above sea-level.	Remarks.
	Between consecutive points.	From San Bernardino.	From Ehrenberg.		
	Miles.	*Miles.*	*Miles.*	*Feet.*	
San Bernardino	0.0	0.0	190.7	980	Town of about 1,800 inhabitants. Seat of San Bernardino County.
Nobbleys Ranch	18.3	18.3	172.4		Near divide San Gorgonio Pass; divide 2,746 feet above sea.
Whitewater Station	23.9	42.2	148.5	1,304	Corral. Water, wood, and grass scarce.
Agua Caliente	10.0	52.2	138.5	725	Sulphur water, temperature 100°. Ranches of Coahuila Indians in vicinity.
Los Toros	26.7	78.9	111.8	203	Water in pool.
Dos Palmas	25.1	104.0	86.7	103	Water alkaline. Grass and wood scarce.
Cañon Springs	11.6	115.6	75.1	1,238	Grass and wood scarce.
Chuchawalla	29.6	145.2	45.5	2,095	Dug for water. Grass scarce.
Mule Spring Station	20.1	165.3	25.4		Well.
Willow Spring	15.7	181.0	9.7	420	Water in pool.
Ferry	9.3	190.3	0.4	408	On Colorado River, opposite Ehrenberg.
Ehrenberg	0.4	190.7	0.0		Mining village on Colorado River.

NOTE.—This road was surveyed in 1876. From San Bernardino to Agua Caliente road good and grade easy; from Agua Caliente to Los Toros sandy and difficult; Los Toros to Ehrenberg road tolerably good. Wells and springs are sometimes filled up by washes from cloud-bursts. The greater portion of this route is through a desert country. The present mail-route to Ehrenberg is from Yuma, on the Southern Pacific Railroad.

ITINERARIES OF ROUTES.

ROUTE No. 40.—*Pueblo, Colo., to Santa Fé, N. Mex.*

[Atlas sheets Nos. 6A, 6aB, 6gB, 70A, and 70C.]

Stations.	Distance.			Altitude above sea level.	Remarks.
	Between consecutive points.	From Pueblo.	From Santa Fe.		
	Miles.	*Miles.*	*Miles.*	*Feet.*	
Pueblo (Denver and Rio Grande Railroad)	0.00	0.00	297.90	4,713	Station on Denver and Rio Grande Railroad; town of 7,800 inhabitants.
Saint Charles	10.24	10.24	287.66		Good ford, grass, and scattered piñon.
Muddy Creek	7.70	17.94	279.96		Ranch and post-office.
Greenhorn Creek	7.90	25.84	272.06	5,860	Good ford; settlements.
Butte Valley	13.60	39.44	258.46	5,894	Water, wood, and grass.
Cacharas (old town)	10.10	49.54	248.36	5,949	Good ford, good water, and grass.
Santa Clara Creek	9.60	59.14	238.76	6,172	Good ford, gravel bottom; grass.
Apishapa	9.40	68.54	229.36	6,195	Good water and grass.
Chicosa Springs	9.40	77.94	219.96		Good water, grass, and wood.
Trinidad	9.90	87.84	210.06	5,990	Town 2,300 inhabitants; water, grass, and wood in vicinity.
Hootens Toll-gate	13.20	101.04	196.86		Water, grass, and wood.
Sayers Ranch	9.20	110.24	187.66	6,292	Wood, water, and grass.
Clifton Station	6.50	116.74	181.16		Do.
Crow Creek Station	11.59	128.33	169.57	6,454	Two and three-fourth miles north of crossing middle and lower roads come in.
Vermejo	11.50	139.83	158.07	6,259	Bridge crossing; good well, grass, and wood.
Cimarron	12.09	151.92	145.98	6,384	Bridge crossing; town; good grazing.
Rayado	10.70	162.62	135.28		Mexican town; good ford; grazing.
La Bahia	8.03	170.65	127.25		Ranch; wood, water, and grass.
Ocate (post-office)	9.60	180.25	117.65		Town 4.8 miles west.
Fort Union	18.30	198.55	99.35	7,077	Military post.
Tiptonville	6.50	205.05	92.85	6,744	Small town; water and grass.
Crossing of Sapillo Creek	3.25	208.30	89.60		Water, grass, and wood.
Las Vegas	18.99	227.20	70.70	6,418	Wood, water, and grass in vicinity; town 6,000 inhabitants.

ROUTE No. 40.—*Pueblo, Colo., to Santa Fe, N. Mex.*—Continued.

[Atlas sheets Nos. 62A, 62B, 69B, 70A, and 70C.]

Stations.	Distance.			Altitude above sea-level.	Remarks.
	Between consecutive points.	From Pueblo.	From Santa Fe.		
	Miles.	*Miles.*	*Miles.*	*Feet.*	
Tecolote	11.20	238.40	59.50	6,162	Water, wood, and grass.
Bernal	5.90	244.30	53.60	5,648	Wood, water, and grass.
San Jose	9.80	254.10	43.80	6,995	Good water, grass, and wood.
Kowzlowskis	18.60	272.70	25.20	7,424	Do.
La Glorieta Ranch	4.90	277.60	20.30	7,023	Do.
Canoncito	6.00	283.60	14.30	6,965	Do.
Santa Fe	14.30	297.90	0.00		Capital of New Mexico, 6,635 inhabitants.

ROUTE No. 41.—*Carson, Nev., to Austin, Nev.*

Stations.	Distance.			Altitude above sea-level.	Remarks.
	Between consecutive points.	From Carson.	From Austin.		
	Miles.	*Miles.*	*Miles.*	*Feet.*	
Carson	0.00	0.00	178.19	4,634	Capital of Nevada.
Empire	3.66	3.66	174.53	4,593	On Carson River; number of mills.
Mound House	3.45	7.11	170.03	5,032	Station on Virginia and Truckee Railroad.
Dayton	5.06	12.17	165.02	4,369	Junction of Virginia and Truckee and Carson and Colorado River Railroads.
Cooneys	16.50	28.67	149.52		Hay Ranch; water; no wood.
Carson River	14.15	42.82	135.37	4,070	Log cabin; wood and water; little grazing.
Ragtown	10.25	53.07	125.12	4,002	Water; little wood; forage for sale.
Saint Clairs	3.87	56.94	121.25	3,989	Bridge; little wood; forage for sale.
School House	6.28	63.22	114.97	3,920	
Hill & Grimes	6.47	69.69	108.50	3,944	Ranch; good grazing; no wood.
Sand Springs	16.51	86.20	91.99	3,926	Water; wood and forage for sale.
West Gate	20.06	106.26	71.93	4,504	Good water; no wood nor grazing.
Middle Gate	3.11	109.37	68.82	4,703	Good water; little grazing; no wood.
White Rock	3.39	112.76	65.34	4,818	Water; no wood; grazing scarce.
Cold Springs	7.11	119.87	58.32	5,418	Good water; no wood; grazing scarce.
Pattersons	10.86	130.73	47.46	5,213	Ranch on Edwards Creek; no wood; grazing.
Antoines	14.37	145.10	33.09	6,517	Smiths Creek; Milk Ranch; forage for sale.
Birchims	22.32	167.42	10.77	5,743	Ranch near Reese River; no wood; forage for sale.
Halfway House	5.08	172.50	5.69	5,726	Well; no wood.
Austin	5.69	178.19	0.00	6,594	Wood and forage for sale.

NOTE.—The lists of variations of the needle intended for insertion in this volume it has not been possible to compile for want of available force, and hence this data must perforce remain upon the original and other MS. records of the survey finally transferred to the Engineer Department.—G. M. W.

o

www.ingramcontent.com/pod-product-compliance
Lightning Source LLC
Chambersburg PA
CBHW021353230426
43666CB00006B/506